Those GloriousTorrington Days
A Collection Of Writings
by Paul Bentley

In the case of any fictional article and/or sections presented here, any resemblance to actual persons, living or dead, is purely coincidental.

Those Glorious Torrington Days. Copyright © by Paul Bentley. All rights reserved. Printed in the United States Of America. No part of this book may be used or reproduced in any manner whatsoever without written permission of the author, except in the case of brief quotations embodied in critical articles and reviews, or brief passages copied for use in educational classrooms.

Cover design by Paul Bentley. Photo is a reverse image of Torrington High School circa 1961.

ISBN-13: 978-1547091140
ISBN-10: 1547091142

About The Author

Paul Bentley is a freelance writer and the author of the sort-of memoir *Sh*t A Teacher Thinks (and sometimes says)*, the novels *All Blood Runs Red* and *August Descending,* and four other compilations of essays and feature pieces: *My Torrington Days: A Collection Of Writings, More Torrington Days (Volumes 1&2), Torrington Days Forever,* and *Ye Olde Torrington Days*. All are available on Amazon. He lives in the Northeast with his wife and the great cat Ivy.

To future generations of Torrington citizens. May the Torrington you experience be as full and as rewarding as the Torrington here.

Table Of Contents

1. Forward - p.1
2. Meet Joe Torrington: Part I - p.2
3. Joe Torrington Revisited: Part II - p.6
4. Vogel School Voices: 1963-1993 - p.12
5. The Night Torrington Exploded: July 4, 1990 - p.44
6. The Warner Hits Home: Grease Paint Strain - p.58
7. Dave Lopardo: A Man On The Run - p.62
8. Torrington People: Us Folks Is Mellow - p.68
9. Banking At The ATM: Growing Older By The Granny - p.72
10. The Dark Brunette Side Of The Wild Blue Yonder - p.74
11. Daniel J. Hoffman: Torrington's Greatest Baseball Player - p.78
12. Frigo: House Of Cheese - p.94
13. Wintering In Torrington: Slip-Sliding Away - p.114
14. Talent, Peter Pan, and The Warner - p.116
15. The Revolving Mayor's Door: A Brief History - p.122
16. The Stars Among Us: Celebrities In The Big T - p.130
17. The THS Football Team Of 1948: Undefeated & Untied - p.148
18. Back To The Future: Torrington 1997 - p.160
19. New Board Of Public Safety Members: Stooges Sworn In - p.162
20. The Berkshire Tavern: An Albert Street Tradition - p. 166
21. The History Of T.H.S. Swimming: Part 3, The Turbulent 1960s - p. 204
22. Epilogue - p. 262

Forward

January 1, 2017. As I sit down this New Year's Day to begin a 5th "Torrington" book, it's with a buoyant sense of excitement and anticipation. Once again I have not planned ahead, so I don't know which old articles I'll be including *or* which new articles I'll be researching and writing. Disclaimer: I know for certain I'll be including the previously published column on the undefeated T.H.S. football team of 1948. AND, I know I'll be writing a new major feature on T.H.S. swimming in the 1960s. Beyond that though, it's literally an open book, the pages ahead as much a mystery to me, the writer, as to you, the reader.

For the first time, I am going to mix old and new articles starting with an old one but followed shortly after with a new. I like the idea of trying something different structurally. *And* I like the idea of interjecting the never-before-seen-and-read with articles which have already seen newsprint, i.e. staggering the discovery factor. Hopefully this mixing will lend an air of excitement to flipping pages.

It's the end of the Holiday, Christmas season. Around me in the Bentley house are festively decorated trees, sprays of fresh greenery, wreaths, and general Christmas bric-a-brac. There's a feeling of joy in the hall, of warmth around the hearth. Of course, all these signs of the season will soon be coming down, put away for another year. But hopefully these gift-wrapped feelings will linger. . . Dickens said of Scrooge at the end of *A Christmas Carol* that "he kept Christmas well." In that same spirit, Torrington citizens, both past and present, have kept our city well. They have given our fair borough a very real past *and* present, i.e. "Those Glorious Torrington Days."

The assorted baubles of our collective Torrington memories can *never* be neatly wrapped up and tucked away in some dusty, space-time attic awaiting a new day, a new season. Torrington is an ongoing 24/7/365. Drums along the Naugatuck, a dynamic flux capacitor. Our past and present merging to become our future: which goes on, and on, and. . .

Peace. And good will to all.

Meet Joe Torrington
Part I

(July 13, 1989. *The Torrington Register*. In the late 1980s the biggest controversy in Torrington was over the building of a new middle school. Vogel was splitting at the seams and the antiquated physical plant no longer fit modern educational needs.. The town was divided: build a new middle school, renovate Vogel – which was the old high school? OR, do nothing? All sides had dug in, much like politics in our polarized 21st century. And progress was at a stalemate. I wrote the below column in response to the many arguments and negativity that were coming from new school opponents, many of whom were senior citizens. And I chose satire/parody as the genre simply because I like that mode. It makes points while offering up a smile [as long as you're not the one on the receiving end of it]. This column also introduced for the first time "Joe Torrington," much to the dismay of many. It would not be the last time I'd use Joe. . . I chose to include this piece in this book because of its 21st century relevancy, i.e. the divide between progressives and conservatives is still very much with us today.)

A lot of people in Torrington these days, particularly those afflicted with an incurable case of intelligence, are scratching their heads over the resounding middle school referendum defeat. They can't for all the money on the Grand List figure out how logic, hard facts, and an even temperament failed to carry the day.

My answer is, as we longtime natives know, simple.

Meet Joe Torrington.

I caught up with Joe the other night at the middle school hearing. He was decked out in his yellow seersucker pants, pink golfing shirt, and matching canvas shoes. He was as tan as a construction worker and about as tired looking.

I got right to the point.

"Joe," I held out my hand, "it's great to see you again. Where've you been?"

"Cheez Paul," he pumped my hand as if pumping for blood, "good to see you too. I just got in from Florida. Damn near missed my spot in the retiree golfing league and this meeting." He sounded exasperated.

"Yeah Joe, I understand." I broke his grip. "Must be tough running back-and-forth between 2 homes, not to mention affording them."

"It is, kid. It is. And now these SOBs want to build a new middle school and raise my taxes even more. Well, they're not going to get away with it." He nodded over his shoulder where I

could see hundreds, if not thousands, of Joe and Jane Torringtons assembled in the background. It was a scary sight.

"But Joe," I protested, "your house in town is only assessed for $100,000 which means the most you'll pay in one year is only $78 more." I started to smile. "Let's face it, Joe. You spend more than that in one month on Lotto tickets, or beer, or cigarettes, or presents for your grandchildren. Wouldn't a new middle school be better for your health and your grandkids' future? I mean," and I gave it my best Henry Fonda sincere look, "how many Care Bears can your granddaughter play with anyway?"

Joe looked little peeved. "Hey Paul, how I spend my money is my business. If I prefer beer to books, or gambling to learning. . ." He cut himself short, sensing the cliff's edge. "But hey, I'm not against education. Didn't I vote for a renovated Forbes School?" He paused. "And the thing's already too small. What a bunch of shortsighted clowns on the Board Of Education." He looked smug.

3

"Come on, Joe," I appealed. "The Board Of Ed wanted a new and bigger Westside school all along, not a renovated Forbes. It was you and your gang who pushed for the renovation."

But Joe wasn't listening. "Look at the crowd," he cackled. "We'll show 'em." He gave a nearby lady the thumbs up and a wink. She giggled. It was a social.

I recalled seeing the same mindless mob in *The Day Of the Locust* and began to feel uneasy. I decided to change direction. "Yes Joe, I guess you're right. You're a regular modern day Socrates, a real Horace Mann."

"Who?"

"How about George Vogel?"

"Darn good man." Joe sighed. "Paul, education just ain't as good as it used to be. You teachers learn these kids almost nothing. These kids are being shortchanged, and now they want to overcharge us, to shortchange them."

Joe seemed momentarily confused by the thought, but drove on. "George Vogel had the right idea. Bolt the desks to the floor, say The Lord's Prayer, and write a lot on the blackboard. Forget dittos!!"

I couldn't resist the temptation and asked, "And what exactly did you learn?"

"A lot." Joe was now rolling. "By the time I graduated from grade school I could diagram a sentence, list the 50 states, give the imports and exports of at least 5 South American countries, do the 9 times table in my head, write both a business *and* a friendly letter, and. . ." he paused dramatically, "recite the Gettysburg Address, well, most of it anyway." He beamed.

"I'm impressed, Joe. You're quite a guy." I decided to appeal to the best in him. "You'd have been a TAG student nowadays, and that's why you should vote for the new middle school. Intelligent people like you dream. They have vision. They don't get bogged down in the trivial and negative. They latch onto grand ideas and soar heavenward with them. They. . ."

But Joe wasn't listening. He was winking at the lady again, and she was giggling again. I was talking to myself. Joe needed the concrete, but the meeting was being called to order, so Joe would have to wait. He wasn't going anywhere. . .

(Above, a promotional flier mailed out to the taxpayers of Torrington. This flier was put out by the Middle School Action Committee, Paul Denza, treasurer. It went a long ways in getting the correct information out there and scuttling many rumors and falsehoods. Other committee members included Mary Ann Borla, Margaret Chadwick, Rita Pacheco, and Ernest V. Cavagnero. Others who worked hard to bring about the school's eventual approval included Mayor Delia Donne, Mike Merati, and Mike Nejaime.)

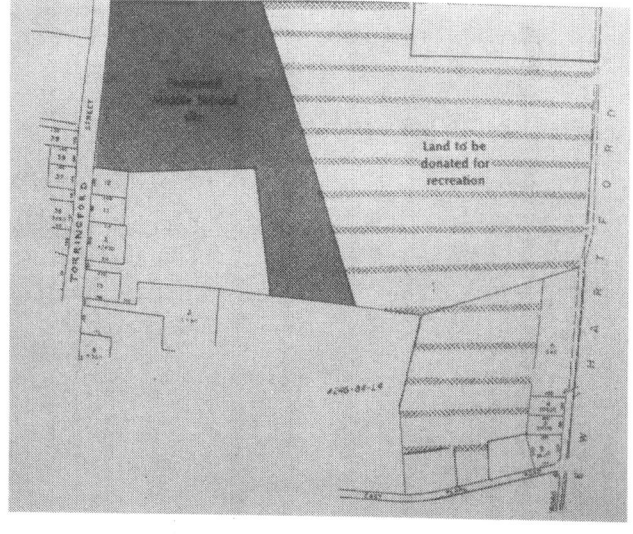

(Right, a drawing of the newly proposed site in 1990, i.e. the Ruwet property. Originally efforts were made to secure the Firtzgerald sisters' property on Kennedy Drive. They didn't want to sell, and when public opinion turned against taking the property through eminent domain, the city decided to take the Ruwets up on their offer.)

Joe Torrington Revisited
Part II

(July 14, 1989. *The Torrington Register*. As the reader might expect, the outcry over the *previous* article was immediate, loud, passionate, and came from many quarters. After the *following* article ran, approximately a dozen letters-to-the-editor were published. I received both anonymous mail *and* nasty/obscene phone calls from people who refused to identify themselves [These were the prehistoric days before Caller ID.]. Had people owned computers and had there been an online newspaper with a "Comments" section, I feel comfortable in predicting that Joe Torrington would have set an all-time feedback record. The column below ran the very next day after Part I, so if people were feeling angered and insulted after the first installment, they had no time to recover.)

Following the middle school hearing, which was a clear cut case of an immovable and inevitable idea meeting an irresistible and inane force, I ran into Joe Torrington again at a local luncheonette. He was basking in the afterglow of adrenaline shock, a typical family condition of the Torringtons caused by excess physical and nervous energy unchecked by any cerebral force. I decided to make a last attempt at communication.

"Joe, I've listened to all the arguments your group has against a new middle school. I agree that grouping could be better, for example just 7th and 8th grade. But besides that, none of your other arguments seem particularly strong."

"No?" he broke in immediately. "Well, what about eminent domain? Why should someone be forced to sell their land?"

"Aren't 2 people being offered $2.1 million for their land on Kennedy Drive, land that even has wetlands on it? I'd like to be forced to sell like that."

"That's not the point, Paul. It's the principle of the thing."

"What about the principle of citizens doing what's best for the town, for the kids?"

But Joe had his arguments, like his Gettysburg Address, memorized and was not to be slowed down. "But even without that land there should be enough room at the high school. Enrollment is down. It only makes sense that if enrollment is almost half of what it was 25 years ago that half the rooms should be empty!"

"I agree, but fortunately the high school now has a handicapped program, special education, remedial reading instruction, and computers. Programs which help many educationally disadvantaged people."

"Then why back a school board that didn't even choose a local for the superintendent's position?"

"The local you're talking about was not the best qualified for the position. Also, he himself backed a policy for years of hiring out-of-town teachers for the diversity of their backgrounds." I was rolling now too.

"Well, what about the fact that a lot of schools have closed in recent years, and now they want to build another one?"

"Migeon Avenue, Southwest, and Forbes are all being used educationally. North and Riverside will serve other municipal needs, while the town made more money selling East and South Schools than those old, pre-code buildings were worth."

"But 8th graders could have gone to them!"

"Yes Joe, if they wanted the same limited educational programs you had in your own K-8 days." Remembering our earlier talk, I quickly added, "But I think it's great you came name the imports of say, Chile. What were they anyway?"

"I forget." Joe was no longer smiling. "But what's so wonderful about learning about Shakespeare and all sorts of other worthless stuff anyway? These kids should be learning more practical things.

That's just good, old-fashioned, common sense. Me, I not only studied, but I played hockey and was an officer in the Rifle Club too." He paused and added, "Back in those years people weren't whimps and afraid of hockey sticks and guns. . ."

(Below, Joe Torrington's yearbook photo from the Torrington High School, Class of 1937.)

Joseph Torrington
"Joe"

"Play today, work tomorrow."

Joe was a happy-go-lucky fellow. We admired his willingness and his high ideals.

HONORS: Hockey 4; Hi-Y Beta 3-4; Treasurer 3; Pep Club 3-4; Rifle Club 3-4, Secretary-Treasurer 4.

"Happy to hear it, Joe. Well, you can forget the Rifle Club making a comeback. Hockey, maybe. But as far as learning about other practical things – you mean things like wood and metal working, sewing, typing, business skills, study skills, baking, cooking, arts and crafts, health, life time sports?"

"You betcha!" The retired Torrington Company machinist pulled on the brim of his T.C.C. golfing cap.

"Many area schools have all of them. And I agree they're wonderful. But you'll never see them in Torrington by putting all the 7th and 8th graders back into the elementary schools, just like in the good old days. There'd be neither the room, the staff, the equipment, nor the money to have those areas de-centralized and placed individually at each school. That's just plain common sense." I was losing my patience and getting blunt with Joe Torrington.

Joe stiffened. "Well, so what then. Let the kids take it easy for 3 years. It's too hectic a life anyway. They'll catch up during their 4 years at THS."

"Catch up? At Torrington High School? Come on, Joe. You're into handicapping races. Does anyone give away the first 3 laps of a 7 lap race, as currently is happening in the 6-12 grade race, and expect to come out a winner?"

"We did for years, and everything was OK."

"It was? SAT scores have declined, college bound has come to mean matriculating at the community college or the beauty academy, while juvenile, family, and young marital problems are at an all-time high. And everything is OK?. . . Maybe it's time to stop talking so much about what our youth are costing us, and time to start talking about just how much they're worth to us."

It was a fitting closing line, but Joe had one final ace-in-the-hole.

"Why should I pay for a school I'm not even going to use? My generation has already built one set of schools. Why should we be expected to foot the bill for another?"

But I had an ace too.

"Because Joe, we foot the bill for people like you."

"Huh?"

"Joe, hasn't your generation over the years received shopping discounts, subsidized housing, subsidized transportation, subsidized food, subsidized medical care, tax breaks, and" it was my final ace, "free cheese from the Senior Center?"

Cheese. The word hung in the air. There was nothing left to say, but I saw hope for the future. . .

✥ ✥ ✥ ✥

Postscript

Ten days after this column was published, I wrote a third and final one in this middle school/Joe Torrington series to explain who *and* what I meant by "Joe Torrington." It went a long ways in soothing ruffled egos, though there were still people who would not talk to me for years. And who never *did* vote for the new school.

Most people today, almost 30 years later, have no doubt forgotten that back in the late 1980s the Torrington Taxpayers Association was formed and that they quickly marshaled their forces against a new middle school. Members, including Joe and Jane Torringtons in force, attended all the public meetings, voiced and wrote about their views, and, in short, fought like hell to maintain the status quo. Nevertheless, in December 1990, after almost 5 years and 2 referendums, taxpayers approved construction of the new TMS. It

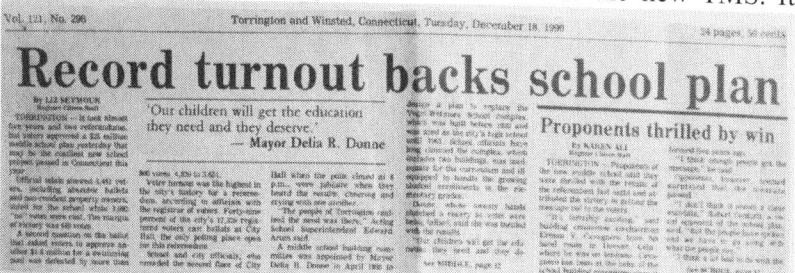

was as sweet a victory for those of us who fought for the school, as it was a bitter loss for those who fought against it, though the latter were gracious in their remarks to the press.

(Right, Vogel principal Tony Distasio applauds the outcome of the December 1990 vote. The same night the voting ended, there was a Christmas concert in the Vogel auditorium put on the middle school musicians. In between musical selections, the voting results were announced by jubilant City Hall and school officials.)

In January 1994, the new Torrington Middle School opened its doors. Though the succeeding years saw structural roof problems and other building setbacks, the TMS was here to stay.

I, for one, could not have been happier.

Vogel School Voices
1963-1993

(New Article. January 30, 2017. Having fought in the press all those many years ago to get a new middle school, I now look back on the years Vogel Middle School was in session with curiosity. Sort of like looking at photos or drawings of a once extant animal. What happened back then, some of the events I personally took part in, would make headlines today. Back then, they scarcely rippled the surface. . . In this article I've attempted to relay some first-hand accounts of the people who were actually there, including myself. I think it's important to do this before those memories are as gone as the first students who inhabited the building in 1915.)

(Above, the Vogel School building as it appeared in the decade before I subbed there. It looked the same in the 1970s.)

Vogel School. A school with a checkered past, a varied reputation. In its earliest years it was synonymous in some quarters with hell-on-earth. Purgatory. A gray-shaded, fire-and-brimstone immersion into the netherworld of juvenile delinquents and confusing education with being a jail warden.

In its later incarnation it evolved and became equated with providing a good general education while offering excellence in many extracurriculars.

What Vogel truly was would depend, I guess, on *when* a person was there and *what* his or her individual experience was.

I was there on-and-off in 1973-'75 as a substitute teacher. I had no problem whatsoever getting as much work as I wanted, since there were a number of subs who simply refused to enter the large wooden doors. I'd occasionally tell the sub finder that I needed more high school gigs before returning to Vogel. A break from the Rogue's Gallery. A little R&R from combat. Fort Vogel. And that request was usually honored. Everyone knew that Vogel was *not* easy money. . . Looking back with the hindsight of 40+ years I wonder now why more students weren't sequestered in an alternative ed program. Was it budget, lack of foresight? There was certainly a need. . . Bottom Line: The worst were thrown in with the general student population, and it made rough going for everyone.

Flashback: It's 1973-'75 in the old Vogel building. I'm in for a Language Arts teacher, and I'm sitting by the door at her desk taking attendance. A student comes in late. I recognize him instantly. A little runt of kid whose mouth is twice the size of his brain. He looks at me, I look at him, and he says, "Oh shit, it's you." I say, "That's right, and if you don't like it you're free to go to the office." He says, "I'll go to the office." He turns, starts for the door, and just as he's passing me says, "I'm not staying in this fucking class with an asshole like you." It's said just loud enough for me to hear.

My reaction is instant. Without thinking, with no hesitation, I jump to my feet, and he sees in a nano-second he's gone too far.

He bolts.

The chase is on.

We're racing down the first floor corridor on the west side of the building. The floor is slippery. He whips around the 90° left-hand turn, almost loses it, and runs past the Main Office headed for the front doors. Assistant Principal Frank Cimino is standing outside the office, and we fly past him. The kid goes through the door, then hesitates and fakes a re-entry. We play musical doors. He fakes re-entry through one door, I jump in front of it, and he fakes another. I think he knows I'm going to catch him in the open field and he'd like nothing better than to get back into the school where maybe he can get lost in a crowd or out-slide me on the corners.

It takes only seconds before he realizes he's not getting back in and breaks for Church Street. He bounds down the stairs, sprints across the grass, and hits the street running like junior Olympic finalist. The kid is quick, but I'm young myself, a runner, and it's only a matter of time. He heads for Main Street. We race across the Church-Prospect intersection not losing a stride. I'm slowly gaining and more determined than ever to catch this little shit.

Fifty yards more and we're nearly at the old Post Office. I reach out to grab the back of his collar, and when I make the faintest contact, the boy abruptly lurches to a stop, throws himself on the ground, and like a turtle on its back, flails his arms and legs and screams till he's redder than the nearby stop light.

I'm standing over him astonished. I don't know what to do. Actually, I didn't know what I was going to do if I did manage to grab him. And I have even less of an idea why I was bothering to chase him at all. It was a spontaneous, POed reaction, sure. But did I think when I collared him he was going to say, "Shoot, guess I was wrong to swear at you, but this chase has really turned my life around. I apologize profusely for my indiscretion"?

(Above, the lower section of Church Street showing the stretch we came flying down. Vogel is the large building in the background.)

Frank Cimino arrives huffing-and-puffing. "I barely touched him–" I start to say, but Frank cuts me off. "I know," he says, "I saw. Get back to class. I'll take it from here."

He grabs the boys under the armpits and starts to drag him back up Church towards the school much as one might tow sack of potatoes.

Seems crazy looking back on it. And not crazy good.

Lots of such incidents. Another time I'm subbing a different Vogel class. A tough group filled with eventual dropouts and Torrington Police Blotter headliners. I'm sitting at the teacher's desk, again by the door, this time with my head down, when someone throws an eraser at me. It hits the mug on the desk holding pencils and pens, and sends it flying. The glass container hits the floor and explodes with a BAM!

I jump inwardly. Look up. Two girls are laughing in the last row right where there should be an eraser on the back blackboard. "Which one of you did it?" I ask calmly. "I did," a young blond says defiantly, her voice implying a so-what? "Go to the office," I say.

My anger's up now. I stand and open the door. I'm not being a gentleman. Some of these weisenheimers at Vogel love nothing better than to slam these old, heavy, wooden doors. Gives them the final word and a chance perhaps to shatter the glass in the upper portion, though I've never heard of that happening. . . As the girl passes me on her way out, she partially turns and says, "Go to hell!"

It is said so mean-spirited that it takes me back for a second. I don't know what to do. If this were a male student. . . But it's not. . . I grab her by the shoulders, hesitate, then. . . (this part censored by my editor). . . The girl starts jumping up-and-down, yelling and swearing. I tell her to hop on down to the office and NOT to come back. I slam the door.

Seems crazy looking back on it. And not crazy good.

There were more inane incidents I was personally involved in, but I wasn't alone. There was plenty of craziness in the old Vogel to go around. A friend of mine was subbing there in the same time period. He got called "a fucking asshole" and in a knee jerk reaction smacked the kid right in the mouth and knocked him to the ground. He got called into Superintendent John Hogan's office, and the super said to him, "Are you crazy? You can't hit students." My friend told him, "You put me back into that same class, the kid calls me 'a fucking asshole' again, and I'll knock him down again." Sidebar: My friend was a wiry little guy; the kid he decked much bigger. . . Outcome: My friend voluntarily quit subbing, eventually got into computers, and happily retired at age 50 with plenty of money and his sanity intact.

I recall students at the Vogel DMZ using one teacher's desk as a landing zone and seeing how many paper airplanes they could toss/ float onto it whenever he was at the blackboard or away from it. . . I remember another male teacher with little class room control having his desk overturned by a couple of hefty angry brothers, and the teacher doing nothing. A PE teacher intervened.

Naturally there were good teachers too. Teachers who *could* relate to the students, *could* control them, and *could* teach them. I think of Mary Cianciolo, Rich Lehmann, Sue Castelli, Mary Zbell, Paul Putnocki, Dick Stomski, Joann Stefurak, and a few others.

The 1970s were nutso times at Vogel, but to be fair, they were tough at many of the area schools.

Later on when I was a Vogel parent in the early 1990s, I saw a different side to the school. So much was going on: art, band, orchestra, drama, an honor society, student council, Invention Convention, Twins' Day, ski club, dances, cheerleaders, basketball, Christmas door decorating contest, mass participation in the Hike For the Handicapped, etc. Cross country, which had always been a strongpoint under Coach Dave Lopardo, continued its decades of winning. And teachers such as Pam Dzurilla, Jeanette Muller, the quirky and fun loving Dave Capolupo (Below, left), everyone's friend Marty Vanek, et al. had raised the level of discourse, student participation, and general academics.

Vogel had become a school to be proud of. A good work place, i.e. one in which a teacher or student could leave at the end of the day happy that he/she did more than just survive.

Other Vogel Voices:

Dave Lopardo: "I was an English teacher at Vogel from 1977 to our very last day there on Thursday, January 6, 1994. Our scheduled last day, January 7, was cancelled by a snowstorm. We opened the new middle school the following Monday, January 10. So, TMS and I share a birthday. . . I was a fish out of water that first year at Vogel, 1977-'78. I had been a THS English teacher for seven years, and believe me, if you got on the bad side of the THS administration, you might be 'transferred' to Vogel. It was the Torrington school system version of being exiled to Siberia by the Politburo. . . (On the right, long time Vogel Coach Dave Lopardo clocks his runners). . . I made the mistake that first year of treating my Vogel students as younger versions of freshmen, and it was a disaster. I needed a lot of help from more experienced language arts teachers like Paul Putnocki, Sayra Poole, and Joanne Stefurak to set me straight and salvage what was left of the year. . . Vogel was a tough place to teach, but what I remember most, and it was something that soon became extinct at the new middle school, was the pride we had in doing a difficult job in a building that lacked just about every comfort and even some necessities. And the biggie: we pulled together and helped each other out unconditionally. Sometimes looking back it reminds me of what it's like to be a camp counselor; you have to do your teaching and have a good measure of obedience and respect from the kids, but you are really one big family. . . And that is my bottom line remembrance of Vogel Middle School: we were one big family."

Jeff Pavan: "I entered Vogel School in October 1978 as a substitute teacher. Ironically I was subbing for Newell Porch who I knew and who at the time was interviewing as rep for a pharmaceutical company (he got the job and temporarily left teaching). I worked with Marsha Olsen that day. My stock as a substitute teacher grew as time passed, but the classes were horrendous. The new assistant superintendent wasn't going to take it, and he pulled the plug and fired several teachers who no longer rated high on the classroom maintenance scale. At that point I had been covering Bernie Corden's classes in English.

I continued subbing for him and eventually became the full-time, noncertified teacher for that class around January 1979. Mrs. Sayra Poole was my biggest advocate. The bottom line was that I could control the classes, and I got along with the kids. I felt both confident and comfortable in that ancient school building. After the end of year in 1979, Charlie Chretien offered me a job as a permanent sub because I was decent with the kids. . . I remember the many fine teachers there: Marsha Olsen, Susan Pagano (on left), Nancy Baldwin, Joann Stefurak, and Irene Landry. Also, the many fine administrators including Charlie Chretien, Bruce Fox, Bob Doyle, Mike Buzzi, and Anthony Distasio. . . My life at Vogel revolved around coaching basketball and working as a permanent substitute. I coached basketball for exactly 100 games and finished with a record of 70-and-30. The players included Gary and Terry Christiano, Brian Anzellotti, Aaron and Justin Lefkowski. At one point we won 29 straight. . . I left Vogel in June 1992."

Deborah Britton Siulinski: "I went to Vogel for 8th grade. I remember in November 1963 John Williams running back into homeroom from the library. He had something he wanted to say and our homeroom teacher Mrs. Grizley took him in the hall. He came back in and sat down. What he had wanted to tell us was that

President Kennedy had been assassinated, and the school didn't want us to know."

James A Gioia: "I remember when Kennedy was assassinated some of us ran to Laraia's looking for a newspaper. . . I also remember in the small basement gym we ran into the wall on basketball layups."

Judith Donna Kennerson: "I remember being in class at Vogel the day President Kennedy was assassinated."

Tom Whittaker: "I was in 7th grade at Vogel in September 1963. We were the first class to do both 7th and 8th grades there. I remember it was $.35 for lunch, and we got one heck of a meal before Christmas vacation. I guess the cafeteria food was pretty good then. . . I remem-

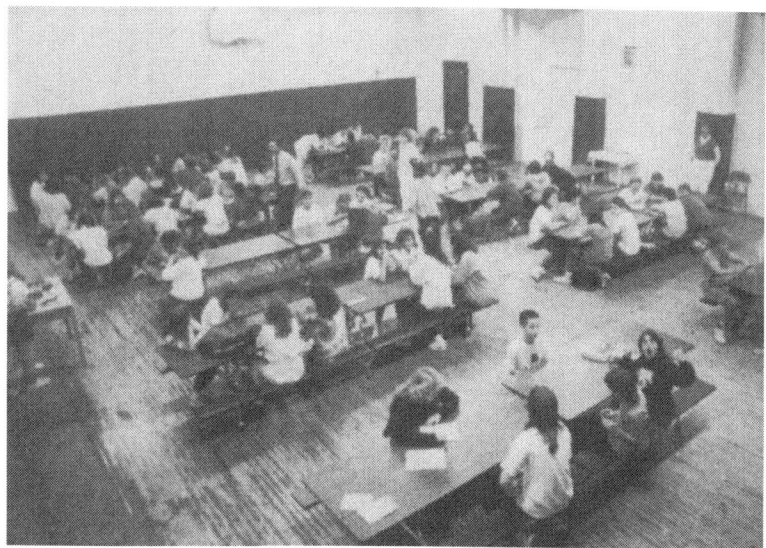

(Above, the basement cafeteria at Vogel in 1989. This is one of 12 eating shifts.)

ber walking to school from the north portion of Benham Street with a great crew of kids from the neighborhood in all types of weather. . . The building had 7th graders on one side, 8th grade on the other. . . One day I'll never forget is learning JFK was shot shortly before dismissal on November 22, 1963. We always went back to homeroom at day's end, and our teacher, Mrs. Healy, spoke to us about it. She calmly explained what was known at that moment, saying to go straight home and be with our families."

Doreen Cellerino: "I was at Vogel in 1963-'64. My mother got called to the office by Mr. Ellis. Lisa R. and I had gotten caught trying to drag a crying 7th grade boy into the girls' lav. He said I shouldn't try to look like Veronica Lake and should hang out with a nice girl, like Adele P."

Marie Kitch: "Mr. Neshko!!! I remember him because of one thing: the large ink stain on his sport coat from the leaking pen!. . . I also remember Mr. Tracey giving us girls a little talk in gym about what to do at that time of the month. He must have been mortified as were we!!. . . We might have had coral gym suits at Vogel. I know we had them in high school."

Bob Parsons Sr.: "One of our teachers had a nervous break-down when I was in 7th grade. That was a bad day."

Ernie Zavatkay: "The teacher who had a breakdown was Mr. Roberts. He had just lost his son in Vietnam. Very tragic at that time, and there was no help for him. . . I remember the lunches at Vogel: English muffins with sauce and cheese, a.k.a. pizza. Mr. Stomki's lab

(Above, a student cartoon from 1991 concerning the Vogel food.)

on the top floor; Mr. Ellis, principal; the gym with the baloney; my introduction to paisley (it was 1964); the old style phones in each room (made of wood with a separate receiver); the basement; and Mr Chretien, vice principal. He was a good man."

(Below, Charlie Chretien just before his retirement in 1990.)

Cynthia Lariviere: "I was there 1976-'78. I remember Star Wars. The cool science lab. Classes like Industrial Arts and Home Economics meeting across the street. Coming to school the morning the church burned down. Freezing wet hair coming back from the YMCA. A feud between kids at Vogel and kids at St. Francis. Being bullied and punched in the jaw. I remember those who stood up to the bullies. The bad girls who had feathered roach clips. Disco. Clogs. School trip to Philadelphia. Selling grinders to pay for a trip. Saturday night dances. Doing the Hustle. Being accidentally tripped by the history teacher doing the Hustle."

Larry Warriner: "I remember 'Birdman.'"

Lori Marino Hull: "Birdman was Mr. Silverstein. I had him for 7th grade Science."

Ray Humphrey: "We used to call him 'The Bird Man,' and he even wrote his own book about birds!"

Darleen Hinrichs: "I was at Vogel from 1974-'76 for 7th and 8th grades. I remember bringing dead birds to Mr. Silverstein for 'extra credit.' He always got so sad talking about them; I don't know why we thought that was a good thing. I guess he didn't like frogs as much because he never seemed sad when we were dissecting them. I also remember Mrs. Burke in 7th grade History. She would always tell us to 'let go,' in other words to put everything down and just listen."

Charlene Mueller Lee: "I had Mr. Silverstein. He believed children are all born with ESP and would lose it as they got older. He would do 'psychic' experiments with us in class. He'd stare at a card with a picture or symbol on it and tell us he was sending out vibes. We had to guess what he was looking at."

(Above, Samuel Silverstein describing to a reporter the extrasensory experiences he said children possess.)

Phil Juhas: "Mr Silverstein used to keep his dead bird-of-the-day outside on the window ledge to keep it cold. He'd bring it in, hold it up by the wings, and tell us all about it. An odd little man, but very enthusiastic. After the first few times, it didn't seem so weird."

Jason Zeiner: "I was there at Wetmore for kindergarten-third grade. I returned to Vogel for 6-8. My last year was 1993. Had lots of memories. One best was skipping homeroom once a week."

David Renzullo: I was there in 1973-'74 on the second floor, Room 22. Miss Santoro was my homeroom and math teacher. Mr. Silverstein was a science teacher. It was pretty wild back then. A lot of rowdiness and fights."

Teri Fuller: "I was there from September 1973 to June 1975. One vivid memory is from my homeroom and math teacher in 7th grade, Richard Lehmann. To keep us in line, he would have chalk-throwing contests. We'd stand in the back of the room, throw the chalk, and try to get it to land in the chalk tray under the blackboard."

(Above, a good natured Mr. Lehmann goes along with a humorous photo for the yearbook.)

Anne Marie Filippini: "I remember pitching chalk in Mr Lehmann's math class. So much fun!! I thought that it was so cool."

Chris Bilosz: "I remember wearing a coral color one-piece outfit with your name embroidered on it to gym class. Miss Moran was the gym teacher. A very small gym. . . I was told I could be a cheerleader or play sports but not both. I remember sports became equal for girls in the 70's for public schools. I also walked to Vogel daily from where Lamonica's grocery store was, rain or shine. Buses ran from farther out on Migeon Avenue; otherwise you walked. We went on a field trip to Washington D.C. in 7th grade. It was a good time."

Cheryl Pecha: "I was at Vogel in 1976-'78. We survived!. . . Very rowdy. . . Fights. . . Dances. . . Being stoned most of the time. . . Mr. Fox or 'Barney' as we called him. . . Class trip to Philly. . . Field trip to Boston. . . School band. . . Sports. . . Mr. Putnoki – that man saved my soul!"

(Left, Mr. Putnoki in 1978.)

Jessie Lee Fogarty: "Mr. Putt was one of the kindest and most insightful teachers I ever had. We were so lucky to have him!. . . Dissecting the frog at Vogel-Wetmore together with Jennifer Palladino forged our lifelong bond."

Annette Jacquemin: "I remember those crazy one piece gym suits we had to wear. Also, Mr. Lestinsky was an awesome math teacher."

Tracy Knibbs: "I went there the last year it was a middle school. Spent half the year there in 8th grade, and the other half at the 'new' middle school (1993). I remember the road between the two schools (Vogel and Wetmore) shut down before school started, and we would

(Above, the section of Church Street running between Vogel and Wetmore. Wetmore can be seen on the right through the trees.)

wait there outside until school started. I also remember the upper cafeteria and the lower cafeteria that was converted from the old gym, which is why we had to walk to the YMCA to go to gym class. We also had to cross the street to Wetmore for classes like Tech Ed, Home Economics, and CAD. My homeroom and English class were in the classroom in the middle of the building that used to be a science lab. The desks were tiered in rows on steps, and when people walked in the hallway, they would bang on the walls."

Fernando Vega: "In 1992 on a Friday afternoon in 7th grade we were dissecting frogs. We didn't finish, and there was no place to store them. So they went in a bag out on the fire escape for the weekend. Problem solved until someone climbed up there Sunday night and flung the bag out onto Prospect Street. Made for an interesting walk to school Monday morning with 40-50 half-dissected frogs everywhere."

Justin Roth: "I remember gym classes at the Y, especially on rainy days.

Lynn Young: "OMG, I did NOT have the best experiences at Vogel during that period of time!. . . I remember walking to the YMCA, which was nice because I was happy to get out of Vogel for that! I remember those hideous gym uniforms – each class had a different color. For 7th grade mine was girl scout green. By the next year they came up with a more modern version that actually was made with material that had some stretch to it."

Heidi Aleman: "I was at Vogel 1985-'86. I remember Bird Man, Stomski, the Space Shuttle explosion, and the YMCA for swimming then racing back to school with soaking wet hair."

(Above, a 1978 Vogel co-ed swim class in the old YMCA 20-yard pool. The teacher is Newell Porch.)

Laurie Chapman Mackinnon: "I remember girls still had to wear skirts or dresses at Vogel in 1968-'69. A few years earlier I remember my brother being sent home for wearing Beatle Boots!!!"

Chris Pond: "Our group was the first class to go through Vogel both 7th and 8th grade. Wearing taps on your shoes was the cool thing back then. If you had the horseshoe taps, they were essentially outlawed in school. My mom cared about the heels. We just wanted to make the most noise walking down the hall when everyone was in class. All the other students would stare out the door to see who was coming. I was sent to the custodian's office more than once to have them removed."

Laurie Zimmerman Canty: "I was there 1975-'76, and I remember the cafe in the basement, the science lab, and having to walk to the Y for gym class no matter the weather. I remember the math teacher Mr. Lehmann saying, 'Close, but no cigar.' The 7th grade trip to Washington DC also stands out, as does the tough English teacher, Mrs. Cianciolo."

(Above, late 1970s. Students line up to turn in papers to English teacher Mary Cianciolo.)

Richard Hess: "I remember in 7th grade Mr. Killiany, a science teacher, smoked Camel cigarettes. He was a real smoking machine, but he told us smoking was bad."

Michael Gruber: "I remember the place was built like a fortress... I remember the female art teacher sitting at her desk the entire class without saying a word... I also remember Lui Collins, the music teacher, at the start of every class playing, 'We will rock you' by Queen."

Lynn Young: "Mr. Purcell, a history teacher, had this cool game he made on a large table in the room – sort of a military type game. I don't remember it too well, but he put a lot of work into it and we each had teams or something... I remember Mr. Gunn who was sort of a hall monitor. Wonderful, kind man. Kept the kids in line in the hallways – and believe me a bunch of them needed it!... One interesting memory: There are murals painted on the walls down in the basement near where the cafeteria was. They were painted during the years Vogel was the high school, and my uncle, Don Rodemeyer, actually painted one of them. He was an amazing artist. When I was at Vogel-Wetmore last year for the Invention Convention with my son, I saw the murals. They're still there. So glad they did not paint over them – they're a real piece of history."

(Above, THS students in the old high school, later Vogel, work on a wall mural in the basement in 1947. L-R: Robert Byrnie, Liligene Horwath Metcalf, Ann Ferrier Szabo, and Alexander Colaciello.)

Kevin Bittner: "I was at Vogel in 1968-'70. My grandfather, C.E. Bittner, taught there. I remember Mr Silverstein as a homeroom teacher in 7th grade, and the strange room behind the coat closet. Mr. Tracey had a Maine accent and was always playing with his pen. There was a tiny library and a dark gym with a wide open 'locker room.' I remember The War Moratorium Protest Day and getting lectured to by a teacher for being 'unAmerican.' "

Christina Byers: "Walking to and from the Y with icicles in my hair during winter. LOL. . . I miss Mr. Putnoki, a.k.a. Mr Putt!! He was my all time favorite teacher. His class had no windows. One day they were painting across the hall, and I got high on the fumes. I slept for a few days and missed school."

David R. Washington: "I remember square dancing in the basement."

Judie Pollick: "Miss Sparrow! Who could forget Miss Sparrow in her dark skirts and buttoned up-to-the-neck white blouses. To this day I remember her saying we were not to sneeze in class! She scared me!"

Claudine Galitello: "I went the first year in 1963. Having spent all of my school years with the same kids at Forbes, this was quite a transition. Only teacher I remember was Miss Sparrow, a tough old bird!"

George Doucette: "I was in Mr. Aveino's class with Bill Zucca, Ralph DeAngelo, Enoch Little, and Rich Bollie."

Frances Bazzolo Louchen: "When I first started substitute teaching, Mr. Lehmann would tell students I was a good teacher because I was his former student. Which was so true!"

Dominic C. Melillo: "We used to be called Vogel mites!! I remember staring at the bricks outside or on a window sill and seeing tiny little bugs all the time. I think that's where the name came from. Also, this is where I smoked my first joint. LOL. Great memories."

Eric Thomen: "I remember walking down into the basement, and there was water dripping on the old stones and lights flickering. It was creepy. . . We were the first class to transfer to TMS."

Loretta Roletta: "Lunch aide Mrs. Brignolo, such a sweet lady! Treated each kid the same. With pure KINDNESS!... Mr. Gunn was cool."

Douglas Barry Jr.: "I was at Vogel from 1988-'89. I remember walking to the YMCA for gym and across the street to Wetmore for the different shops: Drafting, Woods, Home Economics, etc."

(Above, Vogel-Wetmore students crossing Church Street between classes.)

Timothy Strahan Sr.: "It was awesome. You would walk over to the YMCA for gym and swim. You'd have icicles in your hair by the time you walked back."

Andrew J DeSanti Sr: "I went to Vogel from 1975-'77. We called the assistant principal Barney Fife. Loved Mr. Gunn!"

Sara McKenna: "I was there from 1987-'89 for 7th & 8th grade. Besides the way Mr. Buzzi used to greet us daily and the wrath of Mr. Toth (Below, Mr. Toth looking ever vigilant), Mr. Fash 'yelling' in Italian, and trekking to the Y in the winter for swim class (why???), I'd say my favorite memory was when the somewhat gym-smelling gym transformed into an under-the-sea theme for our class night! We were so fancy!. . . Also Mr Purcell saying, 'Even you ca tan on the Yucatán!' And, 'What's the matter? Jaimaica mistake?'. . . I also remember Mrs. Cianciolo diagramming sentences and making us all memorize the prepositions in alphabetical order!"

Lori Arnista Karp: "I still remember all the prepositions! Aboard, about, above, across, after. . ."

Leanne Lefkowski Symuleski: "I went there from 1987-'90. I was in the first class that had 6th grade at Wetmore. I definitely remember walking to the Y for swim class. I also remember all of the bomb scares. They would call Wetmore with a bomb scare, so we would all trek over to Vogel. Then they would call Vogel, and we'd all end up at either the Y or Center Congregational Church. I also remember our 8th Grade Class Night in the basement of Vogel. So much fun!"

Holly Bachle Kitchin Roesing: "I was a student there from 1983-1985. I remember 8th Grade Class Night. Mr. Silverstein and his crazy obsession with dead animals and insects. I remember Mr. Stomski's awesome science classroom. Dissecting lungs in Mr.

(Above, Science with Mr. Stomski. Mr. Silverstein is on the far left.)

Fasciano's class. Wearing those ugly red/white gym onesies. Being an office helper and using the ditto machine. And writing for detention on green pages 'I Will Not Talk In Class' for 100, 500, even a 1000 times and learning how to use two pencils at once."

Jamey Levesque: "The endless green pages. 'I would like to take this opportunity to introduce myself.'"

Tracy Knibbs: "I remember the gym floor and the stairs going down to the lower caf. The teachers used to stand at the top and we would be dismissed from the caf by class. . . It seems kind of funny to me that they let a bunch of 10 to 14-year-olds walk down the street unsupervised in the middle of a school day. Definitely different times."

Phil Zolla: "I liked the feeling of independence walking from Vogel to the duckpin bowling alley on Migeon Avenue. . . I remember Stomski the science teacher. I see Ms. Page every once in awhile. She bought one of my pictures from Acadia National Park. Mr. Fox became an administrator at the senior assisted living center on Forest Street and was there the last time I saw him, which was early last year."

Debra DeDominicis Maher: "I went there from 1967-69. I remember bus trips to New York City and Riverside Park. Back then we wore Nehru jackets, bell bottoms, dirndl skirts, and Trader loafers. And we carried fish basket pocketbooks! Mr. Stomski, Mr. Nagy, Mr. Galgano, Mrs. Watts, and Mr. Wilcox were all fine teachers, to name just a few." (Right, a happy Mrs. Sparks and a dapper Ray Wilcox.)

Mark Pesce: "At Vogel ALL the elementary schools merged. I was awed by that and by changing classes on a buzzer. Slam books, that if your name was in it others would comment about how you were cute, love her, funny, etc. But the variety of girls! I have to mention that Claudia Jarmosik was THE hottest girl not only in Vogel but also in THS. Great memories and times!"

Brian Luhrs: "I remember giving Mr. Fox a hard time, and he followed me to the high school when I graduated 8th and he transferred. I also remember Miss Latch."

Heidi Grant Chappell: "I was there 1985-'87. Mr 'Putt' Putnoki was a great teacher. We gave him Jams for his birthday. He put them on and paraded down the hall to show all the other teachers! Loved his 'Goof Cards' as rewards. If you had one, it allowed you to skip homework, which was a treat!! His favorite colors for kids were black-and-blue. He always made me laugh!. . . I was at Vogel when the Challenger exploded. What a sad day. Mr. Fasciano was so emotional informing other classrooms of the devastating news. There weren't enough TVs so students could view it live. . . Dr. 'D' Distasio issued green pages as punishment. 'I will not. . .' Mr. Patten was a great history teacher!! Probably one of the most interesting classes I had for not really having an interest in history."

Ian Bentley: "I was at Vogel 1990-'93 and was in the band each year. It was a fantastic experience. Mr. Valerio was wonderful, in-

(Above, Mr. Chris Valerio and some band students at Coe Park for the Hike For the Handicapped."

credibly passionate about music and cared a great deal about his students. I think the band was kind of a big deal then (we won several awards at competitions and stuff like that - although I don't recall more specifics). I remember a marching band camp in the summer and a tough competition to be the band drum major. There were lots of school concerts, and trips to Great Adventure, Philadelphia, and Annapolis. Some of my best friends that I'm still in touch with have been friends since those times, and we still reflect back on them to this day. Many of those people are still involved in the arts. . . The drama club was great too. It was run by Ms. Pernal (Above, left) and Mrs. Gall (Above, right). I don't think we ever did musicals in middle school, but we did plays. There was one called *Detente* and a series of one-act plays. We rehearsed in the auditorium right after school, and I always looked forward to it throughout the day. Again, like band, some of my closest friends to this day were part of it, and many are still involved in the arts, some professionally."

Steve Malo: "Sadly, I was in third grade when my family moved to Connecticut, and co-workers told my father to put my brothers and me into Catholic school to stay away from 'the drug school' – Vogel."

Barbara Tousey: "I attended Vogel in 1976-'78. We had swimming for gym class at the YMCA. In 1977 we started classes in the basement of Wetmore for Home Economics and Wood Shop. I remember Mr. Stomski and the science lab on the second floor. I also loved the endless supply of French bread and butter during lunch."

Chris Pepler: "It very different going from East Elementary to Vogel-Wetmore. I remember Church Street was closed to traffic during school hours and waiting outside before school. Every seventh grader was lost as we were learning to take responsibility and be young adults. I have to admit, it was a neat feeling being able to walk to-and-from the Y with no teachers."

✦ ✦ ✦ ✦

Listening to all those "Vogel Voices" and looking at the pictures from that bygone era, I'm reminded what a handsome old building it was, and how a group of educators, support staff, and students maxed out opportunity in the narrow bandwidth in which they found themselves.

If Vogel School was tough at times, it was also home. As Dave Lopardo pointed out, those in residence were, indeed, one big family.

One big interlocking, interconnected, interpersonal family.

Who could have asked for anything more?

Saying Goodbye: Photo Portfolio

(Above, a 1978 band practice in the old auditorium with Mr. Wells.)

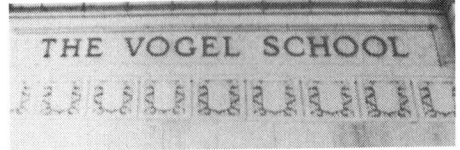

(Left, written in stone above the front entrance.)

(Above, floor level view in the old cafeteria late 1970s.)

(Below, early 1990s. Students entering Vogel with Wetmore visible in the background.)

(Above, late 1970s, the Dance Committee poses with Mrs. Zbell in the stairwell.)

(Above, late 1970s. Miss Stefurak in the background checks over students' work.)

Sayra Poole

Rick Fasciano

Joann Stefurak

Eileen Fahey

(Faculty and staff enjoying a quiet lunch moment.)

(Above, a PE class in the old Vogel basement.)

(Above, the pride of Torrington, the Vogel Viking band in the Memorial Day Parade, early 1990s.)

(Right, a popular bumper sticker) **My child made HONORS at VOGEL-WETMORE MIDDLE SCHOOL**

Bentley   Those Glorious Torrington Days

Bruce Fox   Bob Doyle & Tony Distasio

Mike Buzzi
(Left, Santa discovers there IS a Mrs. Fahey.")

Augie Killiany

Bentley   Those Glorious Torrington Days

(Above, Vogel boys basketball action in 1989 at the Torrington YMCA big gym. Fans Bob Doyle, Barbara and Cookie Anzellotti, and many others root for the boys. Coach Jeff Pavan on the right closely follows the play.)

(Above, the 1979 cheerleaders give it the old, Yea, rah-rah, fight Vogel fight!")

The Last Vogel-Wetmore Class Nears Graduation:

PLAYBILL
VOGEL-WETMORE
A NIGHT ON BROADWAY
CLASSNIGHT '93

PRODUCERS .... Dr. Anthony DiStasio
                                Mr. Michael Cerruto
                                Mrs. Carissa Keepin

DIRECTORS .... Ms. Lisabeth Milewski
                                Ms. Linda Regner

ARTISTIC DESIGN .... Mrs. Susan Pagano

PRODUCTION STAFF
    Cathy Allegrini, Wendy Angelovich, Jerry
    Ayantola, Stacy Banks, Pam Burns, Angela
    Calabrese, Jennifer Cilfone, Jennifer DiLeo,
    Rachel Golembeski, David Hermenau, Jesse
    LeManquais, Chris Neri, Kelly Thibault,
    Carl Thompson, Keila Thompson, Christina
    Weber, Katie Wilson, Todd St. Germain

PLAYBILL & PHOTO COVER DESIGN .... Bryce Lafferty
                                  Tom Herpich

STARRING .... The Class of 1993?

FILMING CREW .... Ms. Sue Ewart

MUSIC .... 2001 D.J.

TECHNICAL STAFF .... Mrs. Mary Kakroski
                              Mr. Richard Lehmann
                              Mrs. Marilyn Adams
                              & cafeteria staff
                              Mrs. Lorene Arsego
                              Vogel-Wetmore Staff
                              Mrs. Terri Reichen
                              & Vogel-Wetmore P.T.O.
                              Custodians

(A final look back at Vogel School from the parking lot which used to border the west side of Wetmore.)

The Night Torrington Exploded
July 4, 1990

(July 16, 1990. *The Register Citizen*. When I wrote this article, the worst fireworks accident in the history of our town, *and* "one of the state's worst fireworks accidents on record" according to the Waterbury *Republican-American*, had happened less than 2 weeks before. In trying to deal with the horrific tragedy, I tried to be optimistic about the future of the holiday in our borough, without negating the severity of what had just happened... Little did I realize just how much time would past before we would once again celebrate the 4th with annual fireworks. I've included in this 27+ year old article new sections: a Recap, Postscript, *and* recently gleaned 4th of July memories from townsfolk. Hopefully, all this adds depth to what was originally a fairly short and narrow piece.)

The misdirection of a 70-pound rack of mortar-like tubes at Torrington's Fourth of July celebration 12 days ago was a fiery tragedy, unlike anything this city has ever seen. Eighteen people were injured, one critically. Life Star performed a Medivac, while Charlotte Hungerford called in 50 additional medical personnel.

Recap: The night of Wednesday, July 4, 1990, was a sweltering 90° in which an estimated crowd of 10,000 turned out to not only celebrate the 4th but also Torrington's 250th anniversary. The show at Fuessenich was bigger and more expensive than in past years. Near the end of the spectacular aerial finale, at a little past 9:30, a rack of mortar tubes was blown out of its 3-foot burial hole (Previous page, the discharged rack). It fell onto the ground pointing directly at the crowd sitting on lawn chairs and blankets in the southwest corner of Fuessenich. (Below, a not-to-scale graphic that ran in the newspaper.)

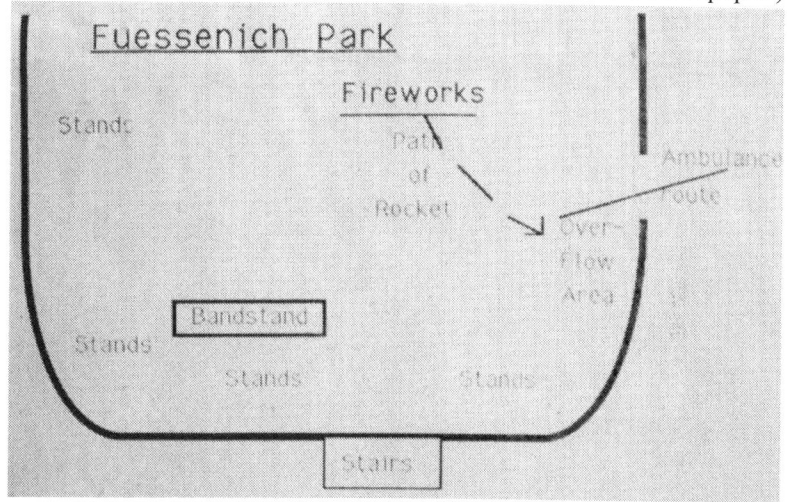

No one saw the rack; eyes were looking skyward. As shells burst overhead, and ohhhhs and ahhhs punctuated the night, a 6-inch shell from the grounded, horizontal rack fired point blank into the southwest throng 300-400 feet away. People described it like a grenade going off. There were 2 explosions, which sent "stars" off in different directions, with each "star" itself sending off even more stars. People were literally blown over. One eye witness described a rocket landing under the chair of a little girl. The explosion sent her flying. Those who had space, dove for cover. The corner was briefly illuminated by the light from the ground explosions, but quickly faded to black. Police and firework employees ran across the darkened field. Far off sirens wailed. Someone yelled for the Park lights to be turned on; they were. Yellow tape was quickly put up. Ambulances arrived. Medics, family, and bystanders attended the wounded amidst a haze of gunpowder in the air. Burns were soothed with cloths soaked in whatever liquid was available. Slowly the Park cleared. The Fourth of July 1990 was over.

❖ ❖ ❖ ❖

Like the where-were-you-when discussions of Pearl Harbor and the Kennedy assassination, the events of July 4, 1990, will be relived for decades. And well they should since Torrington has not seen such war-like ravaging since the 1955 Flood (8 dead, bread lines, water bags, $7 million in damage). Or the 1918 Influenza Epidemic (80 dead, 3,400 afflicted, churches and the high school transformed into auxiliary hospitals).

I was at Fuessenich Park only in a distant way. For the past 10 years I had sat with my wife and children in the very southwest cor-

(Above, July 4, 1988. Southwest corner of Fuessenich. Early loungers, including Joe Ducotey in the center, wait for the start of evening's program. Note the old track at the bottom of the picture.)

ner of the Park where the 6-inch shell exploded. But this year I was bothered by the heat and opted to let them go alone while I lay in front of a fan watching *Yankee Doodle Dandy* on TNT.

As I cooled off watching George M. Cohan, a.k.a. James Cagney hoofing it through such star-spangled tunes as You're A Grand Old Flag, Over There, and the title song, I began to feel patriotic and rejuvenated. By 9 p.m., though the movie wasn't over, I was ready for some real aerial fireworks. So I took The Drifters advice and went up on the roof.

It was quiet and dark sitting high up on the asphalt shingles. But the calm was brief as a 600-foot, multi-colored burst cleared the locust trees in my yard followed by a much delayed "thoomb." I loved it. Torrington fireworks without the hassle of crowds, parking the car, and dragging along blankets and folding chairs. . . Still, not perfect. Most of the rockets did *not* clear the trees, and forget any ground displays. . . I was experiencing mixed feelings by the time the wife and kids came home and told me about the accident. It was then, and listening to the late night news, and reading the newspaper the next day, that I learned just how much I'd missed.

Errant rocket explodes in crowd
Toddler critical; 13 others injured

✤ ✤ ✤ ✤

We Americans love the Fourth of July, a.k.a. Independence Day. And we love our fireworks. Abigail Adams writing from Boston in 1776 after the Declaration Of Independence was adopted observed, "The Bells rang, the privateers fired the forts & batteries, the cannon were discharged. . . & every face appeared joyfull." In 1789 Washington got a similar reception in New York City at his inauguration as president.

Nothing much has changed in 200+ years.

We Americans love noise, detonations, and color. We ignited them at Bush's inauguration, the Bicentennial, the Statue Of Liberty rededication, and we simulate them at baseball games on the scoreboard.

We mail order from the Dakotas and Carolinas for Roman candles, M-80s, sparklers, cherry bombs, bottle rockets, sky rockets, etc. despite the illegality and the danger. In the past several years fireworks have been blamed for destroying a Bridgeport church and a New Haven warehouse, for over 200 fires, and about 10,000 injuries a year.

Yet we love them, and we love them BIG! The more brazen, the better. Americans from all over the country tune into Macy's annual Blitzkrieg, a.k.a. the 4th of July fireworks show on NYC's East River. Hartford has Riverfest, and I guess Torrington is vying to join the big time with its biggest expenditure ever this year: $15,000 worth of force, sparkle, and flame.

Americans are certainly not whiz-bang shy, and never have been. Now *or* in the past.

✤ ✤ ✤ ✤

The Past. I guess I was a pretty typical Torrington youngster growing up as far as the 4th of July went, i.e. no matter what we did during the day back in the 1950s and '60s, the Bentleys always wound up at Fuessenich Park that night. (Below, a July 3, 1961, *Torrington Register* front page with the masthead changed to honor the upcoming Fourth.)

Most of those long ago fireworks shows blur together for me, but one that stands out happened in 1961 or '62. I wasn't with my family, but rather with a male friend *and* a sort-of girlfriend, i.e. a girl I had a crush on though nothing had happened up to this point. We weren't quite "going out," as we used to call it. . . The 3 of us sat in the grandstand behind home plate and watched the show through the chicken wire barrier. At some point my male buddy left. By the time it got dark, the teen girl was pressed up against my side. I could smell her perfume, and we were holding hands. . . That's it. Not much from a 2017 vantage, but back then, it was big time excitement. And it far surpassed the fireworks show on the field, i.e. the real fireworks were in the *grandstand*.

I recently asked some Torringtonians for their memories of the 4th of July at Fuessenich Park back in the 1950s and '60s. Here's what they said:

Maureen McCarthy Kerish: "I loved the waterfall fireworks ground display, and everyone singing 'God Bless America.' The red and blue kazoos – didn't we get them from WTOR? I remember a battle with a tank, can't remember what it was shooting at. I remember the feeling of comradery with the whole town, or so it seemed to a kid. Everyone laughing, singing, and having a wonderful time. No complaining or criticizing. Everyone leaving the park still talking about the show. There was no shoving to rush out. Maybe my memories are clouded by time, if so, let them stay that way. They're some of the happiest memories of my childhood."

Ernie Zavatkay: "The kazoo says it all. In 1956 I remember the first fireworks display after the flood at Fuessenich. It was the first time I saw the the old song 'Bicycle Built For Two' become an animated fireworks display while the entire crowd sang and kazooed, 'Daisy Daisy, give me your answer true' . . . Fantastic."

Louis Cornelio: "Wasn't it hailed as 'the world's largest kazoo band'? I mean, all of us with our kazoos!"

Jay Avallone: "I had my kazoo."

Anne Rothenberger: "My immediate thoughts are of the kazoo playing."

(Below, Cheryl Dwyer and Karen Bentley keep the tradition alive and play their kazoos at Fuessenich Park, July 1985.)

Laurie Zimmerman Canty: "Maybe 1968 or so, I remember there were kazoos. Moving fireworks to music such as 'A Bicycle Built for Two.'"

Tom Piccolo: "If you ever lost the thin piece of film that came with your kazoo, you could always replace it with a small piece of wax paper."

Tricia Frazier: "We would get there late in the afternoon to get our bleacher seat. The Leo many jazz favorites. You could sing along if you wanted to. When it started to get dark, the kazoo party would start with the sing along favorites. There were ground displays such as 'Bicycle Built For Two' and many pinwheels that were lit up with a lot of color. They were animated by the ground workers. The aerial displays would start when it got dark, I want to say around 8:30 p.m. There was a lot of noise and lots of smoke! It was always a great time."

Jane Bastasini: "I always loved the grand finale!!"

Angie Staino-Zav: "I always remember the finale where many fireworks were set off one-after-another!"

Carolann Higgins Pucino: "The Bicycle Built For Two."

Pat Fairchild: "The crowd singing, 'On a Bicycle Built For Two.' "

Karen Parente Beauchemin: "I remember the spinning wheel type of fireworks, lots of smoke, and huge crowds."

John Todor: "Who can forget the two lighted cars racing across the infield. One was always losing until it backfired and won the race."

Roberta Wilson: "Sitting in the bleachers chanting 'ooh ooh aah' feeling the ground shake. Almost scary for a little kid. But oh, so wonderful."

Roxy Adams: "I remember the hoola-hoop contests before the fireworks started and how the contestants would spin the several hoops around their waists for what seemed like forever."

Ray Romaniello: "Loved the cigar smell wafting through the park, just like at the baseball games. John Audia playing the accordion with band members on the bandstand."

Linda Larson: "John Audia played his accordion. We played our kazoos."

Joanne Audia Benedetto: "Those were the days! My uncles John, Mikey, and Sammy Audia were the Homesteaders led by Johnny. They played a lot during the week prior to the fireworks. Every night during that week was a theme. Streets and stores were all so busy.

(Below, a 1961 ad in *The Torrington Register* for a 4th of July sale at the always busy Stars on East Main.)

The Homesteaders also played at the fireworks. The fun was playing our kazoos. They were given to you ahead of time, but they also had them at the Park if anyone forgot his or hers. We used to sing along and have a great time with family and friends. And you also knew just about everyone."

Jean Reid: "If I remember correctly, WTOR supplied the kazoos. It was a wonderful event that everyone enjoyed and looked forward to. There were lots of fireworks. Remember the ones they set off to celebrate Our Lady of Mt. Carmel. There was also a dress up night where the kids got prizes for the best costumes. Oh, such great memories... Johnny Morris and Dick Kilbourne were always there."

Glen Bronson: "I do remember the Lady of Mt Carmel, vaguely. That was probably gone by the 1960s... I remember Al Eyre and Edmund William Waller from WTOR... You had to go real early to sit on the bleacher seats. Mr. DeBrot was always there for every event at Fuessenich Park."

Sheila Martinotti: "My son's birthday is the 4th of July. We always went to the fireworks after his birthday party. When he was a little boy he thought the fireworks were for him. Guess I forgot to tell him why we had them. The good old days in Torrington, 1969."

Lucille Fines: "I never went to the park, but instead all my relatives on my mother's side would go to our Uncle Sonny's (Felix Minnelli) house which was on View Street. He had a huge back yard which, when you went to the edge of it, you could see the whole park! We had our kazoos and our sparklers as we watched the festivities down below. I remember loving the ground fireworks! My favorite were the spirals that looked like giant pinwheels and the cannons facing each other that shot firework cannon balls back-and-forth. Also the finale that seemed to go on forever with the loud bangs at the end that would make your chest hurt and echo throughout the valley!"

(Below, the ground displays at Fuessenich mid-1980s. View is looking east. The lights of Torin Manufacturing across the river are visible on the left.)

Lois Reynolds: "I actually never went into the park on the 4th of July, but heard and saw the fireworks from different views around Torrington. It was always a time for a special spirit of community and excitement."

Rosemary Higgins Dill: "All school playgrounds had talent contests, and my group of three (no talent!) won ours. We got to perform at the fireworks before the big crowd. The director of the show didn't know what to do with us so we sang an old tune, 'Show Me The Way To Go Home' which required little talent!"

Barb Bruns: "Jim Fallon, my father, and we kids lived on Lipton Place. We lived in the grouping of houses right next to the outfield of the park. Even though we kids ran all over the place, we were always back in time to watch the fireworks. I remember watching the guys light and run. It was a source of amusement for an 8-year-old. Never watched from the bleachers because the view from my brothers' bedroom window was much better. We would have relatives and friends with us. I remember burning my hand on a sparkler after it went out. 'Don't touch it. You will get burned.' I learned the meaning of pain that evening. LOL. This was the mid-1960s-to-early-70s."

Delfina Canino McKenna: "I remember attending the Fourth of July festivities under the grandstand. There were ground fireworks. It was just magical to me. I was probably 7 or 8. We had immigrated from Italy in 1967, and I was in awe by all of it. . . There is something about kazoos that I love maybe the connection to the Fourth of July celebration at Fuessenich Park. I actually have a small collection."

Cheryl M. Pace: "I remember my Aunt Mary and I would take my son with us. We'd park in the old Torin parking lot and sit on her car to watch the show. I hope I never forget those days."

Leanne Lefkowski Symuleski: "I remember the accident, when the fireworks went into the crowd. It was so scary. So many people got injured. I remember hearing all of the sirens!"

Jenni Blake Mihalich: "I was down there and remember the accident was terrifying. I don't remember what year though."

Ed Killingbeck: "How naive were we, to shoot fireworks from essentially, the outfield? Took many years, before a mishap! When the Vagabonds finished our show, I remember feeling the falling debris on my face, as we sat right between second and first base! Yikes!"

✜ ✜ ✜ ✜

Danger. It's part of life, and it's a big part of our explosive celebrations and history. And whether the explosions are caused by artillery rounds *or* fireworks symbolizing *artillery* rounds, there will always be a risk factor. We need to learn from this year's 1990 tragedy and to minimize that risk for everyone's sake.

And yet we need to go on. Ron Kovic, a Vietnam veteran and author of *Born On The Fourth Of July*, wrote, "For me it began in 1946 when I was born on the Fourth of July. The whole sky lit up in a tremendous display, and my mother told me that the doctor said I was a real firecracker."

A real firecracker. George M. Cohan was also born on the 4th of July, as were George Steinbrenner, Nathaniel Hawthorne, Gina Lollobrigida, Eva Marie Saint, Calvin Coolidge, and many others. All firecrackers.

In a sense we were all conceived in independence on that day. Every American a firecracker.

Let's keep the conception alive.

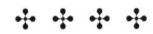

✜ ✜ ✜ ✜

Postscript

Despite my optimistic ending to that 1990 column, fireworks at Fuessenich Park *never* happened again. From 1991-'93 there were no fireworks anywhere in town on July 4, or at any other time. Physically, there was no place within the city limits where crowds could be kept back the new state-mandated distances. Psychologically, there was just not the will. Physical and metaphorical wounds town-wide had to heal and memories soften. In 1994, after a 4 year break, City Hall, in conjunction with the Park & Rec Department, decided on a novel approach. There would *only* be an aerial display, which would be launched from the city landfill, a.k.a. the old City Dump. Townspeople were encouraged to watch the fireworks from Toro Field down the South End, Route 8, the East Side of town, or from any high spot. To ease these less than stellar conditions, a Cruise Night was held earlier on Main Street and there was a polka contest at Fuessenich featuring music by Walt Dolecki. It was a decent solution to a tricky and sensitive situation. But it failed. The fireworks went off on schedule and without incident. But only a small number watched them. Most stayed home or went to other towns to get their explosive fix.

(Above, a mother and her son at John Toro Field watch Torrington's 4th of July fireworks in 1994 being set off high above them at the City Dump.)

It took 10 years and the building of the Vito Colangelo Sports Complex at the Middle School for Torrington fireworks to once again happen. From 2004-to-the-present the annual Independence Day blast has gone off without a hitch. Vendors sell their goods, parents bring their small ones, and all faces light up when fireworks begin.

The future of the 4th of July in Torrington is bright. And loud.

(Right, a 2013 cardboard poster advertising the annual event. This particular poster was rescued from a telephone pole on lower East Main following the celebration.)

One Last Whiz Bang

(Above the Triangle Club kazoo band takes part in the 4th of July festivities at Fuessenich Park in 1970. L-R: Charlie Ross, Ed Killingbeck, unknown, Charlie Ross's son Robert, Ray Carmignani, Larry Marola, and Norman Dubreuil. Photo compliments of Judy Marola Goddard.)

The Warner Hits Home
Grease Paint Strain

(*The Register Citizen*. August 2, 1991. Back in the early 1990s, and for quite a period thereafter, the Warner summer shows were large extravaganzas. The ensembles of children were often double cast which resulted in 100-200 children taking part. With the children came hordes of tagalongs: parent helpers, tech people, set builders, set painters, costume sewers, etc. It seemed as though everyone in Torrington and the area, if not directly involved in the production itself, had a family member or relative who was. . . The Bentleys were no exception. For the Warner's August 1991 production of *Annie*, playbill below, both my sons and wife were in the cast. I was the outsider looking in, and it was in that amused third-person spirit that I wrote the following column.)

Headlines in the summer of '91 have focused on monumental catastrophes: global warming, the ecological disaster in Kuwait, Lowell Weicker's mimicking a governor, etc. But right here in Torrington there is a phenomenon occurring at valley level which, should it get out-of-hand, would spell doom for realism and 3-dimensional advocates everywhere.

I call it the, "Grease Paint Strain."

Anyone who's been to recent Warner productions like *My Fair Lady, Wizard Of Oz,* or *Fiddler On the Roof,* knows that the casts have been getting larger and larger, involving more-and-more star-struck locals who have been weaned on Ed McMahon's *Star Search,* and who believe in Shakespeare's idea that all the world's a stage and all Torringtonites merely players.

(Above, a large hand-painted advertisement that hung on the side of Vitalo's Auto Body on the corner of East Pearl and Main. Back-in-the-day, "signs" of an upcoming Warner production were everywhere.)

Case in point is the Bentleys. We were an Ozzie-and-Harriet type family (call me Mr. Ozzie) until that fateful day in the winter of 1990 when my 11-year-old decided to try out for *My Fair Lady*. Since then it's been Bachelor Ozzie waiting in the wings while the rest of the Bentley troupe hoofs-and-sings its way through Warnerdom, and keeps a future eye on fame, fortune, and casting calls.

✣ ✣ ✣ ✣

Curtain up on yesterday morning. Wife is heating some mush and humming the overture to *Annie*. Hubbie Ozzie hates to be a critic, but feels a Siskel-and-Ebert urge coming on.

"Gee sweetie pie, you and the boys got back from rehearsal kind of late last night. About midnight? And rehearsal again tonight?" Husband risks a chance for cold mush.

Wife, looking a bit like a disheveled Miss Hannigan, "Hey, my little pig dropping, it's a hard knock life, ya know."

"I know, love bug, I know. But I'm feeling like an abandoned orphan myself."

"Leapin' Lizards! Why any kid would want to be an orphan is beyond me?"

"Huh?"

"Sorry. I keep falling into character. Guess I'm not fully awake. But don't worry. It'll be over soon, and the production is great! Another sellout. That old $150,000 Warner mortgage will be paid off before the board has another turnover, and then we'll be on Eeeasy Street." Flips mush and uncontrollably mutters, "Where you sleep till noon, ya ya yaaa," under her breath.

"Uhhh, honey poo, do you think that maybe you'd be better off to start following Albert Waller's advice, you know, the producer of that Torrington pilot. He said to make real life into drama, not visa versa."

"Honestly dear, what *are* you talking about? No partially renovated, old theater could ever kidnap my senses." Wipes off a bead of sweat and looks at outside thermometer which is reading close to 90°. Absentmindedly begins to sing, "The sun will come out tomorrow. Bet your bottom dollar that tomorrow, there'll be sun."

Slowly the boys, who are on their hands-and-knees scrubbing the floor, rise. They grab mops. Do a few intricate dance steps using the handles as partners, toss the mops aside, and join mother at a microphone which has mysteriously appeared. They do 3-part harmony on "just thinking about tomorrow," play it up big to the enraptured cat and hubbie audience, and for a boffo finish pick up the tempo and tap dance off in unison to beyond the refrigerator.

Husband stares open-mouthed and realizes the Great White Way of downtown Torrington has once again woven its spotlight magic. Husband tries to change the topic and yells to unseen performers, "*Annie* doesn't open for days. Why don't we get away for a couple?"

Trio dance back from beyond the refrigerator. They do 2 choruses of "Maybe (far away)" and for an unscheduled encore belt out, "N-Y-C, the whole world is coming."

Husband realizes that the situation is hopeless when wife thrusts her jaw forward like FDR, points to his pajamaed body, and implores, "Everyone sing. Republicans too, Oliver!"

Seeing that the histrionics are malignant, and knowing that it would be impossible anyway to indict a 1931 art deco theater with a 1991 abduction charge (statute of limitations), Hubby gives in.

The quartet is last seen passing into those Torrington lights; that never, never fantasy land somewhere beyond the rainbow. The Daddy Warbucks world where bread lines are short, optimism high, and where, "Annie is the key, yssirree, yssirree, yes sir. . ."

(Above, Brooke Tansley as Annie and Charlie Tirrell as Daddy Warbucks.)

(Above, a small part of the current cast takes a curtain bow.)

Dave Lopardo
A Man On The Run

(*The Register Citizen*. July 24, 1992. Having trumpeted all those bygone Vogel School voices earlier (pp. 12-43), I decided this article was a natural inclusion and followup. No one was more central to the Vogel scene, academic *and* sports, than Dave Lopardo. After the following article was published 25+ years ago, Dave went on to win a Gold T, post many more victories in both cross country *and* track & field, and continue to volunteer for The Torrington Road Race. Since his retirement from teaching he has published several books of short story collections, i.e. Dave Lopardo remains a man-on-the-run.)

Recognition, like fame, can be elusive even when it is highly deserving.

Consider. Vogel-Wetmore cross country coach Dave Lopardo has never won a Gold T, never been roasted, never had a race dedicated to him. Yet, Lopardo is the winningest active coach in Torrington still coaching his original sport.

Dave Lopardo is not the kind of individual to talk about any of this. When Lopardo talks about his team, which has included the boys and girls at Vogel since 1989, sincerity bubbles out from under his ever-present Pancho Villa mustache.

Dave, or "Spider" as his old friends call him, was "into a little bit of everything" growing up in Torrington. He played sandlot sports, Little League baseball, and Torrington High football. Fresh out of Western Connecticut in 1970, Lopardo coached the THS freshmen football team with Ed Evers for 2 years back when Ezio Bonetti was head coach. But then Lopardo slid into physical inactivity. By 1976, the 28-year-old high school English teacher weighed 240 pounds, and Lopardo knew he had to do something.

"I began running to lose weight," Lopardo told me last week, "and I made it my goal to run a marathon (26 miles, 385 yards) within a year."

Such a goal would have been unrealistic for most heavyweights, but Lopardo possessed an iron will that did not register on any scale. Within 10 months, Lopardo had run his first marathon.

"I ran it on a measured course in the THS parking lots in 3:51, even the 385 yards," Lopardo proudly recounted. The unique event was documented at the time by sportswriter John Torsiello, who noted that the students were cheering Lopardo during the last few miles.

Lopardo proved his self-measured marathon wasn't a fluke the following year when he ran in the 1978 Mayor Daley Marathon in Chicago. He pulled a muscle after 20 miles, but hobbled in to finish in a very respectable 3:45. (Right, Lopardo stretches in the autumn of 1978 prior to a road race in Hartford.)

Lopardo trained hard in those years, running 60-65 miles a week from his hilly home in the East End of Torrington. He ran for himself, he ran for others (in events such as the Hike For The Handicapped), and he ran for the competition.

"I ran competitively for four years, 1977-'80, including 4 Torrington Donor Day Races," Lopardo recalled. "The first two I enjoyed. The last two were too competitive, and I finally gave up racing because of the pressure I put on myself."

Ex-THS miler George Pollick was a long time rival of Lopardo's back in those years, and their duels in the 5-mile Donor's Day Race were fierce. Lopardo beat Pollick in the 1978 race, 32:47 to 33:59. It served to intensify the training for both runners for a rematch on a sweltering August day one year later. Lopardo fell behind early, choosing to come from behind. He overcame a substantial gap only to be out sprinted by the quicker Pollick, 31:13 to 31:15.

(Above, some Torrington Track Club members in 1978. L-R: Paul Bentley, George English, George Pollick, Jim Patten, Dave Lopardo, Walt Brothwell.)

As we talked, Lopardo smiled about that loss. Racing was no longer important to him. Volunteerism was. For the past 7 years Dave Lopardo has organized the finish line for that same Torrington race, which he will do again this year.

Also important to Lopardo are all the Vogel teams and athletes he's coached. He fondly recalled his "Bomb Squad" of 1983 and '84, a girls cross country team that went 24-0. The girls on that team were among the best ever in Torrington: Kim LeMere, Beth Sidlosky, Heather Moore, Molly Mueller, Beth Haegert, and Chris Kandefer. A large oil portrait of that team still graces Vogel's downstairs hall.

Lopardo recalled his exceptional male runners: Todd and Brian Mattiello, Steve Goodrow, and the undefeated boys' team of 1980.

He acknowledged the role of Tom Acerbi, the founder of Vogel's cross country team, and how Lopardo's own 1981 team had worn black arm patches in memory of Acerbi's tragic death. And Lopardo gave credit to Jon Hutchinson and Jim Patten for their unofficial help and advice in the early years.

(Below, Coach Lopardo and the 1992 Vogel boys cross country team poses at THS where they used to practice and "run" their home meets. This would be the last "Vogel" cross country team.)

The one thing that Lopardo didn't discuss were the hardships, but I knew he worked under many. With no other fall sports at Vogel, he's had close to 100 students out for the team year-after-year. Those are unmanageable numbers.

Until 1989, when Sue Ewart volunteered for a 2-year stint, Lopardo has had no outside help. The press doesn't cover his meets; Lopardo writes them up himself in the best Grantland Rice tradition.

There is no major booster club, or parents' group, or school support. BUT, Lopardo still manages to have team photos, awards, and an end-of-the-season banquet. He pays for much of it out of his own pocket.

As the years have passed, Dave Lopardo has added the responsibilities of marriage to the lovely Mary Ann, three daughters, two dachshunds, and a house. In 1989 Lopardo instituted Vogel's first ever girls' track team. That team went 7-0 in 1990 and is 22-4 overall.

Track and field is his new love.

"So much depends on the coach being on top of things," Lopardo said. He didn't mention, though I knew, that track and field is a 3-ring circus, i.e. so much going on simultaneously, i.e. tough to keep "on top of things." But Lopardo seems to thrive on being challenged and juggling many activities. He says that it is *track* that he will concentrate on in the future, and that this will be the last year for cross country and him.

⁘ ⁘ ⁘ ⁘

As we talked in Lopardo's kitchen last week with his dog Cookie on his lap, daughter Tammy beside him, and magnets from all over the world covering his refrigerator, I thought of the Frank Capra line, "The richest man in the world."

No one can have it all. But, Dave Lopardo comes close. He's a father, teacher, coach, volunteer, hockey player, and military gamesman.

Running has been an out-and-back course for him. Having made the turn, he's headed home. A man who is reaping what he's sowed.

A man on the run.

Postscript

Dave Lopardo and I recently met for a 2017 morning chat at the Good Company Coffee House on Franklin Street. He had a pot of tea, I had a mug of coffee, and we both enjoyed a pastry. The conversation was light and easy, as it should be between 2 old friends and coaching rivals. Many were the times my cross country teams at Har- Bur Junior High met his Vogel Vikings. It was always a good, close meet.

Dave is still volunteering at the an- nual Tor- rington Road Race. And he con- tinued coaching track and cross country long after Vogel School, i.e.

long after the move to the new middle school.

I frequently see Dave and Mary Ann at "oldies" concerts both at the Warner and Infinity Music Hall. And I see Dave every summer at the Main Street Marketplace selling his books. One year he rented space and a tent for the entire summer. He's still a man on-the-move, still looking ahead, still a tough man to keep up with.

(Above, English teachers Dave Lopardo and Paul Putnoki in the halls of Vogel, 1978, interact with students.)

(Right, author Dave Lopardo sells his books at the 2016 Main Street Marketplace.)

Torrington People
Us Folks Is Mellow

(*The Torrington Voice*. April 1, 1993. On April Fool's Day, 24 years ago I pulled a first. Not only did I have 2 articles published in the same issue of *The Voice*. **BUT**, neither had my byline on it. The other article was the April Fool's joke of Steven Spielberg coming to Torrington to make a movie, which I reprinted in *My Torrington Days*. That column ran under the byline Luap Yeltneb ["Paul Bentley" backwards]. This article ran under the byline "Joe Torrington," and that's the voice I adopted, i.e. that of a wise cracking, older cynic with a hairline of eternal optimism. I've simplified the dialect in this reprint and deleted the *many* dated local references.)

If you've been doing more this winter den fighting your way through humps of snow banks. If you've been occupied with more'n keeping it under 12 items at Stop 'n Shop's express line. Or if yer senses of right and wrong's been shaken up by more'n the potholes on Water Street, den your brains is telling you this town, this Torrington, this little 4-exit stop on Route 8 has had it mighty easy in the great world of international kooks, dips, dweebs, and weirdos.

All you FOJs (Friends Of Joe) know that ole Joe ain't just laying some Bubba City Hall BS on you when he says that Torrington people is mellow people. Sure we get excited occasionally about things like the $13 million renovation to Vogel, or the mayor handing some political crony a $6 million insurance account, or the acquisition of Stillwater deal flowing past us like water over the Brass Mill. (Below, Brass Mill Dam with the spillway on the left.)

But, all-in-all we native T-towners, and all you new immigrants too, keep a pretty low profile. It's just too bad we can't export some of our natural mellowness, our valium what-me-worry lifestyles. If the rest of the world could only take a T-town stress management course, the world might not be wrapped so Danskin tight.

Consider that whacko in Waco, David Koresh, and his standoff with federal agents. Such a thing could never happen in Torrington. To begin with there hasn't been a cult even close to Torrington since the 1970s when Brother Julius said he could walk on the water of Northfield Dam, though of course he bowed out saying if you believe I can do it, what's the point of me actually doing it? T-towners just ain't cult types, though we certainly love our cold cuts: salami, ham, prosciutto, capocollo, even baloney. We love Subway, Blimpie's, Carbone's, and Salerno's (Below, right, in the North End.)

We're not excitable enough to ever go extreme religion, though extreme grinder, yes.

And the shooting of that abortion doctor wouldn't happen here either. Anti-abortionists would never target Torrington because there's simply no abortion here, because there's simply no sex. Nothing. Nowhere. And I have that on the highest authority: the night clerks at Super 8 Motel, Days Inn, and the Pedlar. (Below,

diners outside the Pedlar, i.e. they dine inside, they dine outside, and that's what T-towners care about, i.e. food not sex. . .)

Think about the bombing of the World Trade Center. The tallest building here is the Towers (Right), and Muslim fanatics would never hit that because: 1. Everyone loves our elderly, especially the Beltone/Miracle Ear people. 2. Our Arab population is laid back and more into wrapping food in grape leaves than wrapping columns with C-4.

Yep, the world could use a T-town, nonaggression skin patch. Storm Josh dumps 18 inches of snow and do residents get hyper? No way. We ladle soup, shovel snow, wave friendly middle fingers at city trucks plowing our driveways back in. And we stayed glued to the exclusive WSNG techniweather forecast, being careful, of course to stay within its 3-mile broadcast range.

Shawmut Bank gets robbed, and we laugh about the bumbling crook running around the slopes of Ski Sundown in a t-shirt. We yuck it up more over hospital fundraisers while the CHH president pulls in $196,962 a year. And we roll in the aisles when we hear talk about a Mark Industry union and holding the line on the city budget.

We Torringtonites is so mellow, so full of mirth that if John Brown was alive today, he'e be line dancing at the Water Street Station instead of lining up crosshairs at Harper's Ferry.

We're sunshine in the dark of the world. We're warmth on a planet's cold toilet seat. We're a class act, a top hat and song-and-dance routine. You all know the words. Come on, join in: "Get your coat and grab your hat. Leave your worries on the doorstep. Life can be so sweet. On the sunny side of a Torrington street. . ."

Keep singing.

Who loves ya, baby.

Banking At The ATM
Growing Older By The Granny

(New Article. February 8, 2017. The thing about living in Torrington is that there's always the possibility for adventure, even in the most mundane, routine tasks. You just need to keep your eyes, ears, and sense of humor open.)

So around 11 this morning I decide to swing by the ATM at Torrington Savings Bank on Dibble Street. Figure at this time of day I should breeze through.

As I turn into the bank's driveway I see a car's already in front of the drive-up ATM. Figure these transactions never take long. Pull behind the Chevy sedan. Notice right away that it seems pretty far away from the ATM , and I smile thinking how long the arms of this person must be to have reached the touch-responsive screen.
    Long seconds pass. I now see that it's a small female head behind the steering wheel. I figure she must be stashing the money in her purse. More long seconds pass. Lots of them.
    Finally, the car opens. Slowly. Very slowly as if the driver is afraid of slamming it into the wall. Which would be just about impossible from this distance. Once the door is fully open, it takes awhile for a

pair of legs to swing out. The old gal rises using the door as leverage. I'm practically open-mouthed.

Once on her feet, she lets go of the door and moves slowly around the door unaided. I'm thinking the only way this could take longer is if she had to get a wheelchair or walker out of the trunk, and use it. . . Time stands still. Can she actually see this transaction through to the end before the hearse arrives?. . . Purse opens. Search for the ATM card? I'm figuring even if she finds it, she'll never get it to actually work. Not in my lifetime anyway, which is getting shorter by the hour. . .

It occurs to me that maybe this granny is confused. Maybe thinks she's at Foxwoods or Mohegan Sun and that this gizmo in front of her is a slot machine.

Surprise, surprise. She finds her card, and uses it. . . slowly. . . but apparently correctly. She takes her money. Clutches it like a winning lottery ticket. Moves back around the door and settles painstakingly into the car, ass end first, like the old Queen Mary docking.

More long seconds. No brake lights. Apparently she's stowing her money and possible reorganizing her purse. Finally brake lights, and she pulls away with all the speed of a pedal car.

I pull forward, hours older, but happy that I never beeped or yelled for her to use the ATM that's just inside the front doors. Apparently banking brings out the best in the now older me.

The Dark Brunette Side Of The Wild Blue Yonder
Female Pilots In Combat

(*The Torrington Voice*. May 27, 1993. Back in the 1990s I wrote quite a few articles using the voice of "Joe Torrington." I set him up; he delivered the zingers. This article was the only one that didn't deal with a local issue. I'm reprinting it here because, although the topic is no longer timely, there are *still* plenty of chauvinists around who think a woman's place is in the kitchen. Or, at least on the ground. . . And I still *do* find old Joe amusing. . .)

News Item: May 1993. Female Army pilots begin combat training on Cobra and Apache attack helicopters. Air Force to start female training soon on F-15 Eagle fighter-bombers.

When I read the above AP release, I was struck by the same sense of awe I felt when I saw Flipper perform. I mean, sure, I knew it was possible to train a dolphin to balance a ball on its nose. But why would the dolphin want to? Similarly, why would a female want to go in harm's way and at Mach 1 or 2? There are certainly more pleasant ways of buying the farm.

I knew there was only one person who could supply an answer: Joe Torrington. I found him at that all male bastion, the Elks bar. I came right to the point.

"Joe, you read the news. Why would any woman in her right mind want to fly an Apache chopper in combat? Risk getting blown to tampon-sized smithereens? Smeared like ruby red lip gloss all over a nice clean canopy? Why?"

"Why?" Joe swirled his swizzle stick in his gin-and-tonic. "What do you know about women and flight? Anything?"

I remembered Amelia Earhart, Jackie Cochran, Sally Ride, Meryl Markham, Tinkerbell, Wendy, Supergirl, Mary Poppins, and the Flying Nun. But I said nothing.

"Pay attention," Joe ordered. "Back in my day there were 40,000 Air Wacs in WWII and an elite group of 1074 American females who piloted aircraft, but not in combat. Women in more recent times have been flying military aircraft since 1977. They go on search-and-rescue missions, conduct reconnaissance, etc."

"And all that's not enough? They need combat too?"

(Above, a Paul Hultman, Joe Torrington cartoon.)

"Apparently. It's the natural evolution of the species. Women have chased distance, altitude, and speed records. They've flown in everything from biplanes, to dirigibles, to the space shuttle. It's only natural they'd now want some firepower like Hellfire anti-tank missiles, 2.74 inch rockets, a ventral-mounted 30 mm chain gun, AIM-91 Sidewinder missiles, perhaps a TOW system, some Harpoon or Penguin missiles."

"Women killers? Joe, I may be old fashioned, but I still think a woman's role to give life, sustain it, nurture it. Military nurses and doctors. Support services. Maybe Medivac pilots."

"Come on, Paul, join the 1990s! Women have as much right as anyone to cluster bomb entrenched troops. Why should they be denied the right to seek-and-destroy; to strafe, napalm, incinerate, and if necessary, nuke?. . . These are push button Amazons. Female American gladiators. These are women, America's best." Joe began to sing, "One hundred women, they'll test today. But 3 win the green F-15."

"Sounds reasonable to me."

"And remember, Paul, without combat, where are are the career opportunities? The new policy is projected to open up more than 5000 additional officer, warrant, and enlisted positions. A lot more jobs. A lot more rank."

"More jobs, I understand. But more rank?"

"Sure. Medals and war stories. Who wants some General Betty Broom straight from a career in supply, personnel, or finance sitting around NATO or the Joint Chiefs with her marksmanship medal and Good Conduct ribbon, when the old one-ups-man-ship starts. What's she going to say when the boys start tossing around low level jumps into Grenada, the dog fights over Baghdad, the air-to-ground support in Nam? Well guys, it was really heck getting that last minute inventory of field jackets straightened out?"

"So, she gets some combat time, some medals for valor, and a promising military career is hers?"

"Provided she can get it straight from the beginning and act like a real military pilot. Anyone can learn to fly. Can she swagger? Stand around with hand-on-hip looking as if she just bagged a guy? Forget about being the fairer sex. Can she do shots-and-beers? Can she get a meaningful tattoo like a Tomahawk Cruise Missile with a meaningful caption like, We kill for peace?. . . And finally, she'd have to be able to answer a few simple questions:

7. Will dog fights now be known as cat fights?

6. In a future sequel to *Top Gun*, who will be on top during sex: Tom Cruise or Kelly McGillis?

5. Will approved aircraft nose art now include the Chippendales?

4. Will helicopter blades now be neutral and rotate both ways?

3. Who is the wind beneath your wings? Is the position open?

2. Which one doesn't fit: Eddie Rickenbacker, Chuck Yeager, Jimmy Doolittle, Orville Wright, Mrs. Sky King, or Rin Tin Tin?

1. If you want to be a high tech pilot, why are you reading this nonsense?

Those are my questions, Paul. Sooooo off we go, with that wild brunette yonder. . ."

Daniel J. Hoffman
Torrington's Greatest Baseball Player

(*The Torrington Voice*. July 22, 1993. Torrington has had quite a number of stellar baseball players play in the minor leagues. But, the only two local baseballers to my knowledge to have ever made it to The Bigs were Tad Quinn and Daniel J. Hoffman. Hoffman, by far, had the longer and superior career. . . The information presented here comes from old articles in *The Torrington Register*, clippings sent me from the Baseball Hall Of Fame at Cooperstown, books, and the remembrances from several of Hoffman's relatives. This article was originally a 3-part series, with over a 2 year interim between Parts 1 and 2. What's presented here is a combination of mainly Parts 2 and 3 with many, *many* paragraphs and much extraneous information omitted for purposes of length.)

Daniel J. Hoffman, "Danny" to turn-of-the-century Torrington residents, was simply the greatest baseball player to ever emerge from our borough. It's a claim that bears up well even after 90 years.

Danny Hoffman was born in 1880 in either Canton or Collinsville depending on whose documentation is believed. He moved to Torrington at a tender age and lived here with his family at 189 North Elm (The house is no longer there.). His father worked in the Excelsior Needle Company (Below, a drawing of the old Needle

Shop in 1897), and it's likely the family came here for that job and to be near their relatives, the McLeods.

Danny attended local schools, and like other town boys became greatly interested in baseball. Sports back in those grime-filled factory years provided an outlet for the young and old alike to see a world beyond the back breaking labor of everyday life. It's well within the realm of possibility that the young Hoffman was awe stricken by romantic baseball tales in the popular *Tip Top Weekly* (Right), and later by *The Sporting News* and Richard Fox's *The National Police Gazette,* 2 barbershop and parlor fixtures with their starry-eyed sports pictures and headlines depicting pugilists, horse racers, and ballists. Couple this national elevation of sports, baseball in particular (It was called "the national pastime"), with the fact that life held very few other diversions compared to today, and it was only natural that the sandlots in turn-of-the-century Torrington were filled with youngsters pitching-and-batting.

Danny Hoffman, most likely, in those years played with his cousins the McLeods. The McLeods were a ball playing family, and they represented some of the finest ballists in town. Their influence on Danny would have been substantial.

By the summer of 1899, the 19-year-old Danny Hoffman was playing baseball for the Union Hardware (the old Skate Shop) team in Torrington's Factory League. During that era the mills in most towns had baseball teams: Coe Brass, Hendey's, the Brass Mill, the Needle Shop, et al. And the level of play was fiercely competitive. They'd play evenings and weekends, and the victors furnished prestige for the winning factory.

In a typical game against Hendey's that 1899 summer, Dan Hoffman pitched, balked twice, struck out 8, walked 6, batted 3-for-5, and stole 1 base.

In the summer of 1900, Hoffman continued to play for Union Hardware, while working there, of course. A player had to be on the payroll to be on the team. Hoffman was also the team manager, and in 1900 protested a game against Hendey's saying that pitcher Murphy was not on Hendey's payroll. It is a clear demonstration of Danny Hoffman's sense of fair play. (Below, the old Union Hardware on Migeon Avenue in 2009, looking west through the main gate.)

Danny Hoffman stood 5'9" with a weight that seldom fluctuated over the years from 175. He had shoulders that sloped 45°, a barrel chest, thick wrists, straight powerful legs with calf muscles that ballooned his form-fitting knee socks. He had tremendous eye-hand coordination and undoubtedly a plethora of fast-twitch muscle fibers. In those early years he possessed a youthful, unlined face that would develop lines under the eyes and crow's-feet in the corners by the time he was 28. He always had a mouth that pinched in at the corners, suggesting amusement and the start of a smile. He batted lefty, threw left-handed, and his local play was reported as "gilt-edged." He was also reputed to be *no* wallflower, enjoyed dancing, and one who knew him in later years described him in the relative term "wild."

By the end of the 1900 season, Danny Hoffman finished first place in batting for the Factory League with a .460 average, and Union Hardware won the League. On September 28, 1900, a headline read, "Records Show Dan Hoffman To Be The Find Of The Season." He was said to be a "crack twirler. . . clever. . . with an ability that is not confined to pitching and hitting." A game was played in October, before which Danny Hoffman was presented with a gold watch, then went 4-for-6 at the plate.

In the spring of 1901 Hoffman was playing on the town teams of both Waterbury and Torrington. He was Captain of the latter, while Dave Corcoran managed. As a pitcher he was reported to have a curve that the opposition "was unable to solve." A spectating reporter said of Hoffman's temporary playing of 3rd base, "His work on the sack was a feature of the evening's exhibition. Slow and fast balls were handled by the neatest of fashion, and though handicapped by a left-hand throw, the sphere was sent over to McDermott at first in ample time to retire the best of base runners." Hoffman batted .437 in 1901, and had a fielding percentage of .918. MVP caliber play.

On October 18, 1901, Dan Hoffman lay injured in his North Elm home, ironically *not* from all the baseball he played, but from his job at Union Hardware. He had injured his forefinger, was suffering from blood poisoning, and was confined to home. Hoffman's whole right arm was affected, and though he appeared to be recuperating, it was predicted that it would be "some time before Dan will resume his duties."

(Right, a Danny Hoffman baseball card from when he played with the Philadelphia Athletics of the American League.)

Hoffman's bedridden situation didn't last long. On November 25, 1901, he took the 7:45 train to Millerton, NY and wed Minnie Leaden of Waterbury, "a Brass City belle whose acquaintance the clever southpaw had formed during the summer when he played with that city." Despite his attempt to keep the wedding quiet, Hoffman's many friends gathered to wish the newly wedded couple "hearty congratulations."

One can speculate that the winter of 1901/1902 passed full of high expectations for the newlywed ballplayer. His factory job must have seemed like a dead-end hell waiting to engulf his physical talents. Dreams of making the pros, no doubt, filled his head, and it would seem likely he worried about suffering more future injuries in that deleterious factory environment.

Fortunately, his professional dreams soon came to fruition. On April 18, 1902, Dan Hoffman left Torrington and reported to Springfield where he joined the town team of that Massachusetts city. He was now playing in the semi-professional Connecticut League, a step up from the amateur competition he'd previously faced. He rose to the occasion. He led the league in pitching and finished close to the top in batting.

The legendary Connie Mack (left) of the Philadelphia Athletics met with Hoffman and his Springfield manager Roger Connor in NYC when the season was over. A deal was struck. Mack agreed to pay Connor $1000 for Hoffman's release. Mack gave Hoffman some advance money and told him to report in the spring.

Danny Hoffman was going to the Major Leagues!

Dan arrived back in Torrington, grabbed his new wife Minnie, and they moved to New Britain where they spent the winter. Why New Britain, when his family was living in Torrington? Possibly playing in Springfield had gotten him used to the big city lights. Possibly something else; the reason was never stated in the press. What is clear is that it began a pattern of restlessness for Danny Hoffman that would follow him the rest of his days. He had learned the game in Torrington, as the newspaper pointed out, *but Torrington was now behind him.*

Shortly after signing Danny Hoffman, Connie Mack told the assembled reporters, "This man Hoffman is a fine ballplayer, and if he don't make good, I will be very much disappointed. He is one of the fastest men in the country getting down to first and a good hard left field hitter." Years later in a 1945 biography on Connie Mack, author Frederick Lieb noted, "Connie acquired a great young outfield prospect, Danny Hoffman, from Springfield, Massachusetts. Danny, one of Mack's early favorites, joined the A's with a good pitching record, but the tall taciturn quickly told him to forget about pitching and concentrate on outfield play."

Would Connie's Mack's confidence in Danny Hoffman be justified? Would Daniel J. Hoffman be able to play against the likes of Cy Young, Christy Mathewson, Ty Cobb, *or* would his days on sun-speckled, big city playing fields be just a brief walk-in-the-sun? Glove and spikes in hand, come the spring of 1903, Danny Hoffman would find out. . .

✧ ✧ ✧ ✧

Early in May 1903 it was front page Torrington news when Dan Hoffman got in for the last inning against Boston. Unfortunately, he struck out. On May 12 Hoffman had "4 sensational catches" and hit a triple. By the end of 1903, Dan Hoffman had played in 74 games for the Philadelphia Athletics, hit 5 doubles, 7 triples, 2 homeruns, and batted .246. It was an excellent rookie season, but it was not without controversy. At one point during that '03 summer, Danny Hoffman became restless sitting on the bench (Connie Mack didn't feel Hoffman had enough experience to jump right into big games), and the former Torrington ballist "jumped to the Toledo Club of the American Association. However, Hoffman had a sober second thought before many days, and returned to the Athletics."

On October 14, 1903, following the season, Hoffman returned to Torrington briefly, no doubt to visit his family and friends. He announced to the press he was leaving for Cleveland, but would return to Torrington to spend the winter months if, "I can find a suitable position." It's uncertain if that position was ever found, but it's unlikely. Future whistle stops for him in Torrington would become sporadic, brief, and intended only to hug mom and shake the old man's hand.

The 1904 season started off great for the 24-year-old Torringtonite. In May he participated in a double play "making a pretty throw from the outfield and cutting off a run at home plate."

Shortly after that, against Chicago, Hoffman hit safely 4 times including *two* in-the-park-home-runs. He was, in his time, said to be one of the fastest outfielders who ever wore spiked shoes.

All went well till about halfway through the '04 season. *Then,* disaster struck. Danny Hoffman was batting against Boston's Jesse Tannehill (left) when the left-handed hurler pitched a fast "inshoot." Sidebar: Tannehill was only 5'8" and 150 pounds. But he was one of the best pitchers of his era, and had a fast arm and threw hard. Connie Mack later said that Hoffman, "seemed in a trance at the plate and just couldn't get out of the way of that pitch." The ball struck Hoffman directly under the right eye, almost forcing it out of the socket. It was reported that Hoffman "dropped like a felled steer." Mack would later say that Hoffman looked terrible with that eye out. All night long Connie Mack waited at the hospital until he was told that everything possible was being done for Danny. He would live, and there was a good chance of saving the eye.

Hoffman eventually returned to action for a few games of that 1904 season and wound up with 204 at bats and a .299 average. But it wasn't a total success. Connie Mack: "When he (Hoffman) returned to my lineup, I had to do what looked like a heartless thing. I had to let him bat against Tannehill when Jesse next pitched against us. I hated like anything to do it, and Hoffman was pathetic at the plate. Jesse struck him out 4 times. But I had to do it to restore Danny's confidence and keep him in the league."

Baseball would never again be the same for Danny Hoffman. He would eventually lose sight in that right eye, and the Philadelphia specialists who treated him expressed the opinion that his ball days were over. They weren't. Hoffman played with one good eye for 7 more seasons though according to a 1907 news article, he never again could negotiate left-handed pitching with authority. Because he batted left-handed, the pitch from a left-handed pitcher came down the first base side, and Danny's lead right eye could not effectively pick it up.

Still, Hoffman played in 120 games the next year, 1905, and as if to refute the Philadelphia medics, he batted .261 and led the American League in stolen bases with 46. Yet, manager Connie Mack was not totally pleased with Hoffman. Hoffman was a thinking player and not above speaking his mind. Hoffman and Mack had a "misunderstanding" during games with Chicago, and Mack suspended his star outfielder when Hoffman failed to follow the manager's instructions. It probably involved base running. Hoffman liked to be given some free rein saying that, "Good coaching is a factor, but runners must take the initiative themselves." Connie Mack replaced Hoffman with a chunky Pennsylvania boy, Briscoe Lord, and Philadelphia clinched the pennant not long after.

(Above, the 1905 Philadelphia Athletics, American League champions. Danny Hoffman is in the front row, second from left.)

It was World Series time for Danny Hoffman!

The 1905 championship was the first modern World Series, and it pitted the Philly A's against John McGraw's NY Giants. Unfortunately, Danny Hoffman was only used once as a pitch hitter against the great right hander Christy Mathewson. Hoffman struck out, but his replacement, Bris Lord, didn't fare much better getting a mere 2 singles for 20 at-bats. Torrington fans following The Series were upset that Mack hadn't played Hoffman more, but at least Hoffman had the consolation of being on a pennant winning team, riding in an open barouche for a huge Philadelphia parade followed by fireworks and a banquet, and receiving $823 for the loser's share of The Series purse.

(Left, Daniel Hoffman on the cover of a souvenir program.)

In November 1905, Danny Hoffman arrived in Torrington and, elaborating on The Series, told a *Register* reporter that he'd only been given one chance, and that was in the 9th inning when the game was already lost. Hoffman felt they could have beaten the Giants if, "We'd been in proper form." The reference here is probably to an injured Rube Waddell being unable to pitch, and Hoffman himself sitting the bench. Dan closed the interview by saying he had hopes he'd be playing soon for the NY Americans. Then Hoffman left for Philadelphia where he now ran a bowling alley off-season. His wife was *not* going to accompany him.

In April 1906 Dan Hoffman started with the Philadelphia Athletics, played in 7 games (5 for 22), then, as he'd predicted, got traded to the NY Americans (Also known as the NY Highlanders. They would become the NY Yankees in 1913). He played in 107 games total that year and batted .254. He was back with New York for the 1907 season, played in 136 games, and batted a steady .253. The September 28, 1907, issue of the *National Police Gazette*, which was *the* sporting publication long before there was a *Sports Illustrated*, ran a full page picture of Danny Hoffman in his southpaw throwing stance, with the caption, "Danny Hoffman. The fleet centre fielder of the New York American League Club who has few equals in playing the outer garden."

It was a hell-of-a tribute. (Picture on opposite page).

A month later on October 7, 1907, Danny Hoffman, Kid Elberfeld, Slow Joe Doyle, Tacks Neuer, Rudy Bell – all of whom were stars for the NY Highlanders – along with some substitutes, "put up" at the Hotel Garde in Hartford. They were joined by Manager Doyle of Torrington's Coe Brass team along with some other, old Torrington friends of Dan's. They attended a vaudeville performance at Poli's Theater, and the next day they all set out for the Harwinton Fair in a large touring car. Hoffman had promised to show some of his more sophisticated pro-mates the sights, sounds, and smells of the livestock and country fair. He promised them yokes of oxen and the sight of long-whiskered natives who were only seen once a year on fair day. It was the Hoffman sense of humor.

In the spring of 1908, Hoffman was traded to the St. Louis Browns of the American League. The Sunday supplement to *The St. Louis Republic* ran a close-up portrait of Dan Hoffman with the caption: "He (Hoffman) is considered one of the great outfielders of the game, combining with his speed one of the best and most accurate throwing arms." It was also mentioned that Hoffman was now residing in Bridgeport, Connecticut.

(Left, a baseball card of Danny Hoffman when he was with St. Louis.)

Hoffman played in 99 games in 1908 and batted .251. In 1909 he increased his output and played in 110 games and batted .269.

In 1909 he was voted "Most Popular Member of the St. Louis Browns" by patrons of the Suburban Garden Theatre, and he was given a large, 3-handled, sterling silver cup. The cup is spectacular. It has engraving on 3 sides between the handles and on the base. It has 2 sections in bas-relief: one with a baseball player in a batting stance and the other of crossed pennant flags in the St. Louis Browns colors of orangey brown and maroon.

The 15-inch high cup (above) today is heavily tarnished but still retains the glory of its original owner, who dazzled his fans both on- and-off the field. The cup is in the possession of his relatives.

On September 30, 1909, a baseball game was scheduled to be played at League Park (Fuessenich). It was to pit a couple of teams made up of barnstorming, post-season professionals, of which Danny Hoffman was one. It was never reported if the game was played, but one can imagine the excitement Hoffman must have felt at the prospect of it, i.e. a grandstand of old friends and once again standing on the field where it all began. . . For whatever reason, 3 weeks later on October 25, 1909, Dan Hoffman sold his lone real estate holding in Torrington (376 Migeon Avenue) and moved completely to Bridgeport.

Passing the winter of 1909-'10, Dan Hoffman did some writing and sent a lengthy column to the *St. Louis Republic* on base stealing. Hoffman had swiped 226 bases in the last 8 years and was acknowledged as one of the best in the game. His observations were first rate, e.g. "Speed is a fine equipment, but it is not essential. Few ten-second (in the 100 yard dash) men have blossomed into big league material in the base running department." He talked about watching the fielder's eyes, varying strategies, bluffing, getting pitchers and catchers to worry, being innovative, and he talked about a player making his own breaks... From the article it's clear that Hoffman was a good-humored, literate athlete who valued clear thinking and personal initiative. It's also clear that the same strength of will power and character that allowed him to continue in baseball after his 1904 beaning and loss of vision, was the same strength that inevitably brought him into conflict with tight reined managers.

(Left, a 100+ year-old pinback.)

On that field of dreams in 1910, Hoffman played in 106 games for St. Louis and batted .237. Age and his vision were taking their toll. Finally in the 1911 season Hoffman's average dipped to .210 after 24 games, and St. Louis decided Hoffman's time had come. Midway through the season he was dropped to the minors.

The show was over. Danny Hoffman would never again play Major League ball.

For the remainder of 1911 he went to a club in Indianapolis, while 1912 found him in St. Paul. For the 1913-'15 seasons he was with Wilkesbarre, Pennsylvania, in the New York State League where he batted .316, .250, and .306 in those 3 years and played in a total of 370 games.

By 1916, Dan Hoffman was 36-years-old and was at the very end of his playing days. He began that spring for Bridgeport in the Eastern League, but it didn't go well. After 19 games he was flawless in the field, but he was batting only .222 with 1 stolen base. It was time to call it a day. On June 23, 1916, Daniel J. Hoffman was released from the Bridgeport team. Ironically, his baseball career, which had begun in a Connecticut town that he called home, now ended in a Connecticut town he called home.

It was never a long walk to the ball park.

✣ ✣ ✣ ✣

From here the trail of Danny Hoffman grows cold. It's known his mother and father, along with his brother and one sister, still lived in Torrington, though the parents might have separated; they lived at different addresses. Danny and his wife remained in Bridgeport, though whether or not he enjoyed life away from his adoring fans, whether or not he worked, had any source of income, enjoyed hobbies, enjoyed married life, etc. is unknown. They did not have children.

Danny Hoffman's adult life had been an itinerant one, a journey through many towns, many hotel rooms. It had been a physical life, but one that was now over. Hoffman suffered a general health breakdown, but it was his wife who went first. On January 25, 1920, Minnie Hoffman was buried in a 6-member plot owned by her family (Leaden) in St. Michael's Cemetery in Stratford. She was only 34.

After his wife's death, Danny Hoffman moved to Manchester, probably to the home of his sister Mrs. Louis Drager. His father, John P. Hoffman, who had moved from North Elm Street to Dewey Street to Wolcott Avenue through the 1910s, left Torrington in 1922, I believe, to join Danny and John's daughter in Manchester. The father had been ill himself for a decade.

> **THE TORRINGTON REGISTER**
>
> **DEATH TAKES DAN HOFFMAN, BALL PLAYER**
>
> Daniel J. Hoffman, one time a baseball star with national reputation, died yesterday at the home of his father in Manchester. "Dan" spent the early part of his life in Torrington, attended school here and worked here, and leaves a host of friends in this town. His death was due to a general breakdown and followed a long illness. The surviving relatives include his parents, Mr. and Mrs. John Hoffman, formerly of Torrington; two sister, one of whom lives in Torrington, and a brother, John A. Hoffman, also of Torrington. He also leaves several cousins including the McLeod brothers, who are themselves well known ball players.
>
> "Dan" was born in Collinsville but

Thunderbolt. On March 15, 1922, Daniel J. Hoffman died of chronic pulmonary tuberculosis, according to his death certificate. He was only 42. At the time of Daniel's death, Connie Mack and his Philadelphia Athletics were in Eagle Pass, Texas, for spring training. Mack read the Associated Press news release concerning Danny's death, and after kind words to the press corps, immediately wired $100 to Danny's parents. Over 16 years had passed since Danny had played for him. But that didn't seem to matter. Perhaps Mack remembered an amiable, but stubborn, rookie who had stood toe-to-toe with him on more than one occasion. Him, Connie Mack! One of the greatest, most strong-willed managers of all times. And Hoffman hadn't backed down. A man could admire another man for that.

Or, perhaps he was already formulating the words he would tell his biographer Frederick Lieb two decades later, i.e. that Danny Hoffman would have been one of the League's all-time greats but for an injury which nearly took his life. One of the all-time greats! And Mack wasn't the only one that regarded Danny Hoffman's potential as such. A November 14, 1907, news article said that Hoffman "was considered by many experts the best youngster of modern times until the 1904 accident". . . The BEST!

Could Danny Hoffman have been another Ty Cobb? Could he have been a Hall Of Famer? Probably, but he didn't let it stop him from playing for 12 more seasons when specialists said he'd never even have one more. He accepted that what could-have-been, would *never* be. But, he made what *could* be, good enough for a .256 lifetime Major League batting average and a .951 fielding percentage. . . Daniel Hoffman was human, and it would be unthinkable that he didn't have second thoughts and occasional depressed moments over the what could-have-been. One can easily imagine Hoffman, a left-handed batter, stepping into the box against a left-handed pitcher, and feeling a twinge of frustration knowing that the pitch would be coming down the first base side and that his lead right eye would be worthless to spot it. It would have frustrated the physically perfect gods of Olympia.

But Danny Hoffman didn't let it dictate a lifetime emotional state. His 1909 "Most Popular" trophy is proof of that, as is the fact that when news of his death reached Torrington, it was said to have saddened a large host of Torrington friends.

Less than two years later, on October 10, 1923, Danny Hoffman's mother died, and a little over two years after that, his father died on February 10, 1926. . . Danny, his wife, and his parents were all gone in less than 6 years, almost as if the fates and the powers of destiny had tried to erase all traces of the Torrington legend.

But, I knew it wasn't so. There was Danny's sterling silver trophy, his old baseball cards and pins that even today are prized by collectors, and his relatives (next page) who even after almost a century remember the tales they were told of Danny Hoffman's illustrious career.

(L-R: Joan Kaczynski, Adeliade Cisowski, Janet Benoit, Edna Weingart, and Jeanne Titcomb. These 5 sisters, whose maiden name was Sparks, along with a 6th sister, Grace Milanese of Florida, inherited Danny Hoffman's "Most Popular" trophy. Their father, Joseph D. Sparks, was the son of Danny Hoffman's sister Clara, and as a teenager lived in the same house on Wolcott Avenue, circa 1917, as his grandfather, i.e. Danny Hoffman's father.)

Looking at his trophy recently under a brilliant blue sky with the shadows just beginning to run across a sun parched lawn, I could hear the warmth in the cheers at the Suburban Garden Theatre when it was presented. And I could feel the warmth of his own corner-pinched smile knowing that at last, after 73 years, the Daniel J. Hoffman story was out.

(Above, a warm spring day in 2017. Danny Hoffman's grave with 3 rocks from Fuessenich Park on top along with an old time baseball photo of him.)

Frigo - House Of Cheese

(New Article. February 28, 2017. The genesis of this article falls under the category: Unintended Consequences. A couple of weeks ago I had reason, unrelated to research or writing, to pop in at Stefano Foods on Summer Street. This visit resulted in my seeing the vintage pictures of Frigo: House Of Cheese that hang in the lobby. Later when I was at The Torrington Historical Society on another matter, I happened to mention the Frigo pictures and found out the Society had a recording of Dave Frigo's recollections concerning the business and the 1955 Flood. And, as they say, the rest is. . . Acknowledgements: Thanks to Dave, Mary, Art, and Edward Frigo, *and* Dave's daughter Maria Frigo Stafford, and for their recollections and willing participation. And, as always, to The Torrington Historical Society.)

From Trissino, Province of Vicenza, Italy. To Peshtigo, Wisconsin. To virtually every state in the lower 48, it was a long journey for Stefano Frigo before settling in Torrington in 1939. He'd come to the United States in 1920 as a young man, along with his 4 brothers,

(Above, the 5 Frigo brothers who came to the United States early in the 20th century. L-R: Amedeo, Stefano, Archangelo, Luigi, Pasquale)

$50, and the typical immigrant's dream of making a better life for himself and his family. The Frigo brothers' particular dream centered around cheese, specifically Asiago cheese for which the Vicenza Province was renown.

They went to Illinois first, but the milk was not compatible for Asiago cheese, according to Dave Frigo. Cheesemaker's Creed: "To make good cheese, you need good milk." They continued west and wound up in Wisconsin. Here, cheese operations were set in motion, a factory established, and then, like a cheese wheel spinning, Stefano Frigo's own wheels spun and he journeyed by railroad and bus all over the country selling cheese. He'd send the orders back to Wisconsin by mail, and the cheese would be sent out via railroad express. Pasquale and Luigi ran the Wisconsin manufacturing, while the middle brother, Archangelo, wound up meeting a girl, moving to St. Louis, and eventually becoming a cook.

Ever on the outlook for new markets, new opportunities, the now married Stefano Frigo set up an office on Hudson Street in NYC early in 1939. Hudson Street at that time was a market area for wholesalers. He and his wife, Adelina née Beia, moved to Union City, NJ, and Stefano commuted into the City. The commuting quickly became too much. He talked to his brothers, and they gave him, Stefano, and his brother Amedeo the New England territory, which meant moving north to NE. But where? According to son Arthur ("Art"), Stefano decided Connecticut would be a great area, and the choice of cities came down to Torrington or Meriden.

He chose Torrington. According to son Dave Frigo there were a lot of paisani here, and his father said, "What better place when you have customers right off the bat!" The family in the autumn of 1939 moved to 420 South Main. It was a 2-family house owned by fellow

(Above, 420 South Main Street next to the old Valley Park in early spring 2017.)

Italian Frank Buonocore Sr.

The Frigo brothers, Stefano and Amedeo, quickly set up a little store in the basement of the house, and in 1940 and '41 the City Directory listed Frigo Food Products Co as being at 420 South Main. Early on it was decided the business needed refrigeration, and a concrete basement floor was poured by fellow Italian Julius Bonvicini. This Torrington-Italian network, whereby Italians supported their countrymen, served many local Italians well. It was nothing new; other immigrant groups had done it before the Italians, *and* would do it after them. But the Italians did it as well as anyone, and probably better than most.

✣ ✣ ✣ ✣

The Frigo business continued to evolve and grow. In 1942 the City Directory no longer listed the business on South Main, but rather now at 47 Hammond Passway. Sidebar: Few, if any, post-WWII Torringtonians will remember where Hammond Passway was. OR, remember that before the downtown Torrington Plaza, there was a series of streets where the Plaza is today. Hammond Passway, simply called

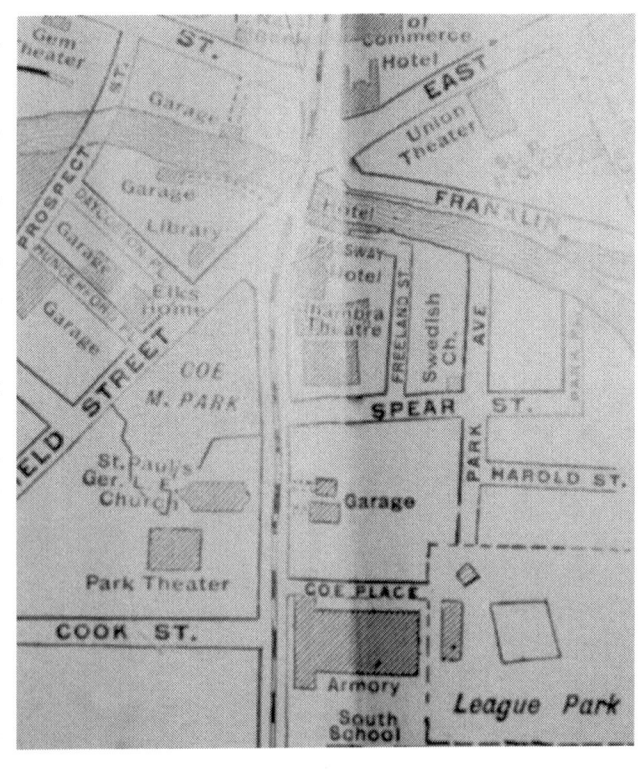

"PASSWAY" on the map (opposite page), was centrally located in the heart of downtown, which was good for business back in the era when Torrington had a thriving main shopping district. *But*, it was bad that Hammond Passway was right alongside the Naugatuck River. Cheese was stored and aged in the basement. Whenever the river would rise appreciably, which it did periodically according to Art Frigo, they would have to form a "relay" to get the cheese upstairs. This was a major inconvenience during small river surges. It would prove a disaster in 1955, but that was a decade+ in the future.

FRIGO FOOD PRODUCTS CO.
WHOLESALE AND RETAIL
Sole Distributor
The Famous Frigo Asiago Gold Medal
C H E E S E
Phone 3260
47 HAMMOND PASSWAY :: TORRINGTON, CONN.

(Above, a 1946 ad.)

The building on the Passway was acquired from the Kirsch family. (Below, an old ink blotter advertising the Kirsch business.)

"THEY SAY IT LOOKS LIKE MY HIDE."

"I'm told that visitors to the famous asphalt lake on the southern Caribbean island of Trinidad say its surface looks like my hide. What's more, that natural asphalt is really tough too."

Barber Genasco Roofings are the only roofings made with genuine Trinidad Native Lake Asphalt... The Vital Element. We are equipped to apply all types of Barber Genasco Roofings on buildings of all sizes and kinds. May we examine your roof and make recommendations? Remember... The Vital Element adds to the quality but not to the price!

C. P. KIRSCH
45 Hammond Passway
Torrington, Conn.
Tel: 6074

It had previously been a garage that did car repairs, but when mention was made of wanting to purchase it, the Kirschs stuck a selling price of $22,000 on it, which the Frigos thought was too high.

The Frigos came in with a slightly lower offer that was refused. Was the Kirsch family looking to soak a prospering business family? *Or*, could it have been a case of discrimination against Italians? Certainly that sort of thing went on, though according to one Frigo family member, discrimination was not as bad in Torrington as in some other places. Possibly, it was a combination of both. . . To get it for the right price was not easy, but Stefano had an ingenious solution. He got someone to front as a buyer for the Frigos. The front successfully negotiated a sales price of $16,000. Stefano paid him $200-300, and the Frigos had their bigger downtown store.

(Above, the new handsome store front at 47 Hammond Passway.)

The retail cheese business in Torrington proved to be a boon. Art Frigo recalled that on payday the old time Italians would come into the store and spend $20 out of a $100 paycheck on Frigo's olives, meats, cheeses, etc. before they went to a regular grocery store/supermarket. He cited his father as carrying premium products and said that people would pay a little more back then for quality, "just not a *lot* more." Stefano Frigo, according to Art, would constantly give out samples, "Try this, try this." Art's sister, Mary Frigo Lach the oldest of the 7 children, echoed that memory. Said that people would not know what a product was or how good it tasted. Mary Frigo Lach: "Father believed in giving samples to taste. People could practically have a lunch on the samples he would give away."

Diane Miasek: "I lived near Frigo's when it was on the Hammond Passway) in early 1950s. Every Wednesday mom made spaghetti sauce. I went to Frigo's and got 32¢ worth of fresh parmesan, and a loaf of Italian bread. Of course Wednesdays were pasta day. That wonderful neighborhood will forever be in my memory bank. Knew all the Frigo sons."

(Above, inside the store on Hammond Passway.)

The teenage Mary Frigo would go to her classes at the old THS on Church Street, then walk down to the store to work. Her father Stefano insisted she take a business course, and she did. Became excellent at shorthand and credited Miss Quinn's class. Mary Frigo Lach: "My uncle's (Amedeo) English was not as good as my dad's (Stefano). My uncle dictated to me in Italian, and I translated it into English in shorthand." The very talented Mary Frigo also helped on the cash register during the busy holiday seasons, but her sister, Angela, was physically bigger and stronger and was able to handle the cutting of meats and cheeses better. Mary worked mainly in the office doing billing, ordering, answering the phone, and a little accounting. "Father depended on me a lot. I came home, and we'd still be talking business. . . I always wanted to work outside the business, but looking back it was the best thing. Even after starting a family, I could work part-time."

Sidebar: All the children would, at some point while growing up, work in the House Of Cheese. Dave Frigo called this "paying your dues." Some worked more than others.

(Above. Behind the counter at the Hammond Passway store, 4 of the 9 Frigos. L-R: Mary, Dave, Stefano, Robert.)

Peter R. Andrighetti: "I can remember many times when my parents, and then I, would be at the glass case ordering cheese."

Not content to merely run a successful retail store, Stefano Frigo bought a delivery truck for a New England sales route that was handled by the second oldest child, Dave.

Dave Frigo: "I'd load up the truck with ice, and leave on a Monday and come back on Friday. Ninety-nine percent of the sales were to individuals, one percent to restaurants. My father had established the network back in the 1930s."

David Frigo would hit the towns with heavy Italian populations He'd speak Italian to some customers, which was a great surprise to them. He loved hearing the experiences of the early immigrants, such as fighting off the Indians while laying the Canadian railroad. He had different New England routes, and he'd drive each one approximately 3 times a year.

(Above, the Frigos pose with the delivery truck.
L-R: Dave, Mary, Robert, and Stefano.)

The Runs. A good example of one of the New England runs was the Vermont one. Dave would go to Brattleboro first where there was an Italian population center. Then he'd head to other Vermont towns where there were stone quarries and hence a lot of Italian stone workers/cutters/carvers/etc. such as in Bellows Falls and Barre. In Barre, Dave Frigo recalls vividly to this day that there was a tuberculosis sanitarium for workers who'd contracted TB because of all the granite dust they inhaled. From Barre he went to Montpelier, Waterbury, Burlington, Rutland, et al. Dave Frigo: "The roads weren't good back then, not like today. And I had to do the business at night when the old man was home."

It was not an easy, on-the-road life.

Maria Frigo Stafford, Dave's daughter, recently told me how it took an aggressive, but also very personable personality to "cold call" on customers/potential customers. She said her grandfather Stefano had that personality, as did her father David. . . Art Frigo added that Dave spoke the best Italian out of the 7 children of Stefano and Adelina, and like his father, Dave was part showmen who loved people. Arthur Frigo said that both his father and Dave could tell a good joke in Italian and that both had a *lot* of personality.

(Left and below: part owner, part showmen, part promoter, Stefano Frigo poses with a 1250 pound provolone, then cuts into it. The cheese was made by the Frigo brothers back in Wisconsin and it took a specially rigged harness to hold it.)

(Right, a promotional calendar from 1950.)

In 1951, the first major shift in the Frigo Torrington business occurred. It was decided that there were too many people for the size of the enterprise. A farewell dinner – attended by many prominent local Italians such as Arthur DeMichiel, Rev. William Botticelli, Frank Buonocore, John Casale, John Speziale, Fiore Petricone, Anthony Toro, John Franculli, Erico Marola, et al. – was thrown for Stefano's brother, Amedeo. Shortly after, Amedeo moved to Springfield and started a downtown store. It's still a popular Springfield stop today.

✣ ✣ ✣ ✣

Business life, and life in general, were good for the Frigo family in the summer of 1955. The 7 children were spread out over a large age range: from Mary who was the oldest at 25, to Edward who was the youngest at 10. This age range meant that their individual interests were diverse. But the commonality of family and the cheese business united them with a strong bond.

The test of just how strong that bond was came on Thursday, August 18, 1955.

Dave Frigo: "When the 1955 Flood hit, I'd been in New Britain that day selling cheese to families. I came home that night, went to the store, put the money into the safe, and knew it looked bad. We had a sump pump and steel sides over the windows, but. . . I got my brother Richard, brother-in-law Bernie (Lach, fireman/fire chief), and Angelo Arsego. We took the cheeses from the bottom shelves in the basement and brought them upstairs. I figured the top ones would be OK. I put my wallet on the top basement shelf. We had power, but water kept coming in, and I knew we should get out of there."

There was a compressor, and Dave Frigo had the foresight to turn it off. They were standing in water, and if the compressor ever shorted out, they could have been electrocuted. The men started going to sleep upstairs, but water was all around and eventually they headed home.

It wasn't easy. Hammond Passway had washed away. Brother Richie fell, went underwater, and Dave grabbed him. The men got to higher ground on Spear Street and from there made it home by partly following the railroad tracks. The Frigos were now living at 21 Tracy Avenue, which itself runs near the Naugatuck River. But the family was OK. Dave Frigo: "When we got home, my father fell to his knees and cried like a baby. He thought we were gone."

In the same general time period, Art Frigo remembered that at 10-11 p.m. his father Stefano shook him and woke him up to tell him, "The dam didn't break!" This was in response to Al Eyre on WTOR announcing earlier that people in the valley should move to higher ground, that the Brass Mill Dam might break. "My father was very emotional," Art remembered. "It wasn't like him."

At some point 14-year-old Art put on his boots and ran downtown. He couldn't get to the store, but saw that part of the Frigo building was down. "It was like a mouse took a big bite out of the corner," he said. He ran home: exhausted, crying, fearing the worst. "I was *so* relieved to see my brothers," he remembered.

The flood waters receded rapidly. When the Frigos got to their business they found the plate glass windows in the front broken, a back corner of the building indeed down, and everything "topsy-turvy" in Dave Frigo's words. All the cheeses, which they had brought upstairs to be safe, were gone. Some were later found in Fuessenich Park. Others as far away as Thomaston. . . The large safe, which had been in the corner that came down, was no longer there. Miraculously, according to Art Frigo, it was found 100 feet down the river, when its top became visible. The money was still inside, and there was now enough cash to recoup. In a strange, random, serpentining contortion of fate, Dave's wallet, which he had put on the top shelf in the basement, was still there.

And the entire family was safe.

Dave Frigo: "The Albreadas took us in. It was unbelievable the number of people who helped."

Art Frigo: "People really pulled together during the Flood."

(Above & below, Frigo's with its back corner missing.)

Initially it was proposed by Dan Farley at City Council that the Frigo building be razed since, in his opinion, it was more than 50% gone. Farley later claimed that Stefano Frigo came at him with a baseball bat, which Frigo used as a cane because of the gout. Friend of the family, contractor Julius Bonvicini, warned the City *not* to tear down the House Of Cheese, unless they wanted a lawsuit. In his opinion it was only 30-35% gone. . . The next day Dick Maine, whose father owned a furniture store in the same area, told Art Frigo that scaffolding was going up. It was true; repairs had begun already. Dave Frigo: "Julius Bonvicini was fantastic."

(Above, the debris and destruction. Early stages of cleanup.)

Bad News: Food inspectors condemned just about all the food, including 100 pound provolones which had been hanging but which, nonetheless, had gotten hit by 2 inches of water. Good News: Family members from Wisconsin and Springfield restocked the Torrington business and cancelled any debts. One of the service clubs gave the Frigos money from a special fund, and in 30 business days, Frigo's *Famous* House Of Cheese was back in business.

Dave Frigo: "Thanks to the people of Torrington and loyal customers, we were able to come back in a timely fashion and to continue our business."

Business continued on Hammond Passway for less than a year before the Flood Control Project decided to widen the river, which would swallow up the Passway. The House Of Cheese moved to 109 South Main (today Joe's Pizza & Wings). The brick building was leased from Larry Rauch. Sidebar: A move would have had to happen in the not-too-distant future anyway as the streets in that neighborhood: Spear, Freeland, Harold, et al. were all bought up and razed for economic development (The Torrington Plaza).

Though the retail business was now a quarter mile south, it was *still* downtown and *still* convenient for its loyal customers to reach. (Below, the House Of Cheese at 109 South Main).

And the customers *did* come.

Shelley DeMichiel Considine: "We went there every Saturday morning. My mother would buy the Boars Head cold cuts and these absolutely wonderful rectangular shaped rolls. . . The luganega sausage we would get for the polenta and chicken, along with corn meal in paper pages ordered by the pound. Frigo's was, at the time, the only place to get asiago cheese. The meats and provolone hanging from the ceiling, the Italian nougat candy at Christmas. . . Ahhh wonderful memories, and although at the time I hated the way we would smell once we left, I miss it now."

Laura Rudolfo: "When it was near Bradlees, I used to go there a few times a week with my grandmother. OMG! It stunk so bad! Now, I would kill for all that stinky cheese, fresh. The luganega sausage was perfect!"

John Todor: "After all these years, I can still remember the smell as you walked in the door. As a huge cheese lover, I thought the place was great."

Jan Roberge Lyon: "As a child raised on Wilson Avenue, I walked to the Y daily after school where my mom worked and I attended classes of all sorts. Passed the Cheese House and always wished the door was closed as the stench was horrific. . . Never ventured inside. RAN past!"

Karol Westelinck Dyson: "Used to walk that way either to or home from St. Francis School as a kid and could smell it a couple blocks away. It was always one of the more exotic shops in town. You could see in the window from the far side of the street and see shadows and 'hanging' items. I don't think my mother ever went in there though she was ½ Swedish and ½ Irish Catholic! Not great cheese loving countries as far as I know."

Louise Manteuffel: "Of course I remember the overwhelming odor when I shopped there. But these days I always smile when I see the family headstone at Hillside Cemetery with that wedge of cheese."

This common motif of "smell" was reinforced by the Frigo children themselves. Art (on left) didn't work there often, as he was passionately involved in school and THS sports (President class of 1959, tri-captain of basketball, co-captain of baseball, National Honor Society, et al.). Art himself remembered that his Friday night and Saturday store hours were often compromised by school activities. But he also remembered that when he did work, he never came up short on the register having invented a "double check system." He also laughingly remembered that it was tough to go to a school dance at the YMCA after working in the store, i.e. the smell had to be showered off.

Mary Frigo Lach recalled that customers either loved or hated the smell. She tells of her "poor dad," Stefano, needing to put cologne on his clothes whenever he'd leave the store on errands such as going to the bank. "I always knew what to buy him," she humorously added referring to gift time and his generous use of artificial scents.

To some non-Italians, such as those quoted previously and (confession) me, the House Of Cheese was a strange and foreign place. We didn't eat that type of food at home, and I don't think many of us

(Above, the front window of the South Main Frigo's during the Christmas season. The holiday sign, according to Mary Frigo Lach, was probably made by her husband, Bernard Lach. Bernie was a non-Italian who was graciously welcomed into the Frigo family despite his initially being a milk drinker...)

knew what some of it was (pickled eels?). There weren't the number of Italian restaurants in Torrington that there are today, and specialty Italian food was not sold in the supermarkets to the extent it is now. I was 19-years-old before I ever knew what pepperoni was or what it tasted like. And I don't think that experience, or lack of it, was uncommon 50+ years ago in this city.

✥ ✥ ✥ ✥

Life changes, and businesses either adapt or die. Frigo's was not about to die. In 1979, the lease was up on the South Main building, but Dave Frigo already owned another commercial building at 46 Summer Street. It just made good economic sense to. . . So, for the third time in 40 years, the House Of Cheese relocated, this time to the corner space opposite the Torrington Towers.

It would not move again.

(Above, an undated exterior shot of Frigo's on Summer Street, with the Frigo coat-of-arms to the right of the door.)

David R. Washington: "We lived directly across the street from Frigo's on 45 Summer Street. Loved the smells."

According to *Register Citizen* reporter Melanie O'Brien in a 1989 article, the aroma at Frigo's was "a blending of cheese, salami, with a hint of sweet, coffee perhaps." Very pleasing. And the Cheese House on Summer Street still sold many of the same products which had endured it to discriminating palates. There was a variety of cheeses: fresh ricotta, Asiago, provolone, cheddar, Romano, Parsesan (and Reggiano), Roquefort, goat, English Stilton, Muenster, blue, domestic feta, and more. There was salami of all sorts: the dry and very hard casalingo, the chunky and coarser abbruzesse, the sweeter soppressata, the garlicky salametto, the cured pepper ham prosciuttini, and more. And, of course, many other delectable edibles: cured beef, artichokes from Italy and California, frozen pasta dishes from a Derby company which made manicotti, ziti, lasagna, gnocchi, eggplant all close to homemade according to Ellen Frigo. Other Italian delicacies: Nutella; cherries in brandy; capers in salt;

anchovies; tubes of strong tasting garlic, onion, pesto; aged vinegar; olive oils; tomato paste, et al.

On the subject of Frigo's food. . .
Mary Lee Cornedi Point: "My father, Andrew, worked at Frigo's weekends and part-time. He'd bring home hard salami; Genoa; provolone; mortadella, which I didn't like; and other great things. At Christmas, he'd bring home lots of food such as candy nougats; we kids would fight over the flavors. And panettone, which is a sweet bread with raisins and candied fruit."

Edward Frigo, the youngest of the 7 children and described by one reporter as a "cheese expert," took over the House Of Cheese in 1983. He posed at the counter in 1989 (above) for a photo, and he recently told me how, generally speaking, it was tough to be on your feet all day. He added that Frigo's had a system akin to "wooden pallets" underfoot, which made it easier. Back in 1989 he told reporter Melanie O'Brien that while Frigo's for many years catered almost exclusively to Torrington's Italian community, that customers now came from all nationalities and from as far away as New York and Massachusetts "looking for good quality cheese." When such distant customers travelled all the way here just to shop, Edward Frigo said they tended to go home with large wheels and blocks of cheese. No cutting necessary. And thus the gospel of good cheese and unique ethnic food continued to spread.

While the products that Frigo's carried were absolutely top-of-the-line, by 1997 times had changed drastically. Dave Frigo said the old customers he used to peddle to had died off, and that people were no longer brown bagging it. Maria Frigo Stafford added, "The big supermarkets today (1997) are taking on so much. A small place really can't compete with what they offer. It's one-stop shopping. And people aren't cooking anymore like they used to because of the fast-food places and the fact that both the mothers and fathers work."
Mary Frigo Lach: "We were a specialty shop, and we had a nice clientele."
But, the clientele was gone. An era was gone.

Dave Frigo said in his Historical Society interview: "We didn't have the ability to go into the catering business. We saw the growth as being in wholesale."

In the summer of 1997, with the strong pleasant odor of provolone still wafting through the air, the House Of Cheese closed. No longer, as in the old days, would the cheese arrive by train at the Torrington depot and be delivered by Daley Trucking to the House Of Cheese, there to be aged and sold at various times. A classic retailer for almost 60 years had succumbed to the shifting, fortuitous nature of life. But not totally. In its place stood Stefano Food Products Company Inc, the Frigo wholesale wing. It had begun back in 1969 and was named after the then patriarch of the family, Stefano Frigo.

Dave Frigo: "The retail store was the mother of the wholesale business."

As the years passed, the wholesaling aspect of business has grown, and today in 2017 it's the last, but healthy, vestige of the once classic retailer. The clients are mainly pizzerias and Spanish restaurants all over New England, though Maria Frigo Stafford says that her father Dave still supplies a few Italian families.

Maria Frigo Stafford: "We're small, but we take care of our customers. We'll make a special run for a small order on a weekend. The service end keeps us where we are today. We have our little niche."

The Frigo *Famous* House Of Cheese is gone. No longer is there a thriving downtown to support it. No longer is there an abundance of Italian patrons to deliver a sales pitch to in Italian. *But*, the Stefano trucks stand ready to roll.

The legacy goes on.

(Above, the Frigo family in an undated photo. Seated are Adelina and Stefano. Behind them, L-R: Richard, Robert, Angela, Art, Mary, Dave, Edward. . . Sidebar: Family friend Mary Lee Cornedi Point happily recalled many good times with this family, including family dinners and how as youngsters she, her sisters, and the Frigo kids would be loaded into Stefano's car to go for ice cream while "he smoked one of those little stogies." She called the family generous, hard-working, & happy.)

There are a few names in Torrington, a *very* few, that once said give rise to roundabout recognition and deep-rooted respect.

Frigo is one.

In Memoriam:
Stefano Frigo: 1904-1981.
Adelina Beia Frigo: 1908-1991.
Angela Frigo Romanczuk: 1936-1970.
Richard Frigo: 1938-2013.

Wintering In Torrington
Slip-Sliding Away

(New Article. March 16, 2017. When the following incident happened, I immediately thought of my senior Facebook friends now living in Southern climes such as Florida. On Facebook during the winter months they constantly point out how they are done with Connecticut winters. And they continually post pictures of the beach, lounging poolside, sipping frosty tropical drinks, etc. Though I consider myself a hardy New Englander who can *still* handle our rough, Northwest Connecticut winters, there are times when I dally with the idea of moving south. *This* was one of those times. . .)

Be prepared, was what I was taught in the boy scouts, back in my Trinity Church, Troop 2, Eagle Scout days. After falling on the snow and ice 3 times last winter, I was determined to be prepared this winter and to stay upright.

I bought ice grippers (below) from LL Bean before the first snow flurries even flew. These particular ones are made by Yaktrax and are advertised as "diamond grip, Ice Trekkers." They stretch out over the bottom of shoes/boots, and they've worked GREAT! so far this season.

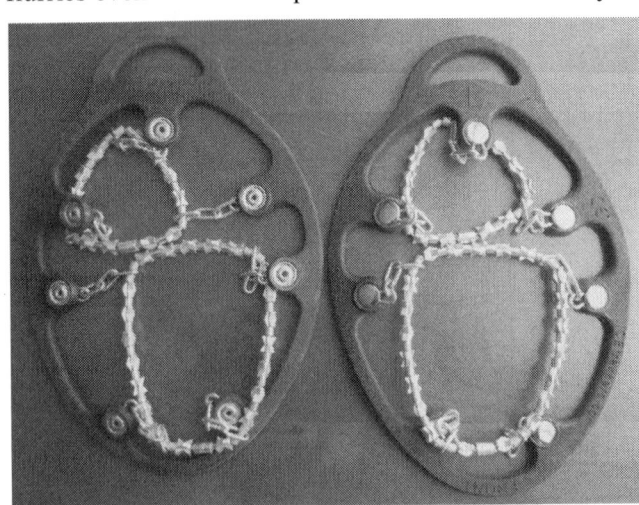

Trouble is, you actually have to put them *on* for them to work.

✥ ✥ ✥ ✥

I went out early this morning to retrieve the trash bin after the USA Hauling truck went by. When I put the bin out last night, there was no ice on the driveway. NOTE: My driveway is in 2 sections: a relatively flat upper portion and an inclined lower stretch.

I gingerly walked out in the dark a.m. testing each footstep in my slippers and bathrobe. Key word, *slippers*, with *smooth* leather bottoms. No problem. No ice.

Then I hit the downslope. ICE! I immediately lost it and started to slide. There was no stopping. Like an ice skater gaining speed to jump barrels, I picked up momentum *fast*!

I slid all the way down and tried to aim for the large trash bin at the bottom, hoping it would stop me. It didn't occur to me in those nano-seconds that the bin was empty now and had no more weight than an inflated lawn Santa.

I hit the trash bin hard like Tom Brady taking out a would-be tackler. Together we slid halfway out into the street; then the trash bin upended and we went down in a pile. . . Stunned silence. Followed by a reflective expletive, followed by painfully getting up. Hands scraped. Knees bruised. Pride down for the ten count. . . I had to walk on the snowy edge to get back up the incline.

Good news: It was still dark. I doubt any of the neighbors saw the pratfall. Bad news: The boy scouts will probably want the Eagle Scout Award back if they ever find out. And I wouldn't blame them.

Talent, Peter Pan, and The Warner

(*The Torrington Voice*. August 5, 1993. Over the years I wrote many Warner play reviews *and* a few previews. This is *not* one of them. In the summer of 1993 I decided to step back as a previewer before opening night of *Peter Pan*, and this article, which is more of an op-ed essay, was the result. Background: In 1993 literally hundreds of youngsters who had landed parts in Warner productions had stardust in their eyes. As did some parents. Though the ideas here seem common sense to me now in 2017, in 1993 the city of Torrington was on a Warner "high." And I felt the thespians and adoring audience needed a grounding in reality. I doubt I influenced anyone.)

When dealing with the performing arts, there are 3 kinds of people: those with no talent, those with a little talent, and those with a *lot* of talent.

Those with no talent are easy to spot. Their idea of hell on earth is having to stand in front of a group to state an opinion, make a little speech, propose a toast. They turn beet red, shake as if an epileptic seizure is imminent: stutter, stammer, and, in general, would be the ones in church mumbling the hymns or just silently mouthing the words. They're the ones who claim to have no rhythm, to be tone deaf, who hesitate to play even a kazoo. Want to see no talent in the singing department? Watch the movie *Paint Your Wagon* and listen to Lee Marvin trying to sing. Thank heavens for the large backup orchestra. And yet, inexplicably, his rendition of "Wandering Star" went to #1 in England when released as a single. It can only be that sometimes when something is so totally bad, it becomes unique. Even good.

At the other end of the performing arts spectrum are those rare individuals with a *lot* of talent: Luciano Pavarotti, Leontyne Price, Laurence Olivier, Dizzy Gillespie, Rudolph Nureyev, Louie Armstrong, Dame Judith Anderson, et al. Those who just plain have *it*.

Then there's the rest. The mean. The large middle. Those of little-to-some talent. I've watched enough school plays, heard enough elementary and high school concerts, seen enough dance recitals to to realize that there are an awful lot of people with *some* performing arts skills.

Having a little talent is like having little knowledge. Can be dangerous. Consider all the children who have appeared in past Warner productions, and those who will appear in *Peter Pan* when it opens this weekend. They all have talent, or they never would have gotten the nod from the casting committee to begin with. Some have more talent than others, but they *all* can act, sing, and even dance to varying degrees. Nothing wrong there; everything right. Gives the youngsters a sense of self worth and sense of who they are. As Peter Pan himself said, "I gotta crow: urrr, urrr, urrr. . . Brag. . . When I discover the cleverness of a remarkable me."

Trouble enters when the young thespians get an eyeful of Pan's magic dust and to start to believe that Broadway, Hollywood, or the London Palladium are around the corner. A sense of self worth is one thing. Far-out fancies another. I'd be willing to bet that there are more young performers in this town dreaming of eventually joining Actor's Equity than dreaming of discovering a cure for AIDS, or being the first astronaut to Mars, or even just starting their own business.

Everyone needs dreams. I think life would be pretty meaningless without a secret longing, an improbable goal that adds comfort to dark nights and lonely beds. I would ask only that, unlike Peter Pan who never wanted to grow up, youngsters in Torrington approach life more realistically and realize that out of all life's professional choices, to aim at a career in the arts is one of the most heart-breaking, frustrating choices available.

There's the audition process, and later directors, coaches, and reviewers. Negativity is always just around the corner. A tough, pull-no-punches world. It helps to have thick skin and callouses on the psyche. But that's asking a lot of anyone, much less those not yet old enough to drive. Still, if children are going to get involved early on with theater, they're going to have to toughen up early on.

(Above, some of the Peter Pan cast give a short, preview performance at Coe Park.)

A little talent can also be dangerous because people with a little talent make it big everyday. I don't honestly believe that Bruce Willis, Rosanne Arnold, Andy Garcia, Debbie Gibson, Garth Brooks, et al. are any great talents. *But*, they've made it. Garth Brooks himself in a recent television interview admitted that there are a number of better musicians and singers on the very street where his office is located. *But* he made it, and they didn't. The young and old see this. They see the marginally talented gain fame, money, and celebrity status. And they see themselves alongside them on that elevated plinth.

It's called *hope*. And rats think the same way. In clinical tests where rats were thrown into tubs of water and let alone till they drowned, it was discovered that if the tester pulled one rat from the water, saved one randomly chosen rodent, the other rats would swim longer before giving up. There was *hope*.

I'm not saying that area youngsters shouldn't have dreams and hopes regarding futures in the performing arts. I'm just saying they should go in open-eyed and realize the odds. Like Captain Hook who was always aware of the ticking clock inside the crocodile who was after him, Warner siblings should hear the tick tock, tick tock of their own futures approaching and have some contingency plans. Crocodiles and futures cannot be escaped.

Peter Pan stayed in Neverneverland and never grew up ("I am youth, I am joy, I am freedom.") He didn't have to. His credits were that good. He was a star with an admiring audience of Lost Boys, Tinkerbell, Tiger Lily, Indians, and the Darling children. Even Hook, Smee, and the rest of the scurvy pirates seemed to begrudgingly admire him. Deserted at the end, Peter was *still* a performer of considerable talent. After all, he could *fly!* And he was right to stay on his own self-made stage taking the bows. With a new generation coming along, it was a long term contract with many more spotlighted performances to come.

No talent, large talent, some talent. Talent can be improved upon, no doubt about that. And if any group can bring it out, it's the Warner personnel. Like the dazzling light of Tinkerbell, Warner productions have, without exception, dazzled area theater goers for a long time.

Peter Pan is next. Overture please. . .

Some Of The Peter Pan Talent Gallery

(Above, L-R: Jessica Durdock as Peter Pan, Ian Bentley, Kyle Bentley.)

More Of The Peter Pan Talent Gallery
(continued)

THE CAST
(in order of appearance)

WENDY/ADULT WENDY	*Christie Williams*
JOHN	*Brian W. Ferry*
LIZA	*Rose Tichy*
MICHAEL	*Dustin Parente*
NANA	*Sharon A. Wilcox*
MRS. DARLING	*Beth Steinberg*
MR. DARLING	*Casey McKenna*
TINKERBELL	*Jeff Schlicter*
PETER PAN	*Jessica Durdock*
LION	*David Cravanzola*
KANGAROO	*Whitney Hamil*
OSTRICH	*Kelly McKenna*
SLIGHTLY	*Ian Bentley*
TOOTLES	*Timothy P. Roscoe*
CURLY	*Erin Fritch*
NIBS	*Catherine Romanos*
BOXER	*Jenna Reichen*
ROCKEY	*Carrie Reeves*
CAPTAIN HOOK	*Alan Anthony Spaulding*
SMEE	*Charlie Gill*
CROCODILE	*Jane Reilly*
TIGER LILY	*Heather Valenti*
STARKEY	*Robert Bongiolatti*
CECCO	*Gabe McMackin*
NOODLER	*Robert Norton*
MULLINS	*Donna Finn*
JUKES	*Scott Schmelder*
JUNIOR	*Eric Story*
JANE	*Lisa Durante*

LOST BOYS .... *Kyle Bentley, Tara Bielawski, Ken Bosley, Anni Bruno, Heather Colt, Damon Cortesi, Justin Dake, Theresa Dumowski, Erin DuCotey, Sarah Handyside, Alex Hudak, Charles Kirchoffer, Kristin McLeod, Tracey Reichen, Claire Reilly, Thea Wirkus-Platz, John Wrenn*

INDIANS .... *Julie Bickford, Kari Boisclair, Jennifer Breen, Liz Capinera, Erin Crossman, Lisa Durante, Kirsten Fredsall, Kasey Gill, Kristen Hafford, Sarah Hafford, Dana Lustig, Jessica Noujaim, Judi Palladino, Katie Rusnak, Liz Salzbo, Hema Shenoi, Jennifer Wrenn, Leah Wu*

PIRATES .... *Terry Breen, Brett Cortesi, Keith Lapotosky, Casey McKenna, Sean Morris, Bob Tansley, Val Vitalo, Paul Whiton*

The Orchestra

Conductor	Matthew P. Valenti
Accompanist & Rehearsal Pianist	Brian Pia
Violin	Jane Pianowski, Joan Dixon, Beth Hochsprung
Flute	Barbara Valenti, Jennifer Lent
Oboe	Nancy Dillon
Clarinet	Theodore Cowles, Annemarie Maccalous
Bass Clarinet	Miles Booth
Bassoon	Renee Ford
Trumpet	Doug Maigret, Rob Fragione
French Horn	Susan Norland, Debby Shaffer
Trombone	Darren Vail, Greg Kawecki
Bass	David Moon
Percussion Set	Scott Kellogg
Bells	Kyle Rhodes
Tympani	Jarred Howe

The Revolving Mayor's Door
A Brief History

(*The Torrington Voice*. October 12, 1995. As the autumn 1995 mayoral election approached, I was heavily into writing about the campaigns. One of my final arguments, and the one I hammered the hardest, was the old political saw: "It's time for a change." I doubt I influenced many/any, but after the votes were tallied in November, the incumbent was out. Torrington's revolving mayor's door once again in the spin cycle. . .)

I like the mayor, I really do. But, enough is enough. Ten consecutive years as mayor. Twelve counting city council time. It's time for new blood, new ideas to step into City Hall and buttress the walls.

Most of Torrington's former mayors have known when their time was up. Most served a term, or two, or three, then gone onto other challenges before their hair turned gray and the citizens gathered outside carrying torches and buckets of tar-and-feather. Most incumbents have stood aside and let a new generation lead the street repaving and pot hole filling. Those who haven't, who never understood that enough-is-enough, have invariably gone down in defeat.

Charles Newcomb was Torrington's first mayor. He beat Frank Coe and George Farnham in 1923 to win the first ever mayoral election. He successfully defended his title in 1925 and 1927, then wisely decided to retire from politics undefeated. At the top of his game. The height of his popularity. He'd served his generation well, though there's no record of the citizenry asking for *more*.

Sidebar: When you're mayor you get invited to a lot of swell functions, as Charles Newcomb learned in 1924. (Left and opposite page, a souvenir program from a banquet honoring

Torrington and Yale legend Raymond "Ducky" Pond. The mayor was in attendance, because he was mayor, i.e, it's *good* to be the mayor. AND, he was there, no doubt, FOC, which is also good.)

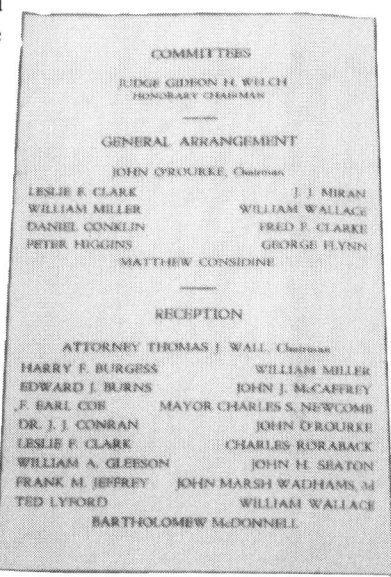

The void in 1929 was filled by Ernest Novey whose primary qualification seemed to be that he was a WWI veteran and a Lt. Colonel in the Army Reserve. He won in 1929, '31, '33, and '35. In 1937 Torrington voters realized that enough-was-enough, and voted Novey out of office. Novey had followed the seminal law of successful Torrington politicians, i.e. be a personality and keep those taxes down! But Torrington voters were following an even older law, one that the Napoleons and Caesars of this world have found out the hard way. Enough-is-enough! and don't let the screen door hit your ass on the way out. Good News: Stay-too-longers in Torrington do not get banished to Elba Island or knifed on the Senate steps. (Below left, Novey as a young soldier in uniform. Below right, a very dapper Mayor Novey in tux. Theory: In Torrington the right clothes can get you into office, *and* help keep you there...)

Next came William Patten in 1937. Good old Bill. Patten stayed in office 4 terms winning his last campaign in 1943 by 20 votes. He got the message. In 1945 Patten declined a reelection bid. Ironically, right next to the election results that '45 autumn was the headline: "Patton Is Relieved Of His Command Of Third Army." The international scene, in a sense, mirroring the local, though to his credit Bill Patten could read the signs that enough-was-enough, long before his homonym-like namesake General George did. (Below left, Patten in 1937 when he first ran for office. Below right, near the end of his 8 years. Apparently being mayor was tough on the eyes. Good News: Patten was an optometrist.)

Democrat George Kilmartin won the next 2 mayoral contests and was mayor from 1945-to-1949. Two-and-done. (Below, at the swearing in ceremony of Mayor Kilmartin in '45. Kilmartin is the tall, white-haired gentlemen, third from the right, who looks like a giant among pygmies. Did his superior height give him a political edge? Did it allow him a view of the future in which he foresaw the '55 Flood and the exodus of industry, and thus caused his I'm-outtahere-move?. . .)

In 1949 a new figure entered Torrington politics who would walk the City Hall corridors for 7 terms as mayor before being booted out by Torrington voters. Enter Fred Daley. Daley won the city's top spot in 1949 and '51 before voters threw him out in a primary against William Carroll (on right) in 1953. Daley was out, but not gone. For some, being called by that titular appellation of "mayor" is a heady, intoxicating psyche boost. Or maybe it's just that some don't have another well-paying profession to fall back on. In any case, Daley left the stage, but only drifted into the wings.

From 1953-'57, William Carroll ruled City Hall. In 1955 he had to defeat a young 39-year-old Anthony Gelormino (on left) Torrington's Street Superintendent, in a primary to get the Democratic nod. He did, then beat Salvatore Rubino by 1700 votes in October to stay Torrington's #1 son.

Two years later in 1957 Carroll was gone of his own volition, and in his place at the head of the table sat a WWII veteran. The now 41-year-old Anthony Gelormino was back. Gelormino beat Gustave Froelich that year by 56 votes, beat Harold Sibley in 1959 by 1700. But he overstayed his welcome. The Wolcottville kingpin girded his political machine for a 3rd term, but it was not to be. Gelormino was beaten by J. Eric Chadwick in the fall of 1961 by 2288 votes. Time for a change, enough-is-enough.

Surprise of surprises. In 1963 the phoenix-like Fred Daley was back. Few believed he could beat Chadwick. Under Chadwick's administration, the "new" THS as well as the development of the Downtown Shopping Center (below) had both been started and finished. Two achievements written in stone, steel, and concrete. *Huge* monuments for the Chadwick team. . . *But* Daley campaigned on the idea (among other issues) that Chadwick (left) had not served *all* areas of the city.

Did the voters buy that idea, or was it just another case of enough-is-enough, time for a change? We'll never know the reason. But Daley got his upset victory.

Two years later P. Edmund Power (right) beat Daley by 712 votes. Daley's career would have given anyone else a nosebleed from all the ups-and-downs. . . Daley seemed to be proving 2 things: 1. Being the incumbent was no guarantee of anything other than having your name and picture in the newspaper a lot. 2. There are politicians, stalkers of a sort, who are just *not* going to go away. Dialing 9-1-1 won't work.

Power won again in 1967, but Daley (on right) was back in 1969. Fred D. had to primary against Fiore Petricone to get his party's nomination, won by 193, then went on to defeat George Klug in the mayoral race by 2399 votes. Once again, Fred Daley was in, and this time he would stay for 4 consecutive terms (1969-'77), bringing his grand total of mayoral wins to 7.

During his 6th term in 1975 (Below, a campaign flyer from '75), Mayor Daley low-keyed his chances by saying, "I never make predictions. If I went by all the people who said they'd vote for me, I'd win by a landslide." Daley was astute enough to know that friends may be friends. But even friends know that there comes a time when enough-is-enough. Sort of a spin-off on the Godfather movies, i.e. change is not personal, it's just good business.

The good business and enough-is-enough kicked in for Mayor Daley in 1977. Running against Hodges Waldron, the ever popular Daley seemed a shoo-in. But Waldron campaigned aggressively, pushed for an industrial site on Kennedy Drive, got union boss Angelo Franculli's labor backing, and beat Daley by almost 1500 votes. Daley was stunned and commented to the press: "It's hard to read the public. One year they love you. The next year you're out." Daley, obviously, had forgotten his own words from 1975. Love, like, and friendship had nothing to do with his loss. Waldron (left) understood his win. His comments to the press were right-on: "From my door-to-door campaigning I knew the people were tired of Daley." . . . Exactly. We love you Fred. You're a helluva guy. Kept our taxes down, filled the potholes. But, it's time for a change. Enough-is-enough.

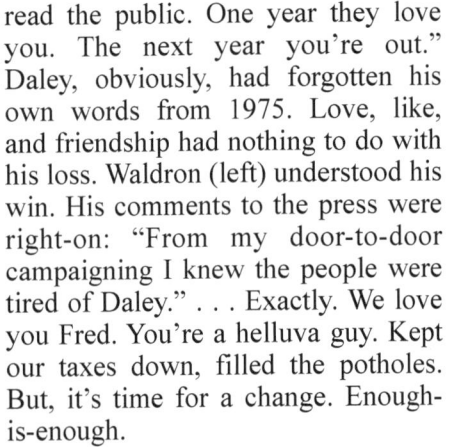

Hodges Waldron did a good job, but after only 2 years it was over. In 1979 the popular Waldron ran against the even more popular Mike Conway. (Left, Conway in 1977.) This was *not* a case of enough-is-enough. Conway had been not only a city councilman but also a THS teacher, i.e. he had major name recognition and a solid proven background.

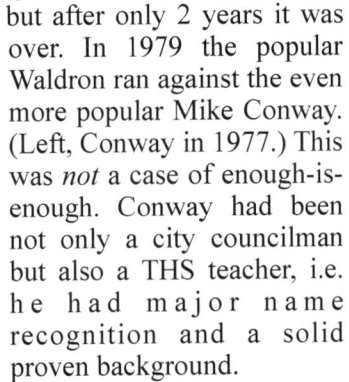

Conway beat Waldron in 1979 by 2735 votes, beat him again in '81 by 3075 votes, and defeated Robert Conforti in '83 by 1814 votes. Undefeated, and by wide margins. . . (Right, a campaign "Conway" giveaway.). . . It'll never be known whether the gregarious Irishman would have overstayed his welcome and eventually been defeated, because a thing called the Grand Jury probe came to Torrington. Though having done nothing officially wrong, Conway and his administration bowed out of an encore run in 1985.

Which leads to the present.

The current mayor has been in power for the last 10 years. A decade of the same top person, the same administration, the same political party, the same ideas. It's time for a change. As history has shown, enough-is-enough.

After all, though the mayor's office door at City Hall may not *look* like a revolving door.

In fact, it *is*.

(Below left, the mayor's door in 1968. Below right, the mayor's door in 2017. Different styles, but the same revolving nature.)

(Left, Charles Newcomb, Torrington's first mayor, looking optimistically forward into Torrington's future. . .)

(Much thanks to The Torrington Historical Society for 5 of the photos used in this article.)

The Stars Among Us
Celebrities In The Big T

(New Article. April 1, 2017. Past readers know that on April Fool's Day I like to have a little fun. In the past I've written April 1st articles which were *totally* fictitious and others which were *mostly* fictitious. The one which follows is something new. First off, I'm telling you ahead of time that this is an April 1st article, something I've never done before. Now that you're guarded, or should be, you'll be reading with a critical mind. Secondly, I'm going to tell you that 99% of what I purport here *is* true, with *one* lone exception. One, and only *one*. Out of all the celebrities I mention here, and all the facts surrounding their visits, there's only one star whom I claim visited Torrington, but who, in fact, never did. And I've made up the details of that visit accordingly. There are enough falsehoods that you should *definitely* be able to spot the *single* poseur. Which celebrity is it? You'll have to keep reading to find out. . .)

It's no secret to longtime Torringtonians that we've been graced with pop-in visits for well over a century from the rich, famous, and celebrated. In *My Torrington Days* I discuss the notables who played the boards at the old Opera House and Alhambra Theater: William S. Hart, Ed Wynn, Douglas Fairbanks, Clifton Webb, Henry Travers, Fred Allen, and the great John L. Sullivan. In later years many newer luminaries have graced the Warner stage: Ray Charles, Jerry Lewis, Shirley MacLaine, Chuck Barry, Tammy Wynette, John Legend, George Carlin, Rita Rudner, James Earl Jones, Stockard Channing, David Brenner, Mark Russell, Frank McCourt, Crystal Gayle (Fuessenich Park), The Beach Boys, Cheech & Chong, Linda Eder, Tom Jones, Melissa Ethridge, Merle Haggard, Paula Poundstone, Vince Gill, Glen Campbell, Wayne Newton, Tony Bennett, et al. Years ago Christopher Plummer was scheduled to play the Warner, and we Bentleys bought tickets. But Plummer cancelled at the last minute and though the ticket price was refunded, we would have rather seen him.

That's the way it is with celebrities. We like seeing them, hearing them, as if they speak from rarified Olympic heights with god-like insight. As if their presence alone, if only for a brief shining moment, can somehow illuminate us, and perhaps give added worth to the town itself, i.e. you *are* worth my time and a stop. . . if only briefly.

One illustrious (infamous?) person who appeared briefly in a Warner play was Governor Lowell Weicker in 1993. He played in the original Warner production of *Robin Hood* in the small role of King Richard who appears at the very end and only has a few lines. It was reported that though he had a minor part, Weicker was very nervous and had the limousine driver cruise around Torrington while he rehearsed. The reason for his nervousness? Probably worried about a hostile reception given the fact that he had recently gotten the first ever state income tax passed. . . His nervousness showed, but he delivered his lines accurately and on cue, and the Warner audience was generous in their applause when he took his bow.

(Right, Casey McKenna and Karen Bentley in the same *Robin Hood* production. Though not as famous as Lowell Weicker, they were both much better talents on the stage.)

Another recognizable name to play the Warner boards was Susan Saint James who appeared in 1995 as Annie Sullivan in *The Miracle Worker*. Saint James was well known to most in the audience from her work in the popular tv series *McMillan & Wife*, *Kate & Allie*, and *The Name Of The Game*. At the time, the Warner was trying to crawl out of a deep financial hole, and her appearance helped assure large audiences. Saint James did yeoman's work. Not only did she put in the rehearsal time and master a difficult role, but she also helped promote the show by visiting schools, doing radio spots, etc. Unlike most celebrities who play the Warner Theater and leave nothing of themselves, Susan Saint James left behind a shining legacy of what can happen when the celebrated and community theater merge.

In that 1995 production a 9-year-old girl, Elizabeth Harris, starred as Helen Keller. Unbeknownst to many, the real Helen Keller had visited Torrington 63 years before on November 21, 1932. . . A reception committee made up of Mrs. Henry Ellis, Mayor Ernest Novey, Mrs. Sanford Wadhams, Louis Tunick, et al. had been at work for some time to bring the internationally celebrated 52-year-old Helen Keller to town. . . Helen Keller was the woman whom Mark Twain once called "one of the greatest figures in the 19th century." She was born in Tuscumbia, Alabama, on June 27, 1880. At the age of 19 months she was stricken with a fever that left her blind and deaf. With the help of a pioneering teacher, Annie Sullivan, she overcame her handicaps to learn to read and write by Braille, to use a typewriter, and to even speak. She graduated from Radcliffe with honors in 1904, and for years served as an international counselor for the American Foundation for the Blind (AFB). It was in that capacity she came to Torrington.

(Left, an undated photo of Helen Keller reading a Braille text.)

On Monday evening November 21, 1932, a large crowd packed the old THS auditorium to see and hear Helen Keller herself. Miss Keller, it was reported, made a stirring plea for the endowment fund for the AFB currently serving 114,000. She wanted those present to realize that the blind were just normal people having the same feelings and ambitions as the audience members. The *Register* reporter commented that, "Her speech, while not clear, is readily understandable when one concentrates closely." . . . Helen Keller said that she enjoyed being with people and said that she "heard" the applause of the audience through vibrations in her feet. She expressed joy when the Torrington audience applauded and said, "It sounded very loud." At one point when the THS orchestra was rendering a selection, Miss Keller kept perfect time with her hands. She repeated one verse of "America" to close the program while Elmer Schroeder played it on his violin. She kept time by resting her fingertips of one hand on the fingerboard of Schroeder's instrument. . . . The evening was considered a great success, and a collection at the end netted $279.72 for the AFB.

One more internationally famous person to cross into Torrington borders was Leon Trotsky (right): the famous Soviet writer, revolutionary, and politician. In the March 19, 1918, edition of *The Torrington Register* it was reported that on the invitation of Joseph Juif of Red Mountain Avenue and a committee of local men, Trotsky had come to Torrington in the past. No date was given, though it was probably in the early months of 1917 when Trotsky was living in NYC. The short news article said that the men, including "many members of the Torrington socialist organization" entertained Trotsky during his "brief stay here." It was said that Trotsky, "until recently the head of the Bolsheviki in Russia" and a man "who has taken a prominent part in the revolution in that country," visited John Brown's birthplace and other places of interest in-and-around Torrington. Sidebar: Joseph Juif's brother, Frank, once ran as the socialist candidate for the office of Judge Of Probate in Torrington. He died in 1917 and wanted no funeral because, as he said, "The boys in the trenches (WWI) do not have any service over them when they die."

At the height of the Depression, in early October 1935, Admiral Richard E. Byrd, famed polar explorer and pioneering American aviator, stayed at the Conley Inn and delivered 2 lectures at the Palace Theatre. It was said in the local press that Admiral Byrd, along with Lindbergh, Roosevelt, and Al Smith, "is easily one of the most photographed, most popular Americans." He was greeted by John Brooks, Mrs. Frederick Braman, Mrs. Sanford Wadhams, et al. upon his arrival and was described as "clear-eyed, youthful in appearance despite streaks of gray in his hair." It was also noted that his face was bronzed and weather-beaten, and that he showed "the effects of his long exposure to the rigors of Antarctic." A group of 10 boy scouts including Francis Oneglia, Carleton Rosenbeck, Felix Cuatto, and James Brewster, were assigned to be Byrd's honorary escorts while he was in town. . . The 2 lectures played to a "capacity house" at the Palace. (Below, the Palace in 1928, 7 years before.)

The talks were illustrated/accompanied by film footage which included scenes of icebergs, whales, penguins, the 2 expedition ships, and the 140 dogs and 3 cows were which brought along. The lectures were described as "most instructive and thrilling, interspersed here and there with humorous incidents." When Byrd finished, "He was given a splendid ovation." All-in-all it was an unforgettable day for those in attendance, and a landmark moment for Torrington.

Over the decades many lesser stars, including many athletes, have graced our town. Among the athletes have been many UConn Huskies: Jim Calhoun, Geno Auriemma, Donny Marshall, Ray Allen, Travis Knight, Chris Smith, Scott Burrell, Murray Williams (of course), Talik Brown, Page Sauer, Maria Conlon, et al. . . Steve Pikiell talked to a Torrington group at the Knights Of Columbus in April 1996. He said his claim to fame was that he'd been the roommate of Tate George, "You know, the guy who made *the* shot." He said when he was interim coach at Wesleyan and saw that 7 out of his 15 players were 5'10" or under, he called his former coach, Jim Calhoun, and asked what he should do. Pikiell said that Calhoun told him to go bowling.

Some UConn players came to Torrington to raise funds. When Rickey Moore sat down in April 1999 at a desk at Wal-Mart after the Husky's National Championship, it was to sign autographs to raise money to benefit the THS basketball team and the Friends Helping Children. More than 1500 fans showed up. Moore was 45 minutes late, but he said he'd stay until "every last person went home happy with an autograph." And he did. The event raised $2,892 after expenses. (Below, Ricky Moore signing autographs in Torrington.)

Not every Husky was so philanthropic, or so it was once initially reported. When Jake Voskuhl showed up the next year, April 2000, it had been reported earlier that the $5/signature fee was "to benefit Jake Voskuhl." Nothing could have been further from the truth. The 6'11" center received only smiles and good will, but 3 local groups did pocket hard cash.

Pioneer sports broadcaster Marty Glickman was here in 1972, while former NY Giants defensive end Jim Katcavage spoke at the Cavallari Post Home in March 1962. NBA skyscraper Yinka Dare bought condominiums for investment at the Warrenton Woolen Mill complex, though whether or not he actually ever visited them I have no idea. It's a pretty certain bet he lost his speculative money. . . Popular Hartford Whaler star Kevin Dineen spent an hour at THS in 1990 talking to students about the danger of drugs, though he undoubtedly skipped mentioning the dangers of professional hockey.

Most celebrated athletes, like Johnny Unitas, came to our valley to sit at a banquet table and give an after-dinner talk. Most, not all. The Harlem Globetrotters and the legendary Marques Haynes played their usual spirited game here in December 1985. . . Pool great Willie Mosconi put on a demonstration of his skills in March 1988. A poster commemorating the event hung for years at the Berkshire Tavern.

(Left, Mosconi with cue in hand, circa 1950s.)

Similarly Ralph Greenleaf, 17 times the world pocket billiard champion, played a 100-ball exhibition match against local Torrington expert Ray Toomaiian in October 1948 at the Central Billiard Parlor. Greenleaf was also a champion 3-cushion billiard champion and an accomplished trick shot artist. Sidebar: A female teacher at THS told my class in 1966 that, "Proficiency in pool is a sign of a misspent youth." Wonder if she would have thought that world champion Ralph Greenleaf misspent his youth?. . .

Golfing great Walter Hagen played an exhibition round at Torrington Country Club (actually in Goshen, but close enough) in May 1936, put together 3 birdies in a row, and later shot the breeze with members in the locker room. He told them that he'd had a chance to turn professional baseball player in 1914 with the Phillies, but gave up the idea when he won his first golf tournament. It was reported by

Register columnist Walter Gisselbrecht that Hagen was "sociable and jovial" and that his golf play was "colorful and carefree." Hagen said he planned on spending several days in the area "attempting to get a few fish." . . . Another golfing great, Paul Hahn, similarly put on an exhibition at the TCC in May 1962. Hahn was said to be the "world's greatest combination of golfer, trick shot artist, comedian, and instructor." No mention was made of how good he was at baseball or fishing.

Three-time Tour De France winner Greg LeMond came to Torrington to neither sign autographs for $5-a-pop nor to put on an cycling exhibition. In February 1995 the world renown cyclist was at Innovative Cycle Concepts Corp. in the Industrial Park to endorse new line of bicycle safety products. He ate homemade pizza and chicken wings cooked by Teresa Canino, tried to compliment her in broken Italian, and signed off on her son Sal's product line. It was a molto bene Torrington moment.

The majority of the celebrities who come here, pop-in-pop-out. Academy Award winner and Northwest Connecticut neighbor Celeste Holm dropped by Nutmeg Ballet in 1996 to view a performance of *Cinderella*. Why? Because she had accepted the role of honorary chair person for the event. Why, again? Because, as she said, "The arts are vital to children." Simple and sincere.

Mr. Whipple, a.k.a. Dick Wilson ("Ladies, please don't squeeze the Charmin!") made a guest appearance at City Hall (below) to say hello to Mayor Delia Donne in June 1990 and smack off a photo-op kiss. Why the visit? The mayor was the friend of a mutual friend, i.e. everyone in the country is only a person or two removed from Torrington. Sidebar: I don't know if "Mr. Whipple" squeezed the Charmin, but he sure looks as if he has a pretty good grip on the mayor. . . Phylicia Rashad from *The Cosby Show* (Claire Huxtable) popped in at the Warner in 2006 to deliver the keynote address to more than 500 women at the second annual Women Of the World (WOW!) Forum. Why? Compatible philosophies. And she was paid. . . In a situation in which real life mirrored art, actress Cindy Williams and actor Paul LeMat, both stars in the classic cruising movie *American Graffiti*, showed up for a real life Meet-And-Greet in July 2007 at the downtown Cruise Night. Why? As Williams said, "I love meeting the people, my fans. It's great. It's outside, it's healthy, it's really American." And, of course, they were paid. . . My brother-in-law once had a conversation with the famous actor Richard Widmark in the waiting room of a Peck Road dentist. They discussed his movies like *The Alamo* and *Judgment At Nuremberg*, and Widmark undoubtedly returned to his home in Roxbury impressed that Torrington people weren't rubes. . . Sam Waterston and Henry Kissenger in the 1990s patronized Dick Cooper TV and Appliance. Why? Simple. They both lived in the NW CT corner, and one would imagine they both had electronic equipment/appliances they wanted to buy and/or needed repaired. Even celebrities are subject to the nuts-and-bolts (literally) of everyday life. . .

Barbara Bush, wife of the future President George Herbert Walker Bush, back in the 1980s walked our Main Street, greeted

Torringtonians, and dropped in at local businesses including Jon Marie and Dee's Restaurant. Why? She was campaigning for her husband, and presumably was hungry. Added Bonus: Dee's was the in-spot and Dee herself was a fellow Republican.

On the subject of hunger, Tom Jones, Stephanie Zimbalist, Christine Baranski and Michael Richards a.k.a. Cosmo Kramer have all dined at The Venetian, according to 2 sources. The Pedlar has been graced by many including Paul Newman (also dined at Tony's) and Mick Jagger. Jagger popped in for lunch, I believe, in 1989 (or thereabouts) when the Stones were staying in nearby Washington, CT at the Wykeham Rise School. Why WRS? The Stones needed 6 weeks of seclusion and rehearsal before embarking on their upcoming "Steel Wheels Tour." Moreover, Keith Richards had a home in Weston and Jagger's daughter Karis was an undergrad at Yale. I'd like to say that Mick played a set, or at least sang a song or two at the Pedlar. But no such luck.

(Above, what Mick at the Pedlar *might* have looked like, if only. . .)

On the other hand, after Three Dog Night played the Warner in February 1999, they followed it up with an encore performance at the Pedlar. They came down from their rooms at around 12:30 a.m. and jammed with the local band Tirebiter, which was already playing. They rocked the house till 2 a.m., the state mandated closing time. I had been there earlier, but left at midnight. Lesson: Don't go home early; celebrity artists sometimes don't come out until the wee, *wee* hours. . . Kelly McGillis, the female lead in *Top Gun*, came to the Pedlar in May 2010 to star in the horror film *The Innkeepers*. Of course, you couldn't go into the Pedlar to see her or watch the filming unless your name was Tom Cruise, Val Kilmer, or Meg Ryan, her *Top Gun* co-stars, none of whom showed. McGillis returned to town for the premier of the finished movie. She looked radiant, every bit the star.

A true superstar who did not disappoint was Lauren Bacall. She came to Torrington in October 1969 for the marriage of her son Stephen (father, Humphrey Bogart) to local girl Dale Gemelli. The wedding took place at the First United Methodist Church. I was overseas at the time, but I remember how people later ohhhed-and-ahhhed when they reminisced how they'd stood outside the church and saw Lauren Bacall. Lauren BACALL! To everyone's credit, no one claimed to have ripped off a lock of Bacall's hair or snagged a stitch of her clothing. Postscript: For a number of years after, Stephen and Dale lived in Torrington, but no one ever gathered again to rubberneck Bacall. Lucky woman.

Celebrity Speculation: I used to hear back in the 1950s that people had seen the flamboyant Liberace downtown. He reputedly had a friend(s) in Goshen and would journey down the hill to mingle amidst the bright lights of Torrington. I was never able to confirm this. . . One might imagine that Woody Allen stood on Torrington soil

(Above, what the author & Woody Allen *might* have looked like together, if only. . .)

back in 1992 when he hired the local law firm of Smith, Keefe, Conti, and David A. Moraghan to represent him against sexual allegations that he abused his adopted daughter. If Allen *did* come to town, there is no rumor of him ever drinking at the Berkshire, buying a round, or hanging out in Coe Park. . . I've also heard that Babe Ruth played baseball at Fuessenich Park with a barnstorming team sometime in the first third of the 20th century. But again, if it happened, I could find no documentation of it. . . Back 20 years or so, word reached me that Meryl Steep would occasionally sneak into Torrington from her home in Salisbury under the disguise of sunglasses, low-pulled hat, etc. to catch a movie at odd hours at the Cinerom. But I never saw her or spoke to anyone who did. . . Probably the most interesting speculation involved who owned the 28-foot stretch limousine parked for 2 days in October 1998 in front of the Yankee Pedlar. It had a front vanity plate with the initials "JC." Was it Johnny Cash? Johnny Carson? Johnnie Cochran? Jackie Collins? Jimmy Carter? June Carter? James Caan? The occupant was never seen. The chauffeur was spotted at one point carrying a Gianni Versace garment bag. Another time holding a champagne glass. The car took up 2 parking spots, and the second day it was ticketed. Celebrity occupant or not, the TPD showed *no* mercy.

World famous author (*A Wrinkle In Time*, *A Swiftly Tilting Planet*, et al.) Madeleine L'Engle lived in Goshen most of her professional

(Madeleine L'Engle at home in Goshen, late 1980s.)

life, though, of course, she kept a NYC apartment and travelled widely. It's an easy speculation that she came to Torrington frequently, and I know she *did* visit Charlotte Hungerford when her husband, Hugh Franklin, was stricken with cancer. Thing is, it's difficult to gather news of L'Engle in Torrington because, after all, who knows what most authors look like, even the famous ones.

Speaking of Charlotte Hungerford, I can state conclusively that the well known character actor Karl Swenson (veteran of many, *many* tv shows) died of a heart attack there in 1978. Reminds me of the old Italian saying, See Naples (Torrington), and die.

Of course it's no speculation that tennis Ivan Lendl bought the Cunningham Farm in Goshen and frequently played golf at the Torrington Country Club. But how many people know that in July 1989, Lendl stopped his Range Rover with 3 German Shepherds in it at Little Caesar's on McDermott Street in Torrington. He ordered a cheese pizza and was reported to have enjoyed it. Sidebar 1: Even the minutia of celebrities gets reported in Torrington. Sidebar 2: Little Caesar's was a stone's throw away from the Cinerom, i.e. could Lendl have been meeting up with Meryl Streep?. . .

Probably the most infamous person to "visit" our town was Katherine Ann Power. Power was part of an anti-Vietnam War, pro-Panther group that robbed a National Guard Armory in Massachusetts in September 1970. They stole weapons, ammunition, and set fire to the building. The group later robbed a bank in Brighton, Mass. One of the gang shot a police officer dead, and they escaped with $26,000 with which they planned to finance the overthrow of the federal government. Katherine Ann Power drove one of the getaway cars. She spent 14 years on the FBI's Most Wanted List. For 3 years in the early 1970s, Power and fellow fugitive Susan Saxe lived on-and-off in Torrington and other area towns working as cooks, clerks, and nursing home attendants. Power went by the alias Maureen Sheila Kelly while she was in Torrington. Apparently the women had no trouble blending in here. Epilogue: Katherine Ann Power turned herself into police in 1993 after 23 years on the run. She served a 6 year prison sentence. As far as I know, she has never returned to Torrington and remains today the only celebrity visitor who is *not* welcomed back.

Not every celebrity associated with Torrington was passing through. A few have actually lived here. Of course, there was the great abolitionist John Brown, but he scarcely needs mentioning. A lesser known was Howard E. Johnson. Johnson was a city resident from 1890-1906 and was a member of the THS graduating class of 1904. His claim to fame? Howard Johnson was a piano player "of exceptional ability" and became a noted song writer. His hits included, "Where Do We Go From Here" and "I Scream, You Scream, We All Scream For Ice Cream." He is buried at Hillside Cemetery.

The world famous journalist and writer William L. Shirer (*Berlin Diary, The Rise and Fall of the Third Reich*, et al.) lived in Torrington for nearly 25 years, from 1947 to the early 1970s. He and

(Above, William Shirer relaxing at home in Torrington, circa 1960s.)

his wife Theresa originally wanted to move to the NW Connecticut corner because of friends like James Thurber and Lewis Gannett who spent weekends in Cornwall. William Shirer told the Waterbury *Republic-American* in 1962 that they wound up in Torrington because it was here that they found a house they could afford. Actually, it was Theresa who found it while William was off on one of his many European trips... The house itself was a 1790's saltbox near the Brass Mill Dam with 100 acres of land.

William Shirer wrote everyday from 9 a.m. to 3 a.m., no lunch break, 6 days a week. He would occasionally use the Torrington Library for research. He cut firewood and did a little gardening for relaxation, had a 6-horsepower tractor to clear snow, and when he needed to go into NYC (kept an apartment there) he'd take the train from either Waterbury or Cornwall. He registered to vote in Torrington and was an Independent. As one might expect from such a busy, accomplished, and preoccupied man (who wrote right up until the time he died in 1993), his impact on Torrington was marginal.

Too busy. With one lone exception. When he and his wife Theresa divorced in 1972 and sold the house and land, they donated 10 acres to the Torrington Land Trust. Like Shirer's books, it's a gift that keeps on giving right up to this day. (Left, May 1972. Theresa Shirer in the center receives an honorary life membership in the Torrington Land Trust. Francis W. Hogan, president of the Trust with his back to the camera, presents the award to Mrs. Shirer. The well known, and land philanthropist herself, Rea King McCarty looks on at the right.)

Another world famous artist who lived in Torrington for many years, from 1927 to his death in 1973, was Paolo Abbate. Many residents will remember Abbate as that eccentric figure who'd walk down Highland Avenue from his home high atop the hill to downtown and back up. I distinctly remember the first time I saw him. He was old, but walked upright, had a white beard, and was wearing a very tall and wide-brimmed cowboy hat. Once seen, never forgotten. World class bohemianism right here in Torrington.

When Abbate moved here in 1927, he was coming from a star-studded background. Living in NYC, he hobnobbed with the great Enrico Caruso and Arturo Toscanini. He sculpted busts of Caruso, the naturalist John Burroughs, and President Warren Harding. He won competitions, taught, wrote, and sculpted.

And he had a vision. He wanted to create an artists' retreat. A peace and cultural center. A complex that would include a library, museum, theater, and work spaces where artists would "congregate to work and promote peace through cultural interchange." To that end he bought the Fowler Place (1750, the oldest house in

Torrington) on upper Highland Avenue complete with its 25 acres and barn.

As the years, then decades passed, fame and fortune eluded him. Almost as if by moving to Torrington, he'd slipped away from the mainstream art world. He became more isolated, but never stopped working and creating. Near the end of his life he was existing partly on milk from his goats which he shared with his stray cats and his Afghan Hound. And he could not pay his $500 property tax.

When he died, his artwork and possessions were auctioned off and went to museums and private collectors. In 1986, The Torrington Historical Society put together a collection of 30 of Abbate's pieces for a major exhibit. A poster for the exhibit hangs in my house today. It's a small reminder of the genius who lived among us and worked unceasingly hard to promote a better world through art.

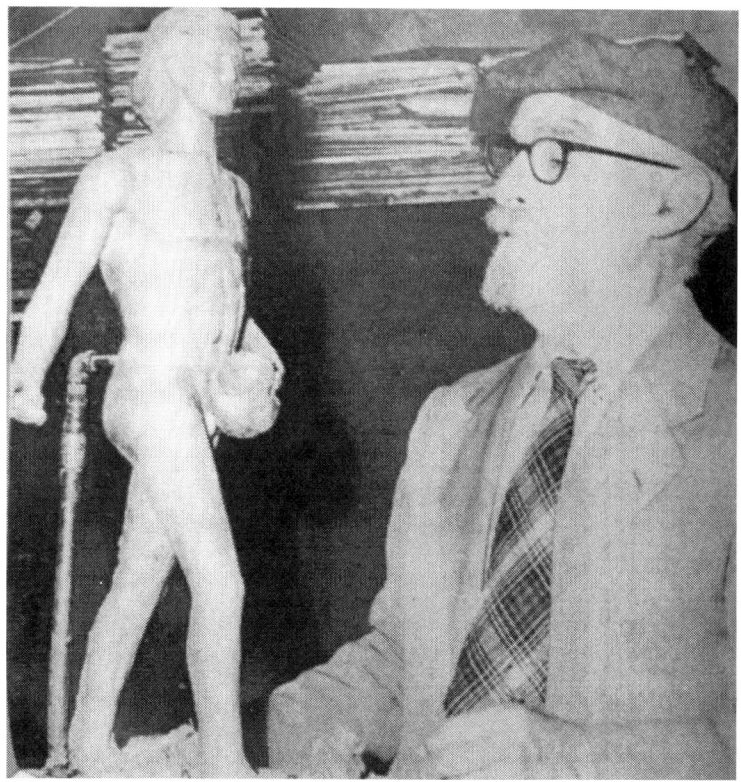

(Above, Paolo Abbate near the end of his life contemplates a small model of his work he called "The Sower" It was a work in progress, and it was his vision to sculpt this same figure into a 50-foot statue.)

(Above, a woman's bust by Abbate cast in bronze. It was rare that his sculptures ever made it to this stage, as he seldom could afford the process of bronze casting.)

✥ ✥ ✥

Postscript I

I know I've missed many celebrities who made Torrington a stop on their life's journey. I failed to mention all the professional wrestlers who were brought in for fund raisers. Grapplers like Brett The Hit Man Hart, The Mad Russian, Diamond Jim Brady, Rocky Jones, Razor Ramon, Dr. D, et al. . . I also neglected to mention celebrities I've talked about in the past like Mouseketeer artists

Jimmie Dodd and Roy Williams. Like Eddie "The King" Feigner and His Court. . . I didn't even talk about Peter Paul, a.k.a. the Armenian immigrant Peter Paul Halajian, and how he started what would eventually become the international candy giant right here in Torrington. He established Peter Paul Candy on the second floor of one of the buildings that was built over the Naugatuck River on Center Bridge.
And I'm sure there are many more whom I've missed.
But, enough is enough.

The celebrities came, and they went. A few stayed longer than others, but it was seldom more than a day or two.
And I like to think we were made better for having seen them. Perhaps realigning our priorities, resetting goals having seen what was, and still *is*, possible.
In any case, one thing is certain. The noteworthy have come to Torrington in the past. And they'll continue to come in the future.

(Below, what Lady Gaga playing the Fuessenich Park "stage" *might* look like, if only. . .)

Postscript II

Some of you are probably thinking about that April Fool's joke and which *one* of these celebrities never came to Torrington. . . FACT: They *all* did. And that's the joke, i.e. there is *no* joke. . . Disappointed? Not amused? Smiles on this end. . .

The THS Football Team Of 1948
Undefeated & Untied
The Glory Of Their Time

(*The Voice*. November 21, 1996. In the entire 123 year history of Torrington High School football, there have been only 2 teams that have finished undefeated *and* untied: the footballers of 1929 and 1948. Sidebar: Last fall, I thought for a brief shining moment the 2016 team was going to roll undefeated. And I went to *all* the games, including the away ones, with that thought/hope in mind. *But*, in 2016 they just couldn't get past Ansonia. . . Flashback now 69 years to the autumn of 1948. Unlike the undefeated squad of 1929 which immortalized itself by forming a club and giving out an annual award which goes on to this day, the 1948 eleven finished their season and quietly walked off into the sunset. Few today remember those post-WWII gridiron heroes. *But*, they were a tough, talented bunch. The glory of their time.)

It happened amidst headlines of Truman defeating Thomas Dewey and a longshoremen strike in NYC. It happened in the first broadcast year of WTOR and the first year Fuessenich Park had permanent lights. Christmas Village was approaching its second season, Torrington was celebrating its 25th anniversary as a city, William Kilmartin was mayor, and Charlotte Hungerford was in the throes of baby boom labor pains.

Down in the 30-year-old Church Street School, Richard Hughes was principal, and the faculty included the redoubtable Catherine Calhoun, Yale man Tracy Conway, Rose Brennan, scholar Everett Wood, future superintendent John Hogan, rookie Seymour Franklin, Ethel Johnson, steely Nellie Sullivan, and the most popular teacher Harold Rich. . . Students that fall, the Class Of 1949, chose Tyrone Power and Gene Tierney as their favorite screen idols; and Vaughn Monroe, the Mills Brothers, and Frankie Lane as favorite musicians.

And they chose football their favorite sport.

That football was #1 with the student body and Torrington fans as well was no surprise to anyone. Football was everywhere. Sportsmen's Paradise sold junior-size footballs, helmets, shin pads,

Bentley   Those Glorious Torrington Days

The 1948 Team. (From L to R) Front Row: Sam Mele, Anso (Moose) Bergonzi, Julie Palliuzzini, Bill Drozdenko, Jim Morzella, Don Santoro, Harold Pedlick, Charles Gebrian, Roy Borzansky. 2nd Row: Lou Zanderigo, Stan Nawalaniec, Tom Avampato, Tom LaPorta, Joe DiPippo, Peter Mazzaferro, Bill Mougenot, Andy Basile. 3rd Row: Joe Bianowicz (in shadow), Phil Kearney, Henry Bianowicz, Ted Averill, unknown, Bob DelVecchio, Herman Renzullo, Donald "Doc" DeDominicis, Lou Giotcile, Assistant head Coouch Anthony Apitzs. 4th Row: Manager Frank o'Meara, Dick Clark, Arnold Barnum, Tom Danaher, Leonard Bonini (in shirt), Jim Lepage, Leforge, unknown. Top Right: Jack Walsh.

149

football jerseys, and pants for ages 6-12. Older players played on the Torrington Redskins, a semi-pro team that averaged 190 pounds a man and featured the likes of Shy Samele, Lou Revaz, Cecil Best, and Ray Borzansky. And the THS team of the past year, 1947, not only won, but also at times looked invincible. Pete Mazzaferro: "We lost 2 heartbreakers in a row in '47 to the 2 best teams in the state. Then killed everyone. In one game (Coach) Pete Dranginis had the starting team put their civilian clothes on at half time." Stan "Stach" Nawalaniec (on left): "That '47 team was a tough, tough, tough team."

September 1948 dawned with a 6 game winning streak intact from 1947, but reporter Art Perret was not optimistic. Going down to Fuessenich to watch the team practice, he reported, "And once again we find the season's outlook blemished by the same old problem: a dearth of material." Head coach Pete Dranginis: "A lot of big guys were working afternoons and evenings in factories, driving good cars, making more money than teachers."

Still another problem: enrollment at THS had declined from 915 in '47 to 873 in '48. The backfield that September averaged 140 pounds a man; the line a 185. Needless to say, a question mark hovered in the air over the team's chances, though the students themselves went about life at THS (below) with smiles and laughter.

The September issue of the X-Ray, the student newspaper, ran the upcoming football schedule, a small article that the cheerleaders had added 4 new yell leaders (Beverly Norton, Lorraine Mossiman, Margie Patrick, and Susan Lucas), and profiles of the football co-captains: Jim Morzella and Danny Santoro (below).

INTRODUCING

Jim Morzella

Eng. IV, Art II, Physics, Typing II are the subjects which Jimmie is struggling with this year. His favorite teacher is Miss Johnson, and he also is a member of Varsity.

Jimmie's opinion on the New Look? "Well, it depends on who wears it. Some need to!" His opinion on short hair cuts for girls: "No, emphatically no!"

Cary Grant and Larraine Day are his favorite actor and actress. "Maybe You'll Be There" (not you!) is his croon song.

His secret ambition is to be a boat builder and his Pet Peeve is teen-age girls smoking.

IN THIS CORNER

Danny Santoro

When this little bundle was delivered, little did mama know that what she held in her arms was to be one o the most spectacular guards T.H.S. was ever to have. You all know by now the little babe was Danny Santoro, co-captain of the 1948 softball team.

Danny has well earned this title he has played varsity football since his freshman year. In school he carries an academic course and admits Mr. Conway's tops on his list parade of teachers. But football and school does not take up all of his time, he frankly tells us he is searching for an ideal girl. She is 5 ft. 4 inches tall and must be proportioned like Esther Williams, her hair brown, and her eyes, green, but most, she must like football.

We discovered that Danny is also very talented for on Saturday night you'll find him playing the accordoin in the "Bee Are Trio". I'll let you in on a secret: In a few years you will probably be crooning tunes arranged by none other than Danny, for he plans to be a musical arranger. Best of luck, Dan, we'll be cheering for you all the way.

On September 21, 1948, THS scrimmaged state powerhouse New Britain and fared well. Andy Basile (in 1996): "We kicked the shit out of New Britain. They were supposed to be hot, but they couldn't catch us."

THS opened 4 days later against Crosby. Not much rest, but The Big Red won that opener 20-7 with senior Julie Palazzini (on left), who had come out for the team only one week before, throwing 3 touchdown passes.

Stan Nawalaniec was the regular QB, but he had injured his knee in the Crosby game, and Palazzini would be relied upon in the future when a passing arm was needed, usually going in at left halfback.

One week later, on October 1 on a Friday morning, a Pep Assembly was held in the THS auditorium in preparation for the biggest game of the year: Ansonia. Torrington hadn't beaten The Chargers for 15 years going back to the Sonny Nevin team of 1933. In 1947 THS had lost to the Ansonia 7-6 in the last 2 minutes. But this year they were ready. At the assembly the cheerleaders led by Captain Phyllis DiLullo (on right) and supported by seniors Elsie Muraro, Madeline Kish, Mary Maville, Rosann DeCroce, and Stach's sister Helen Nawalaniec (later to marry center Tom LaPorta) were introduced. Coach Pete Dranginis gave an illustrated blackboard lecture, and the band played. There was magic in the air.

The next day 2500 fans showed up at Fuessenich for the opening kickoff. In their first possession, the THSers drove to the Ansonia 15. The field goal attempt hit an upright but just managed to fall over the crossbar. THS 3-0. (Below, a place kick at Fuessenich in 1948 in an unknown game. The ball can be seen rising in the center.)

In the second half Ansonia scored to make it 6-3, and the Torrington stands went glum. But then Lou Zanderigo, a speedy sophomore, returned the ensuing kickoff to the 38. Andy Basile: "Lou Zanderigo was the fastest." Lou Zanderigo: "With Vinnie Drake and Allen Webb chasing me, I had to run fast." And then Julie Palazzini faded back, could not find a receiver, shook off 2 tacklers (Pete Mazzaferro: "A guy had Julie by the shirt, but he pulled away."), and got a pass off to Len Bonini. Bonini was in the clear down the right sideline. Palazzini's pass traveled 50 yards in the air. Bonini took it in, outran his pursuers the remaining 20 yards, and just like that it was THS 9-6! Ansonia coach Pop Shortell broke his pencil, a fight broke out in the stands, and a cheerleader cried. . . The game got rougher. Andy Basile and Harold Pollick hit first team All-Stater Vinnie Drake so hard on a double team with their forearms that they had eye shadow on their sleeves. The game finally ended 9-6, and a low key Pete Dranginis told his players, "I'm happy we won, but make sure you've got your equipment on Monday." Julie Pallazzini: The most outstanding memory I have of our undefeated season on the playing field was beating Ansonia. Throwing a touchdown pass wasn't too bad either."

Nine days later, THS met Naugatuck on a Monday night under the new permanent lights at Fuessenich. THS had played under portable lights in '47, as had the All-Torrington team for years. The portable lights in reality were lights set atop wooden ladders held in place by guy wires. For the Naugatuck game the Recreation Department also set up 7 new sections of bleachers to accommodate an additional 1000 people. Two thousand people showed up. Good News: Tom LaPorta (below) was returning after being out since the second day of practice with a bad knee. It had been damaged on a clip during a scrimmage. Tom LaPorta: "I was hurt, lying on the ground, and Pete (Dranginis) came over and said, 'You hurt?' It's never fully healed, and I've been limping for the last 40 years."

Torrington dominated Naugatuck and won 31-6. Lou Zanderigo scored 3 TDs, two of them on runs of 54 and 30 yards, and Coach Dranginis substituted freely. Bob DelVecchio: "Pete would play his players. He'd try to get us in." A highlight occurred when Tom LaPorta intercepted a pass and raced 60 yards for a TD only to have a penalty nullify the play. Tom LaPorta: "I intercepted the pass at linebacker in the middle of the field. I ran right down the middle. I was so scared I didn't know what to do." Don "Doc" DeDominicis: "I ran down the field with him. Jimmy Smith clipped someone."

October 15 saw the win streak extend to 10 games when THS defeated Bristol 28-6, scoring in the first half on every possession. Comic relief was provided by assistant manager Billy Danaher when he trotted out onto the field during a timeout, got tangled with a cheerleader, and fell into the water bucket.

The season was half over and THS was 4-0. Coaches shared in the success. Pete Mazzaferro: "Tony Apizzo, the assistant coach, was a hard ass, a tough guy, and a good line coach. He taught shop." Bob DelVecchio: "Pete Dranginis could coach anything. The best." Doc DeDominicus: "I remember how Pete D. always made it a point to make every player feel that he was an important part of the team, even if he were only 3rd string. Pete always smiled."

And the season was successful because of the players themselves.

Doc DeDominicus: "Jim Morzella was tough." Tom LaPorta: "Pollick was a bull. Geez, he'd come around that corner!" Andy Basile: "Harold Pollick talked with a hairlip and would threaten opponents if they touched his one-bar helmet." Stan Nawalaniec: "Sam Mele, what a kicker! And he could run! Pete M. (Mazzaferro) kept us laughing. He knew more about sports. Dan Santoro was one of the biggest guys, along with Roy Borzansky. Harold Pollick, oh man, you put him on the line and no one was going to get through. Same with Santoro. Tom Avampato was small, a little runt, but boy could he catch a ball. And Billy Drozdenzo!"

The season resumed on October 23 against Wilby and was described by sportswriter Art Perret as "a contest that was anything but interesting." Too one-sided. Zanderigo scored on the reverse from 10 yards out for the first score. Andy Basile: "That was the old 782 on 3, our favorite play. We'd run out of single wing, and I'd hand it to the fullback or tailback, spin, or keep it. We had that play timed perfect." Anso "Moose" Bergonzi: "782 on 3. That was Andy Basile's play." THS beat Wilby 28-7 with Pollick kicking 4 for 4 on extra points.

Against Sacred Heart Nawalaniec and Mele both scored twice, 3 different bands played at halftime with Robert Cook leading the THS musicians, and 2000 chilled Friday night fans saw THS win 39-0. Pollick's string of consecutive point after reached 10. Basile: "Pollick could kick a ton. He got better as the year went on."

(Below, a photo of some 1940's THS football fans in the bleachers.)

The 6-0 Big Red traveled to perennial state powerhouse Danbury the next week on November 6. THS was now rated #2 in Class A, while Danbury, having a rough year, was unranked. Danbury's 40-foot portable lights made distinguishing players difficult, as did the fog. But one didn't have to see much to be aware that THS was in trouble due to injuries. Andy Basile, whose dad played with Coach Dranginis on the 1929 team, injured his shoulder and had to be taken to the hospital in an era in which no medical personnel were stationed on the sidelines. Stach Nawalaniec was knocked out of commission after a shoestring catch, and Lou Zanderigo twisted a leg early in the 1st quarter. (Sidebar: In one game Zanderigo's father went out onto the field to escort his son off because he felt the game was too rough. The police escorted the father off.) . . Luckily against Danbury the defensive line rose to the occasion, as it had all year, while Sam Mele, "the pride of Southwest School," averaged 45 yards on 3 punts. THS prevailed 26-7 in front of 3000.

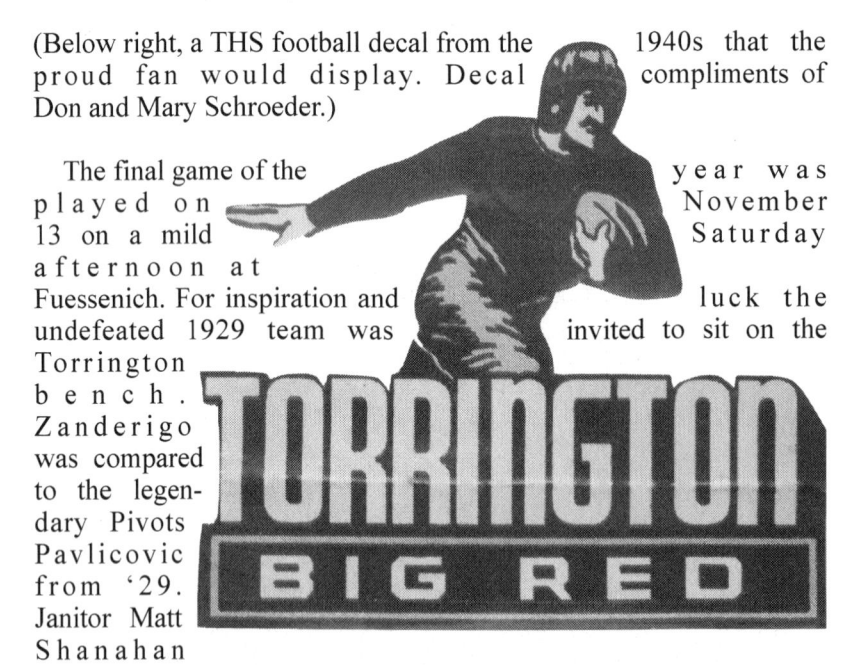

(Below right, a THS football decal from the 1940s that the proud fan would display. Decal compliments of Don and Mary Schroeder.)

The final game of the year was played on November 13 on a mild Saturday afternoon at Fuessenich. For inspiration and luck the undefeated 1929 team was invited to sit on the Torrington bench. Zanderigo was compared to the legendary Pivots Pavlicovic from '29. Janitor Matt Shanahan taped the running backs' an-kles before the game as he always did. In later years he'd collect admission at the gate. Fred Short handled the PA and called for a moment of silence to be observed for Assistant Principal James A. Smith who had recently died at the young age of 49. Sidebar: Smith had died at his desk while on duty at THS. A memorial assembly would later be held in the THS auditorium for the sophomore, junior, and senior classes, and would feature the singing of hymns by the high school chorus and short speeches by Superintendent John Murphy, Board Chairman Fiore Petricone, et al.

But for now it was time to play football, and try to finish the season undefeated and untied.

It was kickoff time.

Andy Basile: "Weaver was a tough game. We broke a runner's back leg. Four of our guys hit him, and you could hear it snap all over the place." Joe Interlandi's Weaver center was taken to the hospital with a fractured ankle, and Lou Zanderigo also went to have his hand put in a cast.

Roughness aside, THS just had too much talent and won 33-6.

Cheers. Hoots. Hollers. Pandemonium on the Fuessenich Park field. Undefeated. Untied. The winning streak, which started in '47, extended to 14 games.

> **James A. Smith Dies Suddenly At H. S. Office**
>
> James A. Smith, 49, assistant principal of Torrington high school and president of the Y. M. C. A., died suddenly this morning in his office at the school.
>
> Death, according to Dr. H B. Hanchett, medical examiner, was caused by a coronary occlusion.
>
> Mr. Smith was seated at his desk and slumped over just after Clifford D. Mignerey, a member of the school's faculty, started to talk to him.
>
> Death was almost instantaneous, and he was beyond human aid when two physicians who were hurriedly summoned arrived at the scene.
>
> Mr. Smith suffered from a heart

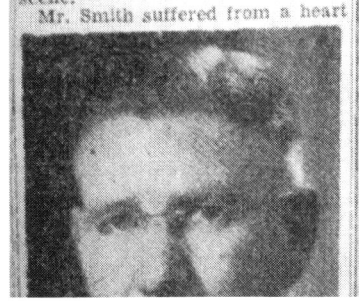

Sad News: The CIAC announced it had no intention of trying to select a state champion in post season play, then turned around and gave Norwalk the Waskowitz Trophy (symbolic of being state champion) despite one tie and despite the fact that Norwalk had defeated Danbury 25-7, i.e. slightly less than THS had defeated Danbury, their one common opponent. And as to any Turkey Day game, as is the tradition now, Pete Mazzaferro said, "We didn't play a Thanksgiving Day game because the THS basketball team played the alumni on Thanksgiving night."

It was time for basketball; football was over.

On December 9, 1948, the THS football banquet was held at the Elks. Players were honored with gold football charms, Jim Morzella got the '29 Club Award, Dan Santoro the Service Cup, and all watched home football movies taken by Matt Shanahan (the whereabouts of those movies today is unknown). Hank O'Donnell from the Waterbury Republican was toastmaster, and the event was sold out.

In a fortuitous turnabout, the CIAC finally decided to award *both* THS and Norwalk championship plaques. The 14-game winning streak came to an end with a 14-6 opening loss to Crosby in 1949. The team went on to win the next 5.

Co-captain Dan Santoro went on to the University Of Washington and played freshman ball. He hurt his Achilles tendon preparing for Notre Dame and never played again. He became an optometrist. . . Pete Mazzaferro has been the head coach for the last 28 years at Bridgewater State. He would like to coach into his seventies. . . Harold Pollick went to Fork Union, but is deceased as is Len Bonini. . . Joe Bianowicz played at post-THS at Cheshire and Brown University, and later played service ball with Lou Zanderigo at Ft. Dix. . . Andy Basile played both Navy football and baseball, while Tom LaPorta played football at Lackland AFB. . . Julie Palazzini went on to play minor league baseball with the Braves and currently works at a golf course in Port St. Lucie, Florida. . . Stan Nawalaniec boxed for 7 years, fought Golden Gloves, semi-pro, pro, made all-Navy, and today is a hair stylist. . . Moose Bergonzi plays senior softball 3 times a week in California where he now lives. And the rest. . .

(Below, some members of the 1948 team in 1996. Front Row, L-R: Lou Zanderigo, Don "Doc" DeDominicis, Tom Laporta. Back Row: Andy Basile, Bob DelVecchio.)

In a golden vision, amidst the yellowed autumn hardwoods of Church and Prospect I can see the gang now. They've changed into their football togs in the basement of the old school and are coming through the oak doors into the sunlight. The underclassmen are starting the mile or so walk to Fuessenich: up Prospect, left at the alley opposite the Brass Mill, through Coe Park, helmets swinging at their sides, townspeople and teenage girls smiling and waving and wishing them luck. The upperclassmen are piling into Stach's 1929 Oakland convertible, guys in the rumble seat and tottering on the running boards, while others hop into Avampato's green Model A pickup.

The caravan heads south spilling over with bodies and dreams. Ahead lies 782 on 3, the clash of pads, the rivened cleated earth, the mercurial foot races to the end zone, the bone jarring tackles, and Titanic excoriated warriors standing triumphant amidst a vortex of megaphoned cheers, streamed pom-poms, blaring bands, and the

(Above the 1948-'49 THS Cheerleaders. L-R: Janet Roberts, Maggie Kish, Diane Zappulla, Phyllis DiLucco Cardegno, Rosann DeCroce Fitzpatrick, Helen Nawalaniec LaPorta, Mary Maville Scoville, Marlene Burghoff, Elsie Muraro, Edwina Bartley.)

adulation of a school and town.

The 1948 THS gridsters. Then, and always, the glory of their time.

Back To The Future
Torrington 1997

(*The Voice*. January 9, 1997. Past readers of my column, or of any of these "Torrington" books, know that I used to enjoy putting out an annual prediction of what Torrington would be like in the upcoming year. As always with these rewrites, I've deleted or edited the most dated predictions. Sidebar: I used to base these predictions on what had come before, and I'd mix it with a healthy dose of wisecracking sarcasm. I'm happy to report that I didn't change that "voice" in this rewrite, *nor* did a single prediction here ever come true...)

It's once again that time of year for pushing aside the empty beer cases of the past and for staring into new depths and a new future. Armed with only a freshly fermented Ballantine Ale, "America's Largest Selling Ale," full of "Purity, Body, and Flavor," I once again fixate on the emerald green depths and see our common 1997 destiny...

1. *The first vision that greets my eyes is that of our new mayor, Mary Jane Gryniuk. She'll be all smiles when LaMonica's renames their classic bacon sandwich the MJG BLT in her honor. "At least it's not baloney," she'll tell reporters.*

2. A statue of Gryniuk will be erected at Columbus Square on East Main. Initially there'll also be a movement to rename the wedge of land, "Gryniuk Square," but it'll fail when no one on the Council can spell "Gryniuk."

3. *Several shoppers will die from exhaustion in Walmart's parking lot after driving around for several days looking for a parking spot.*

4. Christmas Village will hold a Truth-In-Christmas night whereby slightly older adolescents will be told that there is no Santa Claus. Members of the Torrington Taxpayers will break the news.

5. *The Main-Water Street block housing the old Howard's and the Wasteland Gift Shop will be sold and torn down to make way for a strip of national outlet stores. Parking stickers for Trinity's lot will be scalped for thousands.*

6. Displaced by the outlet stores, the Nutmeg Ballet will take to the streets. Tiny dancers dressed only in frankfurter buns will eke out a living pirouetteing around the numerous hot dog carts.

7. *By February WSNG will begin broadcasting Talk Of The County again. Several seniors will suffer heart attacks from the excitement.*

8. Luciano Pavarotti will visit Torrington just to dine at the Venetian, Anthony's, Salerno's, Roma's, and Bachi's. When the food runs out, Pavarotti will gobble down Joe Quartiero and Art Mattiello too, lick his fingers, and announce, "Now, that's Italian!"

9. *First Night will result in a sex orgy in Coe Park when youthful revelers misinterpret the phrase "first night."*

10. City water users, objecting to the Water Company's rate hike of 16.5%, will protest and fast. But their all-water diet will fail to impress Water Company officials, obviously.

11. *Residents in Torrington on Laurel's new fiber optic cable will begin receiving transmissions from deep space. The signal will be roughly translated as, "John Brown come home. Leave axe."*

12. Having raised $850,000 in their capital building fund drive, and spending it all, YMCA executives will unveil 2 new treadmills, new soap dispensers, and a rooftop full of Adirondack tents for residents. The terrific view of the newly renovated Vogel-Wetmore complex will silence critics.

13. *Seniors from the Sullivan Senior Center will use fake IDs to start hanging around the newly refurbished Teen Center across the street. They'll take hostages and hold out for buns of steel, ripped abs, juicers, and a Candystripper bus, fully fueled.*

14. Torrington will get a website on the internet. Nerds from all over the world will visit here electronically, causing creepy, psychic vibrations and an outbreak of pocket protectors, keys on chains, and moist towelettes.

15. *Steven Spielberg will not come to town to make a movie.*

16. The mayor will win re-election with the slogan, "Mary Jane, she's more than a synonym for marijuana."

And that'll be Torrington 1997. Cross my ale bottles.

New Board Of Public Safety Members Stooges Sworn In

(*The Voice*. January 9, 1997. I like bobbin' head dolls. And, I used to like to use them in articles to add humor and take the edge off. . . Background: Without dredging up too much of a controversial past, I'll just say that the Police Chief in 1997 was being re-investigated regarding the illegal wiretapping of phone calls from the cellblock between prisoners and their lawyers. A settlement had been reached under the previous Republican Mayor, but many in the city were not happy. Under the new Democratic Mayor in '97, a hearing was called, and 3 GOP Safety Board members resigned because of it.)

The Mayor in a move that caught even the most astute City Hall pundits off guard, announced at a press conference on City Hall steps this morning that Larry Fine, Moe Howard, and Jerome "Curly" Howard were being appointed as new Public Safety Board members

(Above, new Public Safety Board members, L-R: Larry Fine, Moe Howard, and Jerome "Curly" Howard are sworn in in front of City Hall. The slapstick masters have pledged an unbiased attitude towards the Police Chief, though none have ruled out a squirt of disciplinary seltzer in the face or an eye poke should guilt be proven. "Hey!" said Stooge leader Moe, "It's good enough for any true stooge. . .")

effective immediately. They'll be replacing the 3 members who recently stepped down over the hearings involving Torrington's current Police Chief. The Mayor told the assembled reporters, "When the 3 former members realized that their self-imposed disqualifications meant that the Board no longer had a quorum, they magnanimously resigned permanently so that the hearing process could go forward, and so that the truth regarding the Chief could be reached."

The Howard brothers and Mr. Fine, known professionally as The Three Stooges, recently bought condos at Lakeridge and were sought out by the Mayor because of "their clear thinking, their communication skills, and the fact that Larry is usually armed with a seltzer bottle." Asked if she felt there was any danger at the hearings due to the preponderance of heavily armed police, both in the audience and on the stand, the Mayor would only say, "I think that in the unlikely event that violence should erupt, the Board Of Public Safety will now be able to handle that emergency."

"They're nothing but a bunch of stooges," the defense attorney for the Police Chief fumed to press members. "Just a bunch of political stooges."

"Soitenly, we're stooges," Curly shot back. Then barking like a dog, "Arf! Arf! Arf!" and running fast in place, Curly windmilled his left arm in giant circles and punched the defense lawyer in the stomach with his right. As the legal expert bent over, his client, the Police Chief, stepped forward to help, but was interrupted by Moe who quite distinctly asked him, "What're ya doin' birdbrain?" As the Chief opened his mouth to respond, Larry stepped forward and squirted it full of seltzer, at which point Moe turned to Larry with a "Oh, buttin' in huh? Whatcha think you're doing, frizzlehead?" Moe then fluttered his hand up-and-down rapidly and poked Larry in the eyes. Larry retaliated by blindly swinging the seltzer bottle at him, but hit the Police Chief instead, causing the Chief to lose his balance and fall backward into several Republican town committee members. Once again the GOP members supported the Chief.

When order was restored, the Stooges were asked by the defense attorney, still holding his stomach, what their qualifications were for an administrative post. Safety Board initiate Moe answered that they had little leadership experience, were emotional question marks, and were oftentimes given to bad judgment. "In other words," he reasoned, "we're perfect for this, or any City Hall position in Torrington."

The defense attorney asked if the boys thought they could control their aggressive instincts in the staid confines of the Board environ. Their movie *Disorder In The Court* was cited as evidence that they probably could not.

Stooges' leader Moe lost no time in responding to the attorney's sarcastic insinuation. "Sooo, trying to moider us before we even get started, huh? Listen, lamebrain, I ought to. . ." Moe's forked fingers shot forward but were stopped at eye level by the attorney's quick, anticipatory reflexes. Defense attorneys know about Stooge behavior and sneaky tricks. Curly stepped in, as did the Chief and Larry. Curly palmed his own face several times, pulled down on it, then started slapping himself. He began his patented, " Woo, woo, woo, woo!" in front of the Chief, while Larry knelt behind the attorney. Neither the Chief nor his lawyer knew or saw a thing. A push, and Mr. Attorney went tumbling down the City Hall stairs, while the Chief, distracted, got crapped on by the City Hall pigeons. As he staggered around, the Mayor bonked him with her gavel. He tumbled down the steps and fell into the DAR fountain.

EMTs quickly revived the pair, who, along with certain key Republicans, limped off toward the parking lot, the day a complete loss. In the the background were a cacophony of reporters "n'yuk, n'yuking," and a kaleidoscope of citizens "Curly Shuffling" in the street.

The Three Stooges themselves took it all in stride. Board member Moe commenting, "To deal with knuckleheads, you need Stooges. We're happy to help out."

(Left, Curly, not letting the City Hall fracas bother him, enjoys a meal at the Venetian. Restaurant.)

(Above, Moe admiring the Civil War statue in Coe Park. When this reporter asked what he liked about the monument, he replied, "Listen Puddinhead, if a dumbbell like that can strike gold, so can we." Asked if he was referring to the Stooges someday getting a statue of their own in Coe Park, he said, "It's a big park." Then he gave the author an eye poke, twisted his nose, called him a dimwit, and hopped a Torrington cab already occupied by Curly and Larry. They were last seen n'yuking it up and driving west into the sunset. . .)

The Berkshire Tavern
An Albert Street Tradition

(New Article. April 20, 2017. There are not many old time Torrington watering holes and eateries left. But the Berkshire Tavern is certainly one of them. Thanks to the many people who shared many memories with me, almost more than I could use, and apologies to anyone whose reminiscences did not make print here. . . Special thanks to Mary Ann Woiciechowski Kennedy who not only furnished 4 of the photos used, but also was invaluable in providing background and general info, as well as anecdotes from 1950 forward. . . Some of the most damning and embarrassing anecdotes and memories that were shared by people, I've chosen *not* to repeat, as it was *never* my objective to embarrass anyone. Certainly not the business itself. . . Nonetheless, I feel that what's here is an accurate depiction of what the old *and* new Shire was-and-is like. If you've never been, or haven't been in years, now's as good a time as any. . .)

It sits comfortably at 71 Albert Street, a throwback to saloons with tin ceilings and well worn floors with exposed nail heads made smooth by the shoes and boots of generations of hard working, thirsty people.

When a person enters, the bar is to the left, the dining room to the right. If it's not crowded, heads at the bar are sure to turn at the sound of a new arrival. Like any bar, there are the regulars who could be in any chair, but on weekends tend to crowd on the immediate left, e.g. people like Mike Stefurak, Mark "Ziff" Richenberg, John and Carmen Indomenico, et al. In the old days there would have been an army of shot glasses alongside a regimented line of beer glasses all flanked by scattered cigarette packs. And the drinkers would have been only men. It was the law, i.e. no females allowed. And it was the custom even when the law was eventually dropped.

All that is changed today. Women may now outnumber men at the bar, and there are as many wine glasses as beer mugs/pints/glasses. It would be unusual to see a shot glass.

✢ ✢ ✢

I first went to the Berkshire (also called the Berk and the Shire) around 1961. Back then it was a "Tavern," not a "Cafe." And the interior and exterior were both physically different too. The interior, especially, was plainer, which befit the working men from the factories, foundries, and construction trades who frequented it.

(Above, The Berkshire circa 1960s.)

In 1961 a few of us: Todd Benjamin, Tony Costa, et al. stopped for a pizza and soda after a Friday night, 7th & 8th grade dance at the old YMCA. The thought of stopping for pizza was not mine. Pizza did not exist in my world. My family never made pizza or ordered it. It was not something my father would eat, so my mother deferred to him, and we kids to her. . . I remember that in 1961, as now, there was a divider between the bar and dining room, but unlike now, the old partition was solid and could not be seen over. (It's visible in the above picture just inside the door.) I lived on Blake Street, approximately a quarter mile away, so in a sense The Berk was our neighborhood place.

It had been there for a long time.

Susan Reynolds McKennon: "Not really sure if this is true. My grandfather, Pete Crowley, said that in years long before any of us, it was a stagecoach stop. Pete died mid-1970's at the age of 93. So it's very possible that he heard the story from a family member."

Jeffrey Stevens: "Had many a great pizza there. I think that building was my grandfather's (Joe Mubarek) grocery store before I was born. They may have even lived upstairs."

Jeff Stevens is right. The building at 71 Albert Street most likely was constructed in 1909 (the first year it was listed as vacant) and was designed by the architect C.D. Janssen, later of New York. The next year, 1910, it was listed as Mubarek Brothers Grocers. The building stayed Mubarek's till 1934, when it was listed once again as vacant. It stayed unoccupied till 1946 when it became the Berkshire Tavern. NOTE: There had been an earlier "Berkshire Tavern" owned by John Avampato in 1934 at 24 Winsted Road. By 1937 it was listed as Brownie's Tavern owned by E. Fray. Did John Avampato move his business and business name in 1946 to 71 Albert Street? Was Avampato the original owner of the the Berk? No one I contacted knew, and the State Liquor Commission does not have records for those early post-WWII years. What *is* known is that around 1950 Peter Woiciechowski bought it, and it was under his family's ownership for the next half+ century. (Below, the bar circa the 1960s. NOTE: A large pizza was $2-and-change.)

Peter Paul Woiciechowski, known simply as "Pete," was in charge on that Friday night in 1961 when I had my first ever pizza. Pete was originally from Newtown, Connecticut, but lived most of his life on Route 118 in Harwinton, later moving to Harmony Hill Road after his children were grown. As a child he went to Harwinton schools, but his daughter, Mary Ann Kennedy, told me Pete got thrown out at an early age for putting a snake in the teacher's desk. . . Before buying the Berk he had worked at New Departure, according to Pete's other daughter Diane Landucci, and had no tavern or business experience whatsoever. There *was* a tradition of farming in the family, and I was told that Pete saw himself as a farmer at heart. In later years he kept his own garden, but the produce was for family consumption only, i.e. not for sale or to be used on the Berkshire pizzas, burgers, etc.

Around 1950 Peter Woiciechowski bought the Berkshire Tavern, and the rest, as they say, is history. But it was a history that took time to develop. For example, pizza did not come with the tavern. I was told by one family member that Pete developed his own formula/recipe through trial-and-error for the pizza dough, sauce, and sausage. Another family member said, No, the Berkshire pizza recipe was a combination of tradition and tinkering. That Pete paid a man from Winsted $500 for the recipe, and it was *this* recipe that he experimented with. Irony #1: From Pete's perspective from the beginning, the idea was that pizza would be a good enticement to attract-and-keep customers. But that pizza was only going to be offered until Pete recouped his $500, i.e. pizza and the Berkshire were never seen as a permanent coupling. . . Irony #2: Pete was Polish and spoke Polish, i.e. it's ironic that a person so cultured in Eastern Europe should develop the best *Italian* pizza in Torrington, especially given how many Italians there were, and still are, in town. . .

I don't remember Pete waiting on us back on that night in 1961. In the 1960s and early 1970s the two I remember who took pizza and drink orders in the dining room were the bartender Harry Banziruk and the longtime waitress Mildred "Millie" Thrall. Harry was a machine operator at the Torrington Company while Millie worked at Fitzgerald Company and Torin. Bartending and waitressing were something they, and many others, did over the decades for extra money. Harry himself was close to Pete and also did work at Pete's house.

Neither was a man that anyone looking for trouble wanted to mess with, certainly not me. In 1961 I was only 13-years-old, and my

drink of choice was Coca Cola. That was what we ordered, and we weren't the only youngsters coming to the Berk for pizza and soda.
Richard Bartku: "My buddies from Scoville Hill and I used to go to the Berkshire Tavern (not Cafe) to watch the Friday night fights on TV. Yes, Joe Louis. They would serve us their fabulous pizzas, but no beer. I loved that place. Have not been back in over 60 years. I hope it's still as good. Of course, nothing tastes as good as when you are 13."

Older teens in the 1960s, and beyond, however, preferred stronger drinks.

Hartley "Bud" Connell: "I used to go to the Berkshire underage back in the sixties and I was not alone in that libation liberation. Always thought the Berkshire saved a number of lives keeping the lads home instead of driving to NY. Did my fair number of drives to Amenia and Millerton, but after THS in 1964 graduated to the Berk! Went something like this. Always went to the tables on the right as you walked in with usually 2 to 4 guys and sat. The owner, Pete, took our order of a large pizza and pitcher of beer. If you acted like you'd been there before, no problem. Act like an obnoxious kid buying rubbers for the first time, and you were carded or just asked to leave. I didn't look 21 till I was 31, but I was never carded at the Berkshire unlike most bars/taverns in Litchfield County. Don't know why. Never asked. Just enjoyed the cold ones and ambience only the Berkshire could offer a young guy with a full future ahead of him."

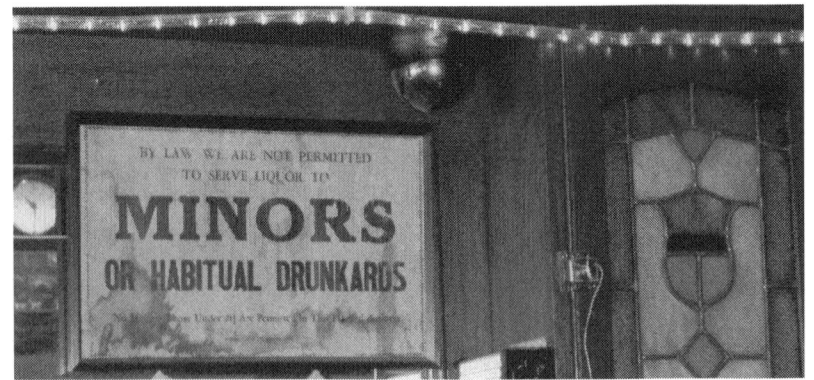

(Above, a framed warning, stained by decades of hanging over the Berkshire bar, still proclaims that, "By law we are not permitted to serve liquor to MINORS OR HABITUAL DRUNKARDS. No Minors [Those Under 21] Are Permitted in This Place Of Business")

Frank Bentley: "I have fond memories of the Berk from my younger days. It was one of the establishments that would serve you without checking for an ID. Couple that with the best za (pizZA) in town and going there was a no-brainer. One of my cherished memories was the times I went with Chick Baltuskonis, Fred Reichen, and Tom Husser. There was a partition separating the bar area from the dining area. One night while waiting for Millie to bring our bill from devouring 2 large pizzas and 2 pitchers of beer, we decided to bolt without paying. We escaped unharmed. The next week we were brave enough to return. Somehow Millie didn't remember a thing. Again when she went to the other side to get the bill we split. Wow! This was a great thing we had going! The 3rd time was not the charm. This time Harry, the bartender, confronted us with the unpaid bill. When he slammed his fist on the table, I was quaking. I feared he was going to haul off and belt me or maybe even have us arrested. When we paid up, he shocked us by saying, 'All right, *now* what are you having?' We were quite shocked but very relieved, of course. We said, 'Two large mushroom and sausage pizzas and 2 pitchers of beer.' And with that, life was good again and we spent many more times at the Berk. It's a great memory, and to this day I still hit the Berk regularly even though I live in Wallingford."

Carmen DeAngelo: "I remember when I turned 18. Had my first legal drink with my father at the Berkshire. Something I will never forget. Good times and memories."

NOTE: The drinking age in Connecticut was lowered to 18 in 1972 and stayed there for 10 years. It was raised to 19 in 1982, raised again to 20 in 1983, and finally returned to 21 in 1985.

Susan Borrelli Poley: "The Berkshire is where we all had our first drink. Pete knew us and would serve us beer."

    Other than going for pizza occasionally in the 1960s, I never went into the Berkshire to drink when I was underage. We could drink legally in New York State and did at places like the Tally-Ho, Log Cabin, Rumpus Room, Berkshire Lodge, etc. When we wanted to stay in town and drink *illegally*, we'd hit Teddy's A Go Go and Cindy's, both on the Litchfield Road before the driving range.
    All that changed in 1970 when I got out of the Army and was now of-age. From 1970-'74 I worked off-and-on at Hillside Cemetery, the

Wire Mill (part of the Broad Street plant), and Booth's Foundry a.k.a. Torrington Casting. These were all dirty, physical jobs, i.e. they all built up a thirst. And all were in the Berkshire Tavern neighborhood. It was natural on some days after work that we'd gravitate to the Albert Street watering hole where cleaning up first wasn't necessary beyond washing the face and hands. My mother used to tell me, "Your father never drank at taverns. If he wanted to have a drink, he'd dress up and go somewhere nice like the Pedlar." It made sense, but it just wasn't always practical, especially when your co-workers said, "Let's stop for a couple." Sidebar: There was an old worker at Hillside named Charlie Baker who had worked at the cemetery forever and lived just down the hill on Walnut Street. Charlie in his circumnavigations around the cemetery would pick mushrooms. Then later trade them with Pete at the Berkshire for draft beer. I don't know if Pete used them on the pizza or for personal use. But no one died or got sick that I ever heard. . .

Back in the 1960s and '70s the Berkshire was a plainer, rougher place. The walls were hued a light tan by cigarette and cigar smoke. The word "dingy" comes to mind. And I have no memory of any wall hangings, plants, or what some might call the woman's touch. It was a place of boisterous talk and laughter, shots-and-beers, and dirty fingernailed men. On the dining room side there were a jukebox with yellowed selections, an old bowling machine in the corner, and booths with a wall buzzer, that theoretically should be used to summon the waitress. I don't know if the buzzers worked; I never heard one go off. A pool table would come later.

Karol Westelinck Dyson: "I was not allowed to go there when I was young, and only ever went with my boyfriend Jimmy Lehmann. I did not tell my parents. I think the seedy reputation was before the '80s. Seemed like there was always someone going in or out who looked inebriated! My young impressionable mind I guess."

Cindy Casal Zack: "Gosh, I remember when 'decent' women didn't go in!"

Shawn Fogarty: "I remember riding in from Harwinton with my dad to get our pie. There was no such thing as delivery in those days. It was a rough kind of atmosphere at the bar for a kid. I was kind of impressed that some of the guys would say 'hi' to my dad and shake his hand while we waited for our pizza."

Richard M. Knapp: "My grandfather was Arvid Levin. He arrived here shortly after 1900 and worked as a blacksmith at the Anaconda Brass Co. He walked to work from McKinley Street. On occasion my mother and aunt in the 1940s and 50s would wonder why he was late. I remember how embarrassed they were when they had to go to the Berkshire and get him home. He found it a very relaxing and friendly place."

Will Point: "I once saw a man exit the Berkshire holding a pizza *vertical* like a book. I imagined he was thinking to himself, 'I know I'm drunk, but when I get home this pizza will get me off the hook. My family will be so happy!' "

(Above, owner Pete Woiciechowski tending bar in 1964. On Sundays the Berk opened at noon, and Pete wore a shirt-and-tie to go along with his ever present cigar, usually an Evermore or Moneymaker. His daughter Mary Ann Kennedy: "On Sundays he liked his shirt to be ironed just right.")

Mary Ann Woiciechowsi Kennedy: "A guy came in late one night and got a pizza. He was on a motorcycle, and he carried the pizza sideways like a briefcase... Another time a guy out front backed into a parked car. There was a fellow sleeping in the parked car with his feet hanging out the window. The first guy thought he'd killed him. He was very upset..."

Back in those golden 1960s and '70s, there might have been over imbibing at the Shire by some, but most held their liquor well. I never personally witnessed any fights or physical confrontations, though others did.

Mary Ann Kennedy (on far left with father Pete in center and mother Elizabeth on right): "Ernie Jasch was the guy who knocked out my father's 2 front teeth. Sucker punched him. . . Ernie seemed to get inebriated pretty fast. Pete would pour him one drink, then without Ernie knowing it, Pete would serve him ginger ale. And Ernie would *still* get drunk!"

Anonymous Old Timer: "Ernie Jasch lived upstairs back in the old days. To say he was a regular at the downstairs bar would be an understatement. He was such a barfly that he had his own special bottle – a half gallon of Calvert's. Pete would keep it in the refrigerator because Ernie liked it cold. Neat, no ice. One evening Ernie showed up as usual, sat down, and Pete got Ernie's bottle to pour him a drink. Ernie looked at it and without batting an eye said that there was less in the bottle than there should be. Accused Pete of drinking it himself, or selling it to others. . . Understand that Ernie was swizzle stick thin. A wizened man with glasses who looked like he hadn't had a good meal in decades. Pete, on the other hand, was a hulking bear of a man. Huge with the stump of a cigar usually hanging in the corner of his mouth. He saw red. Came around from behind the bar, grabbed Ernie by the scruff of the neck and seat of his pants, and carried him to the door. He paused before throwing Ernie out. But he *did* throw him out. Literally. It seemed as if Ernie soared like a bird all the way to the sidewalk, though in reality it was more a matter of Pete just dropping him on the sidewalk. When asked later why he paused – was it conscience? – Pete said he was waiting for a car to come along. . . No one messed with Pete."

Dave Frigo: "Peter was one of our earliest customers. We go back over 50 years. He was a hard, *hard* worker. He didn't take any crap from anyone. It was his way, or the highway."

Pete could be an intimating person. Mary Ann Kennedy tells the story how whenever Pete would stop by Christy's Tavern on High Street and Vivian, the owner's wife, was working, she'd phone her husband to come in. And she'd leave when he did. Pete intimated her that much, probably more by his gruff manner and physical presence than anything he actually did or said.

Glen Bronson: "Friday night. Place jammed, young kid out of control. Pete told Harry not to serve the kid anymore. Like most any young kid he got hot and started the shit: 'Who said that? I'll kick his ass.' Pete came out from behind the bar with the cigar hanging out of his mouth and said, 'You wanna see me?' The kid still mouthy said, 'Yea. You're an asshole.' So Pete, with Harry right behind him, with his Adam's apple twitching as it did when he got excited, started backing the kid up one step at a time. He was jabbing him with his finger at every step? Said, 'So I'm an asshole? You've been coming in here since you were 17. You didn't think I was an asshole then. I like your old man so I let you in here.' Now they're almost to the door and Pete said, 'Here's your chance. If you want me, you better do it now cause you're not coming back here.' The kid fell over backwards on the steps. Harry went out, picked him up, shoved him, and said, 'You heard Pete.' Then it was back to business as usual."

(Above, L-R: Pete Woiciechowski, Leon Woiciechowski, Tom Jerrykitz, and Glen Bronson circa the early 1980s. Photo compliments of Glen Bronson. Note: This picture is pre-renovation and was taken in the back corner by the men's room which is on the right. The pool table can be seen at the bottom. Note also that Pete and Tom are smoking cigars. Smoking in bars, taverns, and restaurants was legal, and it was certainly done at the Berk.)

Glen Bronson: "Harry (the bartender) would have a few but never appeared drunk. A real find for Pete. In the liquor business you don't find many who won't rob you blind. . . Pete, on the other hand, drank and sometimes had one too many. I can see that if a person wasn't around him that much, the person might not pick up on it as easily as I did. The way I could tell Pete was drunk is that he'd be more full of bravado than ever. He'd buy drinks and strike up conversations where he didn't belong."

I myself never saw Pete drunk, but maybe I just wasn't savvy or regular enough. One cold sober, take-no-prisoners thing of Pete's I did witness many times back in the early 1970s was his love of cutting a deck of cards for money. Sad to say, I witnessed the Berk owner on several occasions take my brother-in-law Kenny

Perzanowski for what seemed like a lot of money. And it happened so fast! I mean how long does it take to cut a deck of cards multiple times? They'd start cutting for $5 a flip, and increase it usually when one fell behind. It would take no time at all to get up-or-down $100/$200+. Of course, no one was twisting Kenny's, or anyone else's, arm to gamble with Pete. *Still*, not everyone lost.

Ray Lanthier (Berkshire cook for 25 years): "I sometimes cut cards with Pete for $100 a cut. And I usually won."

<u>Sidebar</u>: Pete was an interesting character. A larger than life person whose talents and interests went beyond the confines of the Berkshire Tavern.

Erin O'Meara Clark: "My Dad grew up next to Pete and his family (in Harwinton). I remember him telling me Pete was also a pilot and used to buzz the neighborhood with his plane, a little too low!"

Klaus Gorski: (related to Pete through marriage): "Pete owned a 4-seater plane."

Susan Borrelli Poley: "Pete was a bondsman at one time; plus, he used to fly his own plane. He bought my father's bar, the Village, in Lakeville in 1962 to expand his business. One of the daughters (Diane Landucci) ran it."

Tavern owner, entrepreneur, cook, bartender, gardner, pilot, and bondsman = Pete Woiciechowski. He was a well rounded man. A street smart, hands-on owner who kept the customers happy and kept them coming back. Mingled with them. Set them up. Listened to their woes and imparted his knowledge. A user friendly place. Going there for a drink and/or pie was usually a pleasant, uneventful hour or two. With great food.

Sara McKenna: "We went every Friday night as a family. When I was really little (probably 9) my parents ordered pizza from there and my grandfather (DiLaurenzio, not Doc) went to get it. We, of course, went with him as we were grandpa's girls. When he got there and realized it was a bar, he made my sister and I stay in the car, lie back in the seats, and wait for him because a bar was no place for kids! Little did he know we were there every Friday with Mom and Dad!"

Claudia Bruno Castle: "When I was young in the 1950s and '60s we always got our pizzas from the Berkshire. They were the best! Sometimes my father would pick one up and bring it home to West Goshen, but more often, in nice weather, the whole family would ride to Torrington to get it. Then my father would drive us to the Brass Mill Dam where we would sit and enjoy it. It was a big treat for all of us!"

Diane Woiciechowski Landucci (daughter, picture on the right): "The Berkshire was a nice place to go. The people were very cordial."

Peter Diulio: "Many great memories growing up and going to eat pizza there, while hearing Pete talking real loud behind the bar. Always a friendly tavern."

Jane Borovy: "As a child I only remember Dad getting pizza at the Berkshire and when I was older and I'd come home over the years. Yup, Berkshire pizza please!"

Jean Sterling: "That was my Mom's favorite place to get pizza."

Gary Versari: "Great spot growing up in the 1970s for pizza, 25 cent beers, and some pool."

Arthur Surdam: "Like everyone I well remember the excellent pizza. But as a kid, I also remember the jukebox which I would always play while my dad and I waited for the pizza. It was the 1960s, and the music was great. I remember the bar was packed, and a lot of guys who worked at O&G would be in there on Thursday nights (pay day), and Pete would cash their pay checks."

Bob Parsons Sr.: "They had 'Cryin Time' on the juke box."

Bill Celadon: "I remember under Pete's watch stopping late one night for a slice and a beer, maybe 40-45 years ago. Johnny Cash was playing on the jukebox, while we played the bowling machine in the narrow area near the men's room."

Dave Frigo: "Peter had a big following with O&G and payday. In the early days, O&G paid the workers with cash. When they went to checks, Pete would cash $8000/9000 worth of checks. This way the guys didn't have to let their wives know when they got a raise."

Sidebar: For decades there was a framed cartoon that one of the regulars drew hanging to the left of the bar next to the front window. It featured a rowdy O&G crew cashing checks on payday. Pete, naturally, was behind the bar. The cartoon is no longer on the wall in 2017, and no one I asked knew what became of it.

Mike Barbero: "My Dad brought me there many times, and I later went there regularly with friends. It was Torrington's Cheers. Best pizza in town and great salad dressing!"

Dottie May: "The Berkshire was the only place we ever bought pizza, at least while I was living at home. The best anywhere!"

(Right, a large Berk pie with cheese, sausage, mushrooms, and half anchovies.)

Eunice Froeliger: " It was a real treat in my family to either go to the Berkshire Tavern or have my father bring a pizza home from there. There wasn't much going out to eat in those days. The sausage was the best, but I hadn't developed a taste for anchovies yet so we always had to get a pie with half anchovies. My brother is rarely in Torrington, but he always goes there when he is!"

Joyce Satanski Jacques: "I remember back when I was about 4 or 5-years-old living on Clarence Street, my dad used to pick up 3 or 4 pizzas, and my much older sisters and their husbands would come over every Sunday night for dinner and family time. It's funny because as an adult I ended up dating and eventually living with Ray Lanthier who used to work in the kitchen. He would always bring something home to eat after work whether it was a pizza, salad, or sausage grinder."

Jennifer Suthowski Hardwick: "Crazy fun! Walking in and knowing every person sitting at the bar."

NOTE: The old Berkshire Tavern was not only a meeting place for family and friends, but other "groups" liked rendezvousing there too.

Roxanne Gianni: "When I worked at the Torrington Company in the Finance Division (cost & general accounting), we had almost all of our parties there. We always packed ourselves into the place. Best pizza in town. Miss those days."

Sandy Richard: "I used to work at Social Security, and some of us would walk to the Berkshire occasionally for lunch. We'd sit in a booth and have one beer. Their hamburger and sausage sandwich with the works were fabulous! I think 4 p.m. was the cutoff. After that you could only get pizza. In work later, we'd silently mouth, 'I'm so thirsty!' It was because of the beer and and sausage, but we didn't want the others to know."

Jason Williams: "What I remember most was going there on Tuesday nights after the Torrington Company softball games with my dad and his teammates back in the late 1980s and early 1990s. It was the best pizza."

Edwin Ben: "When I went to the UConn Torrington Campus, my U.S. History class and I went to dinner one last time before the unfortunate closing. It was a lot of fun. We've been going there ever since as a 'UConn' reunion."

While comradery is desirable, and it was great at the Berk, the crux of keeping any tavern going is the *food*, i.e. booze is booze, people are people, but it's the *food* that determines whether or not a tavern's doors stay open. In the case of the Berkshire, it's not only the pizza that kept most people coming back, but also. . .

Diane Pappalardo: "My former brother-in-law, Gary Cooper, worked there. We ordered many pizzas and salad from the Berkshire. Oh that dressing! Everything was available for either dine-in or take-out."

Joy La Mere: "Best salad dressing ever! Still stop in to get a salad whenever I'm back in town."

Katie Patterson: "I used to live right around the corner and would go there often for their delicious burgers. Always a treat."

Hartley "Bud" Connell: "My wife and I have been once-a-week regulars for decades. In her frisky youth, wife enjoyed scotch and soda, but now it's white wine with ice. Me, I liked Double Diamond in the early years, Smithwicks (always draft) now since DD is no longer offered. We split a salad: olives and dressing on the side."

And even for the many who have tried *only* the Berkshire pizza, there's one memory that stands out above all others, and gives every pizza regardless of its toppings a common denominator:

Diane Bruneau: "Best pizza. The only one that comes in a bag, not a box."

(Right, the author with a large Shire pie to-go in the famous brown paper wrapping.)

Doug Grieco: "When I think of the Berk, I always think of the brown paper bags they put the pizza in. I've never seen pizza put in anything but a box, other than there. You just can't recreate that crust they have. It's gotta be those old pizza ovens and a secret recipe. Best sausage and roasted peppers around!"

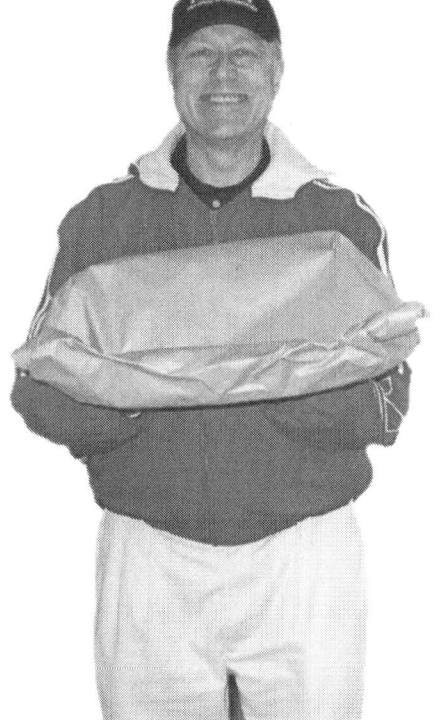

Dave Ferrato: "Still make the best pizza, and they still put it in paper bags. We go there every time we visit from Florida. My wife's Uncle Alphonse Woiciechowski was Pete's brother."

Cheryl M. Pace: "My dad used to order us pizzas from there when we were kids. I can remember the taste and smell to this day. (I can't wait to get back home to enjoy it again.) They wrap it special in a paper that doesn't let it get soggy. Amazing hometown goodness. I hope they keep it going. P.S. - I continued the tradition with my kids too."

✣ ✣ ✣

As the years passed, the Berkshire stories: the stuff of local legend, continued to grow and expand (sometimes close to the facts).

The Legend:
Dennis Santore: "There was a story how someone rode a motorcycle up the steps, through the bar, around the booths, and went out from door. It was Buddy 'Zeke' Zaharek who became a preacher in Florida the last years of his life."

The Fact:
Mary Ann Woiciechowski Kennedy: "Dad (Pete) didn't like motorcycles. One day he said something, and the guy (Zaharek) went out, drove his motorcycle in, and drove around. Dad had him arrested, then bailed him out. He was a bail bondsman."

The Legend:
Klaus Gorski: "There were stories of a cow in the bar."

The Fact:
Mary Ann Woiciechowski Kennedy: "It was a horse, not a cow. And I don't know if it was actually inside or just on the premises. I know my dad (Pete) rode it home to Harwinton at 1 a.m. and parked it in the garage. The next day he rode it back."

The Legend:
John Todor: "I remember a story that someone told me about a patron telling the bartender about his pet python, which was about six feet long. The bartender didn't quite believe the size of the snake,

so the guy left and showed up a while later and laid the snake out on the bar. Emptied the place pretty fast."

Chris Pond: "I'm pretty sure that snake belonged to Pete's daughter Mary Ann."

The Fact:
Mary Ann Woiciechowski Kennedy: "The snake was a 3-foot boa constrictor, and it belonged to Peter, my son, who loved exotic animals. He'd gotten the snake from someone at the Junior Republic, and I named it 'Stretch.' When he brought it to the Berkshire, my son didn't lay it on the bar. It was wrapped around his neck!"

The Legend:
Joyce Satanski Jacques: "I don't remember his name, but there was a bartender that worked there who played the bagpipes. One St. Patrick's day Ray Lanthier (the cook) had him walking up the street playing the bagpipes. All the neighbors came out of their houses to see what the heck was going on. It was one of the best things ever!"

The Fact:
Ray Lanthier: "I paid Scott Cawley $20 to go up-and-down the street playing bagpipes. It was St. Patrick's Day. People came out of their houses, and they really liked it. He also played inside. . . Speaking of inside, we also used to light off M-80s inside."
(Above right, bagpipers playing inside the Berkshire. Photo credit to Kerri Anderson Ouellette.)

Most of what went on inside the old Berkshire wasn't the stuff of legend. It was just plain fun. Good for laughs, with no malice intended, no laws broken, no dangerous byproducts.

Ray Carcano: "We had ordered pizza one Sunday evening in the summer. My wife, Brenda (the niece of bartender Harry Banziruk), dropped me off to run a quick errand. After having beer and grabbing our oily pizza, I went outside to wait for Brenda. Ten minutes passed, and she still didn't show. I decided to go back in for another beer. As I walked back in carrying the pizza, I shouted out, 'Who ordered the pizza?' You should have seen the faces at the bar. It was definitely a priceless moment."

Glen Bronson: "There was one Sunday night about 10:30 (the bars closed at 11 at that time) when Jim and Lisa Hudson (names have been changed) came in (they had moved away) to see everyone. They also wanted a pie, a few pops, etc. Leon made the call that we would all pitch in, get the place cleaned up, then we would turn the lights down low and have pizza and a drink or two. Amazingly that was agreeable by all. LOL Well, we had the pie and commenced to drinking, talking etc. I was behind the bar, Leon and Lisa were sitting on the stools, and Jim was standing at the end of the bar by the opening. After a few, Jim said, 'I have to pee.' He backed up, turned toward the bathroom and went down, face first. Didn't try to put his hands out or anything. Lisa screamed, jumped off the stool, and proceeded to feel for a pulse. Anything. Side Note: We were all scared shitless. The next thing was a big snore out of Jim! It was such a relief that we all laughed uncontrollably. Finally Leon said, 'What are we going to do with him?' I said, 'He's tired. Put him on the pool table and he can rest.' We put him on the table and he snored happily away. The next thing I saw was Tony Languell, a Torrington cop. He was looking in the window and pointing to the back door. We let him in. He had a couple slices and said, 'You need to be out of here by two o clock.' We took George and put him in the car. Leon, Gloria, and Jim vanished. And I went home."

Ray Lanthier: " Bob Sprague used to come in. He'd complain that he didn't like driving a garbage truck. He'd talk about where else he was applying for work, and I'd overhear it. I'd call his home. Make like it was one of the places he applied to, like Midas Muffler. His mother would phone the Berkshire and tell him to, 'Stop drinking and get to your interview!' And he would."

Glen Bronson: "There was a couple from the Hemlocks trailer park who came in daily. His name was Tex, cowboy hat and all. Six foot, 118 pounds. Always a Lucky on his lips and his wife Alice, on his arm. A missus 5'x5'. Alice was sweet on me, and Leon would tell Tex to go home. That she would get a ride with one of us. She would pour the drinks, and eventually we would take her home. This one

(Above, friends Leon Woiciechowski and Glen Bronson circa the early 1980s shaking hands and clinking beer bottles. This is the old Berkshire, pre-renovation. Note the simplicity of the booths, the lack of wall hangings, and the wall buzzer.)

night she was like a kitty cat rubbing up against me and all the rest. When it came time to leave, Alice said, 'Leon, can I sit in the front between you and Glen?' Leon looked at me, and I said, 'Well, the car rides better that way.' It was quite a sight, Leon rolling around on the sidewalk laughing his fool head off. . . Same Scenario, only this night she wanted to dance, specifically a polka. Leon loved to polka, so I put a dime in #10 but played a waltz, The Rangers Waltz. We both danced a little with Alice. I was hopeful that that would end it. But no! Now they both wanted to polka. I played In Heaven There Is No Beer, and off they went: 6'4" Leon and 5'x5' Alice. About the 3rd time round the pool table, down she went! And we couldn't get her up. She probably weighed 350-400 pounds. Again Leon said, 'What are we going to do?' I said, 'Have another drink. She'll come out of it.' . . . Finally we got her up and into the car and back to the Hemlocks. We got her out of the car and to the steps, but she couldn't navigate them. This was a problem because once we had her lined up, we could not get around her to open the door. Finally I called out to Tex, and all 118 pounds of him opened the door. He assessed the situation and said, 'You push and I'll pull.' Side Note: Back then, I was a really rugged guy. Anyway, Leon was on one cheek, I was on the other, and it was 1, 2, 3 − PUSH! It took 3 tries but finally with all our strength and Tex pulling, she went through the door and knocked Tex ass-over-tea-kettle. We never saw her again, but I'll never forget her or that night. We've had many beers and scotches laughing about it since."

(That Old Gang Of Mine. Photo credit to Glen Bronson. The old Berk circa the early 1980s. Pizza sign quotes $4.50 for a large pie. . . Included in this gathering are Glen Bronson, Leon Woiciechowski, Stretch McDonald, Earl Johnson, Tom Jerrykitz, Tony Languell, Chet and Mike Tomascewicz, Dan Fisher, et al.)

Anita Vedovelli (waitress, kitchen help, bartender for 15 years): "Ray (Lanthier) used to tie my apron to things. . . They hid my brother-in-law's truck. When I went to leave work, it wasn't there. They moved it down the street. . . After my first day, one of the long time workers told me, 'I can be your best friend, or your worst enemy.' It was very intimidating. . . After a week I thought I'd leave.

The people were crazy. Why did I stay around all those years? It was family. We helped each other."

(Above, Ray Lanthier and Anita Vedovelli in 2017 in front of the pizza ovens at Scarpelli's where Ray still makes pizza and where Anita herself once worked after the Berkshire years.)

Out of all the incidents that ever occurred at the old Berkshire, the one that old timers remember best, and the one that even newer/younger patrons have heard of, is the day the tavern was robbed at gunpoint, and a shot fired.

Klaus Gorski: "There's a bullet hole in the ceiling, above and to the right of the cash register. It's still there. Geez, maybe the slug is still in there."

Mary Ann Kennedy: "My father, Pete, cashed O&G paychecks on Thursdays. The robbery was on a Thursday, April Fool's Day (April 1, 1970). The robber hit Pete in the head with his gun and shot a hole in the ceiling. Pete had a kink in his neck before the robbery. But after getting whacked in the head, the kink was gone!"

The Particulars. At around 11:10 a.m. on April 1, 1970, a lone gunman entered the Berkshire. He was described in the newspaper account as "tall, thin, with a reddish mustache, a blue cloth jacket with a hood, and wearing dark sunglasses." He ordered the 8 patrons

Bandit holds up Berkshire

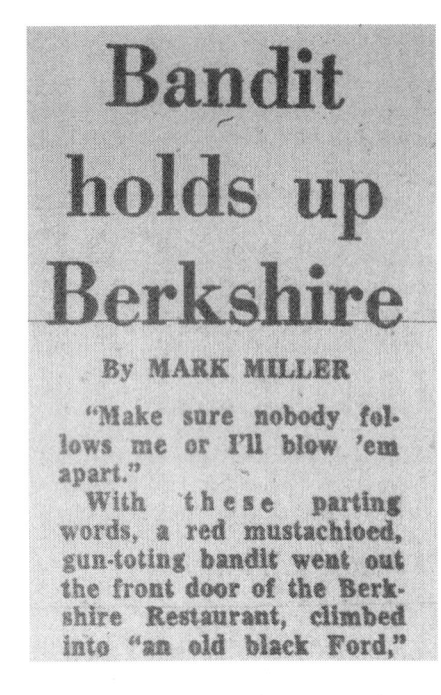

By MARK MILLER

"Make sure nobody follows me or I'll blow 'em apart."

With these parting words, a red mustachioed, gun-toting bandit went out the front door of the Berkshire Restaurant, climbed into "an old black Ford," to put their foreheads on the bar, and told Pete to fill a paper bag with money. Pete thought the gun was a toy, hesitated, and the robber fired a warning shot into the ceiling. It was only then that Pete began filling the bag with money, while the robber had the 8 customers lie face down on the floor. Out front an accomplice had the getaway car, "an old black Ford," waiting. When the bag was filled with "an undetermined amount of cash," the pair sped off. The car was last seen heading south on Rt. 25. They were never captured.

I remember the robbery well. I'd only been out of the Army a couple of weeks and thought I'd returned to a combat zone. As far as the robbers getting away scot-free goes, I was told by one knowledgeable Berkshire insider, "There are different forms of justice." That Pete found out who the 2 men were and that, "It was taken care of." It would make sense, i.e, frontier justice for the old saloon. But who knows for sure. (Below, the circular bullet hole is *still* visible in 2017 in the old tin ceiling.)

Sidebar: While it was certainly possible that someone could have easily lost his life/her life during that robbery, there's a story exactly the opposite, i.e. how the Berkshire might have actually *saved* a life.

Jan Roberge Lyon: "Not sure the year this happened but it was sometime after my 1967 THS graduation. Fall of '68 maybe. . . My grandfather, John W. Scoville, walked to the Berkshire Tavern daily in the morning for a shot of brandy. At 82-years-old and a heavy cigar smoker, he had been warned by his doctor to quit. But he told the doctor that he'd been smoking cigars all his life and wasn't about to give them up now! In the morning in question, he went to the Berkshire from his home at 98 Wilson Avenue, which was right across the street from the tavern. Upon returning home, he was struck with a heart attack. Neighbors saw him staggering across the street back to the house and called my mother who lived in the upstairs flat where we were raised. By the time she made it downstairs, grandpa had made it to the front yard and dropped dead. The coroner said that the only reason he made it to the yard was the shot of brandy! Rest in peace 'Bomb-boo,' our favorite name for Gramps."

On the subject of criminals and the Berk, Glen Bronson tells a more uplifting and amusing story than the robbery one.

Glen Bronson: "It was a slow Monday night, and there were only Leon and I in the place. A young couple came in. They were good looking and very happy. Turns out they'd just gotten married and were celebrating the occasion 'honeymooning' at the Berkshire. In the course of conversation told us, 'It'll be awhile before we're back.' Confessed that the fellow was going 'up-the-river' and that he was leaving the very next day to do his time. Leon graciously contributed a pizza and a few beers. It was not only their honeymoon, but also *his* last night of freedom. And they chose to spend it at the Berkshire. To my knowledge it's the only wedding reception ever at the Berk."

✜ ✜ ✜

In 1972 Connecticut passed a law that it was now legal for women to both sit *and* stand at a bar. I'm not sure exactly what year the room divider came down. But one source said it was to allow females easier access to the bar. Another source, that the divider came down to open up the space for a pool table. . . Personally, back then, I preferred the Berk with the partition *up*. Why? Simple. I just liked the look of the room better, though the old divider was certainly *not* a thing of beauty. Also, I don't know if the lighting was changed, but it seemed harsher, brighter with the wall down. Mark McEachern of the Torrington Historical Society remembers the same thing and recalls that there were florescent lights.

Along with the physical change to the room, things seemed to get rougher over time. Edgier.

Randy Brothwell: "When I used to go there in the early '80s, it had become kind of disreputable."

Ted Dunn: "Back in the 80s a friend of mine and I were in the Berkshire drinking beer, and I was shooting pool. We both had shoulder length hair. We drank a lot of beer and spent a considerable amount of money. As we were leaving, someone called out 'Good night girls!!' I turned around and was heading back in when my friend grabbed me and convinced me to let it go. I just thought it was funny that not one of the rednecks said anything while I was holding the cue stick."

Susan Strand, in a *Torrington Register* column circa 1986, said of the slightly older time period: "The Berkshire had a certain atmosphere about it that invited excitement, or mayhem depending on your point of view. I was sitting at the bar the night someone set off a cherry bomb inside the building. . . (Another evening) We weren't there very long before a fight erupted and the fighters ended up right next to our table. They didn't think it was funny when they saw us laughing uncontrollably; but Leon came to our rescue and didn't let the situation go any further than it already had. It was definitely a night to remember."

Whether or not these impressions were correct of a tougher, edgier Berkshire evolving through the 1970s into the early 1980s (and they *were* shared by me), there can be no doubt that in 1983 a seismic shift occurred. Pete sold the business to his son Danny. And life at the Shire, as the saying goes, would never be the same again.

Change didn't occur immediately. Danny himself had worked there, as had all Pete and Elizabeth's children to varying degrees, and Danny no doubt was well inured to the way things had traditionally been. By 1986, however, his vision of what the Berkshire needed to be matured, and he decided it was time for the dusty old "tavern" to evolve into a "cafe." Perhaps recapture some of the magic Danny remembered from his youth. Sidebar: Danny once wrote: "When I was a young boy and Torrington had its spectacular Fireman's Day Parade, a man, a friend of my father's, came into the cafe after the parade with his set of bagpipes and proceeded to march around the partition, wailing away on that beautiful instrument, reducing the din of a very crowded establishment to an almost inaudible whisper. The performance was more than stunning, and even after he left it took some time for the combined conversations to return to the previous level."

Could this be the sort of magical moment that Danny wanted to recapture again? He was willing to try and to put his money where his dream was. The change would start with the physical.

Mary LeBlanc: "My ex-husband, Vernon, refinished the bar when Danny took it over from his father."

Not only was the bar refinished, but the interior was painted a darker color, wainscoting added to the walls, wall hangings above that, new booths put in, new lighting, and a partition once again added separating the bar from the dining area. This was no plain plywood barrier like the old one had been. This one featured wainscoting, turned newels, and stained glass. If customers were going to be separated, it might as well be in style but not be so opaque as to not allow one side to see the other.

(Above, the bar area in 2017 in the mid-morning hours before opening. Though different than the 1960's space as seen on p.168, it is still laid out the same and still retains the bones of the old Berk.)

Sidebar: The pool table was gone. Danny later told the press that it killed the pizza business. But in the back corner there was still entertainment, updated for the late 20th century. . . **Karen Czerwinski**: "If I really remember correctly, my brother and I would argue over who would get to play on the PAC-man video game there!"

I remember the first time I was in the newly renovated space back in 1986. I was stunned. Suspicious. Didn't know what to make of it. Suspected that the factory, construction, and trade crews would abandon it. Knew for certain that life at the Berkshire would never be the same again.

So what *were* the short term results? Answer: Danny built it, and they came. Families, singles, working people, professionals. Old timers were slow to abandon it, many never did, the regulars stayed. Long term effect: A younger generation discovered it, and the Berkshire Cafe was here to stay. In the words of Susan Strand, "Business was booming."

Kathleen Goodwin: "Danny was such a good host. I moved away 14 years ago, but I remember it well! The best pizza."

James Lombardo: "Danny was a good friend. I still go there all the time, though I miss the old days when they had a pool table."

Gayle Adorno Campbell: "I worked at the Torrington Company, Needle Bearing Division. We would go there for a special lunch, i.e., someone's birthday or someone getting transferred. Danny always made sure we had a big enough table and we could be back by 1 p.m. He had the pitchers of beer waiting depending on who was attending (no supervisors). This time frame was in the 1990s."

Hartley "Bud" Connell: "I enjoyed the late owner Danny, who enjoyed sitting down with us and discussing past, present, and future travel plans. When we went to Ireland, many of our stops were on his recommendation, and we were never disappointed with his suggestions."

Mary LeBlanc: "Danny was a good friend of my family and was close to my brother, John Waldron. They traveled to Ireland together. John also bartended there."

I myself remember Danny showing me black-and-white photographs he had taken on a trip to Egypt. Professional caliber shots, many portraits of the Egyptian people. He also talked about some of the sizable expenses he incurred there, and I remember thinking, *Business must be damn good.*

To this day I think of Danny possessing the soul of an artist who should have *never* been running a tavern, though there's *no* doubt he did it well for quite a few years. (Right, a painting signed by "Byrley" and dated 1978 that was hung by Danny decades ago above the entrance to the men's room. It's still there today. I think it combines his love of art with the quirkiness that was the old Berkshire.) A big part of Danny's success was due to the fact he liked people, and people liked him. He was tall, but non-threatening with a ready smile and conversation worth listening to.

One of his first hires was Ray Lanthier.

Ray Lanthier: "When I came in that first day, Pete looked at me and said, 'What do you want?' I told him that Danny had hired me and that I was here to work. He told me, 'Then get your fucking ass in the kitchen, and get to work' . . . I learned that Pete's bark was worse than his bite. I thought he was a great guy. *BUT*, not at first."

Danny was quieter than Pete. Totally different personalities with the common thread of attracting good workers. Between the 2 of them, many local people worked long, hard shifts at the Berk. People like Ray Lanthier and Anita Vedovelli. Harry Banziruk and

Millie Thrall, mentioned earlier. A couple of the earliest bartenders were Red Briggs and Tony Torsiello. Later would come staffers Louie Variengo, Tony Pucino, Charlie Cawley, Susan Poirier, Mike Arlen, Mert Davis, Robin Gath, Gary Cooper, Jay Winegar, Eddy Earle, Leslie Reznick, Lisa Hogan, Anna Miasek, the friendly Amber Macary, et al. **Floraine Consolini**: "I remember in the early 1950s, maybe late 1940s, my friend's father worked there as a bartender."

Many did. Some were better than others. Most were honest, a few were not. I remember one bartender over charging a friend of mine twice, and not long after the second time it happened, the friend complained and the offender was gone. The friend received a $25 gift certificate from Danny. . . A Different Time, A Different Bartender: It was a slow Monday night with few customers. After the last customer and the bartender left, Mary Ann Kennedy found $75 left near the bar. The next day, the bartender, who'd been on duty the night before, came rushing in and said he'd left his tip money. Mary Ann showed him the $75, he said it was his, and she asked how he could have *possibly* gotten $75 in tips when there was almost no one in the night before? The bartender was eventually fired.

Not all the help stole, of course. There were, and still are, gems.

Mary Ann Kennedy: "Hau Bentley was just the sweetest bartender. She'd clean an ashtray even if there was only one ash in it *and* almost as soon as the ash hit. My father, Pete, knew this. He'd miss the ashtray intentionally. She'd fly over, wipe it up, go away and he'd do it again. Sometimes she'd hover near him just for this reason. Everyone knew about it, and everyone got a kick out of it. The guys loved her." NOTE: Hau Bentley was the Vietnamese wife of Henry Bentley from Harwinton, a retired Lt. Colonel in the US Air Force, who served as a combat pilot in WWII and Vietnam.

Gayle Adorno Campbell: "Bill and Gretchen Ross worked there. Bill used to own The Spaghetti House. Carol Dean also worked there when Danny had it."

Ray Lanthier: "Billy Ross fell in love with Gretchen, who worked in the kitchen, and they got married."

Diane Addison: "I've been going there for over 50 years! My dad, Billy Ross, worked there as a bartender and waiter for years. He was the head schmoozer. LOL"

(Above, March 1998. Berkshire owner Danny Woiciechowski with retiring bartender Billy Ross. Ross was retiring after 14 years, and Danny said of him, "Billy was always here on Friday nights. He was really the nerve center of the whole operation.")

Good bartenders, good waitresses, *should* be good schmoozers. Have an active sense of humor and a moderate threshold of tolerance, even when the feet ache and the unexpected happens.

Jocelyn Archaski: "I was sitting at the bar and saw a rat running behind the counter. Told the bartender and he shrugged and said, 'Yeah, he's around, but he doesn't bother anybody.' If I recall the bartender even had a name for him. I want to say it was 'Arnie,' but I might be off. . . Another time it was really busy and either my dad (Dale Bronson) or Bud called Leslie who had become their friend, on the phone to ask her for another round."

Ray Lanthier: "One bartender would rent limousines. Danny would tell him, 'How stupid are you?' So one day he rented a limo and sat in the Berkshire parking lot just to piss off Danny."

Funny joke, funny sense of humor, though expensive. . .

Unfortunately some bartenders at the "new" Berkshire definitely did *not* have much of a sense of humor. Or perhaps it was more of a low tolerance for anything other than discrete, sedentary talk. I recall going in there one Saturday afternoon and having a beer while I waited to pick up a pizza. Must have been the late 1980s/early 1990s. While I was sitting enjoying the draft, I was joined by a fellow who I'll call Jim. Jim had a loud voice and a louder laugh and he stood alongside me. He had just started his first beer, wasn't drunk, and certainly was no rum-dumb. A suit-and-tie professional. We were talking, Jim was laughing, and the bartender came over and told us in a haughty, disdainful manner, "This *isn't* the old Berkshire anymore." Jim and I looked at each other. Gave it a puzzled WTF shrug, and Jim left shortly after. Guess our volume was too high. I was stuck waiting for my pizza, kept my thoughts to myself, but it was awhile before I ever went back.

Bill Celadon: "After being told to 'get the fuck out' years ago, any good thoughts of the Berkshire have faded from my memory."

Thought: Civilization can be a damn pain-in-the-arse. In some respects, when the Berkshire Tavern became the Berkshire *Cafe*, along with the elevated name, came a heightened sense of expectations from the patrons. They got it. Got families. Got more salad and club soda types. And perhaps lost something in the process.

✤ ✤ ✤

The years passed. Pete died on a Thursday in July 1993 during a heat spell. He was 75-years-old. Gone was the founder and legendary

(Above: Happy Days Are Here Again. September 26, 1959 at Deer Island Gate. L-R: Red LaRosa, unknown, Peter Woiciechowski, Red Briggs, Bill Heacox, Tony Torsiello. Sitting in front, unknown, but could be Ernie Jasch.)

bar keep. A man who in his later years used to like to open up early for the old timers, such as his really good friend Red LaRosa. Who saw himself as a farmer at heart, but who knew little about farming and liked to go to Las Vegas. Who rolled the dice in the biggest gamble of his life when he turned a tavern into a big-time pizza house. And won.

While the inimitable Peter Woiciechowski could never be duplicated, he could be replaced, and it was his son Danny who now kept the cafe going.

From 1983 to around 2010, i.e. 27 years Danny Woiciechowski was THE man at the Berk. Like all of us, he had his faults. But unlike the vast majority of us he no doubt felt the day-to-day pressures of keeping a family business going where the work day was typically 12-14 hours long, and the work week all 7 days. And keeping it going when I'm not sure the artistically inclined Woiciechowski was a natural fit. Example: He once turned off the tv set in the bar during the 7th game of the World Series with the score tied in the 9th inning, because he wasn't paying attention and just wasn't swept up with baseball. Even at *the* climatic moment. **Ray Lanthier**: "Danny was always mad growing up because he'd get stuck working at the Berkshire. His brothers played sports. But he was never into that." Fact: As a student at Lewis Mills High School, Danny was in the Camera Club and on the Yearbook Staff for 3 years. . . But despite his natural leanings elsewhere, Danny worked hard and put in the hours. Why? I'm not sure, but probably in part because he felt a responsibility to all those he employed. He told the press in November 2008, after a temporary state-mandated shutdown was lifted, "It's real, *real* nice knowing our family here is going to be back where we all want to be." He added, "Family, that's a phrase that could be considered corny or overused. But it's exactly like that."

Family. The owner, his employees, and patrons. The customers from all over the state who phoned Danny, concerned over the state-mandated shutdown. The local police and firemen who routinely celebrated promotions there. The two former employees who split off when they thought the Berkshire was going under and started Berkshire West *with* Danny's initial blessing. And *with* a stack of free thin-edged pizza pans Danny gave them. . . Danny once said that he thought of the Berkshire as "a small bar, on a side street, in Torrington." Nothing more, nothing less. That is, until the shutdown in the autumn of 2008 when there was such an outpouring of sympathy and support from all over Connecticut, that Danny Woiciechowski told reporters, "I'm surprised. And moved."

I'm not going into the Berkshire's problems with the state; there were many. The state had its hand in Danny's pocket, and so did thieves. Ray Lanthier: "There were a bunch of robberies. Danny never reported them. He didn't want to report the amounts." . . . There was also a marriage gone bad. . . Life was a bitch. . . Still, Danny fought hard to keep the Shire open and said in a letter to Judge Vincent Roche, "I pray I might retain the business so as to honor my father's name and tradition." But try as he might, the odds, and perhaps the Olympian fates themselves, seemed aligned against him. He himself called the matter, "a perfect storm." It was. Business and life. A heady confluence of bad luck, bad decisions, and. . . A former Internal Revenue official, a man familiar with the Berkshire and its tax situation, told me that it was the state of Connecticut and its state tax department that ultimately did in the Berkshire back then. And perhaps its owner. . .

On August 16, 2010, Danny died unexpectedly. He was only 57-years-old. Many mourned his passing, and I was among them. (Below, Danny and the author in a frozen moment in the autumn of 2009.) When I think of Danny, I think of simpler times like these. Of men *and* women, *and* sometimes their children, smiling, laughing, and bonding at *his* cafe. Though I didn't know Danny when he was a youngster, it's a happy image I have of him as a boy, enjoying the countryside where he grew up. **Bonnie Gangell**: "I lived in the same neighborhood in Harwinton and went to school with the Woiciechowski boys. Leon, Danny, and I used to ride our bikes together." It was a time when Danny, no doubt, believed all things possible. Work hard, peddle hard, reach for the horizon. And with a little bit of luck, and an outstretched hand, life can be. . .

❖ ❖ ❖

These 2017 days, the Berkshire Cafe is no longer under the ownership of the Woiciechowski family. For a time it looked as if the Village Restaurant from Litchfield would buy it, but I was told they dropped their offer at the last minute. Then for a time it appeared that Danny's sister-in-law would close on it, but that too fell through. . . **Lloyd Agor**: "I talked to Leslie (Reznick) about buying it, did a walk through, and finally used every dime I had, and then some, to buy it and make it work. Failing was never an option."

Agor had to deal with both the state and federal governments 6 years ago to close the deal and admits that the whole process was "convoluted and confusing." But it finally *did* happen.

Today, in the Woiciechowski vein, Lloyd Agor puts in long hours. He commutes daily from his home in New Milford (an hour away), and is usually at Albert Street by 9:30 a.m. and frequently stays till closing. Agor himself didn't know anything about bar-restaurant business when he took a leap of faith and bought the Shire. He came from New York state and had raced and been around cars for 34 years. Though his family had owned a bowling alley with a bar when he was growing up, it was sold when he was 13.

Question: Aside from Agor's dedication to the Berk, a place he first patronized back in the 1980s, and his willingness to work hard, how has the Berkshire survived, and even thrived, since an admitted neophyte bought it?. . . Answer: Lloyd Agor says that there's a lot of continuity; nothing much has changed. The pizza is still made using the same 67-year-old recipe. Sidebar: For those who think it *has* changed, one old timer told me, "The sauce no longer has Pete's cigar ash in it." The sausage is still made on the premises the same way, and there's even continuity of staff. Anna Miasek has been there 31 years, Eddy Earle 20 years, Lisa Hogan 17 years, and Leslie Reznick 32 years. Proprietor Lloyd Agor credits the latter,

Leslie, as "the only reason the Berkshire has been going the last 4 years."

Business is very good, and Agor credits the restaurant portion for that, saying that food furnishes 70% of the revenue. Adds that the "to-go" business is "huge." That they go through 140-150 pounds of beef a week, 220 pounds of sausage, and 500 pounds of mozzarella. Sidebar: The cheese is still bought from the Frigo family, now Stefano Food Products. **Dave Frigo**: "In the old days we went through an entrance in the front and carried the cheese downstairs. It would have been too far to carry it through the back door. Now, there's a large cooler upstairs, so it's no longer necessary to store the cheese in the basement." (Below, the "Frigo" cheese that many places use today.) **Lloyd Agor**: "We only use quality products. A lot of meat comes from Litchfield Locker."

Agor admits the Berkshire has been demanding and says humorously of the 6 years he's owned it, "Those years are measured in dog years." (Below, owner Lloyd Agor in the late-morning stands ready for that first customer of-the-day.)

The Berkshire Cafe in 2017 is a well run business that employs 16 people. Cash or check only, but if you're a plastic person, there's an ATM. Only one bounced check was never made good on, and it's seldom that orders get switched, though Lloyd Agor admits it happens occasionally especially when two different people have the same first name... A new concern is iPhones that sometimes refer the caller to a "Berkshire Cafe" in Massachusetts.

But these are all minor things. The Big Thing: The Berkshire Cafe in Torrington goes on. A legend got a new lease on life. And its future is as golden as the crust on one of its pies.

POSTSCRIPT:

I've often thought that if a person ever wanted to reconnect with the past, if he/she desired to see old friends, old acquaintances, all that person need do is to sit at the Berkshire bar every Thursday night-Sunday for a year. Eventually, it seems to me, most locals wander in, if only for take-out. Even those natives who have moved away, always seem to pop in when they return to visit family and friends. Question: Why? Are the returnees looking to once again inhale the warm, unique, redolent smell of a Berkshire pizza cooking? And perhaps to sample a slice or two? Or are they actually hoping to run into some old familiar faces, and to hear once again a remembered voice or two?

If it's only the old styled pizza they're looking for, they *can* reconnect with that. It hasn't changed. But the old timers...

Most of the old, *old* timers are gone, passed over Jordan. Gone too are the days when young Woiciechowski daughters Mary Ann and Diane cleaned the back of the bar on Sundays while the mother Elizabeth cleaned the bathrooms, then did the books at night. Gone are the days when Mary Ann and Diane stuffed cigarette packs with 2¢ change before putting them into the vending machine because the machine only took quarters and a pack was 23¢. Post Berkshire Life: Mary Ann moved to Seattle for 30 years, Diane has resided in Lakeville for decades, and Leon became an air traffic controller and no longer lives in Litchfield County. Mother Elizabeth died in August 2016 at 95-years-old. Though there was no mention of the Berkshire Tavern in her obituary, she was an integral part of it and was said by daughter Mary Ann to, "have kept Pete in line, to some degree."

Other Berkshire Characters 2017 Patrons Won't See: I remember Harry Banziruk's brother John, the well driller. He had beefy forearms and would position a coin over the large artery/vein in his wrist. He'd twitch his hand sideways, the blood tube would pop up, and flip the coin. He'd start small with a dime, and work his way up to a quarter, all the time wanting to bet someone, *anyone*. . . Jackhammer man Phil Heacox who stuttered, almost like his jackhammer, and could barely get his beer and shot order out. . . One of the regulars, who will go unnamed here, who after a few drinks would proclaim to have the biggest penis (he said "dick") ever and would try to get others to put theirs on the pool table to determine the winner. Not a nasty drunk, as someone said, but a real pain-in-the-ass. . . . Louie, one of the cooks who made pizzas 7 days a week, was a factory worker, and probably didn't get a lot of time to socialize. Whenever he wasn't making a pie, he would come to the door by the end of the bar and chat with the patrons. **Glen Bronson**: "One of those days my brother Dale and I were at the end of the bar playing cribbage with Leon. Louie came out several times, and one time he tried to strike up a conversation about the news-of-the-day, which was about a serial killer in Chicago who had murdered 28 people, had put them in cement walls, yada yada. No one was really listening, but undaunted he came out yet another time and tried again. 'He killed 28 people!' Louie said all excited. 'Twenty-eight people, can you believe it? Twenty-eight people!' Dale, sitting next to me, commented, 'And he's gonna do it until he gets it right.' I had a mouthful of scotch and water which ended up all over Leon. Louie was ordered to stay in the kitchen." . . . The wisecracking drunk who tried to order a beer, and when bartender Mert Davis told him he'd had enough beer, asked for a shot. . . The day of the Belmont Stakes in 1973 when Glen Bronson bet some character $100 that Secretariat would win. Pete held the money, and of course Secretariat won. Pete then told Bronson that he owned him $50 because, as he reasoned, "That guy would have never paid you if I wasn't holding the money."

Legendary times. Great people. Left, the Berkshire Cafe rests, ready for a new generation, and many *more* convivial times. . .

(Above, part of the Berkshire kitchen showing the pizza ovens. On the far right is the grill. Back before delivery and franchise pizza, according to Anita Vedovelli, they'd sometimes cook 250 pizzas a night, and if they cooked over 200, Danny would give them a bonus. Below, *half* of the 2017 expanded menu which also features chicken wings, chili, homemade soup made fresh daily, taco salad, salad, garlic bread, and, of course, pizza to include a pineapple topping that was added after a customer requested it.)

★★★★★ THE BERKSHIRE CAFÉ ★★★★★
71 ALBERT STREET TORRINGTON, CT
~ We do not accept credit cards but we do have an ATM ~

SANDWICHES $6.95   WRAPS $8.95   GRINDERS $8.95

CHEESEBURGER   HAMBURGER   SAUSAGE   MEATBALL   HAM SALAD
TUNA SALAD   TUNA MELT   ROAST BEEF   HAM   TURKEY   SALAMI   BLT
PASTRAMI REUBEN   GRILLED CHEESE, TOMATO & BACON
GRILLED CHICKEN BREAST (Regular, Lemon Pepper, Buffalo Style or Parmesan)
BRATWURST SANDWICH   FRENCH DIP ON GARLIC BREAD   ITALIAN COMBO

MUCKE'S HOT DOG $3.50   DOUBLE HOT DOG SPECIAL $6.00
SMALL SIDE OF POTATO SALAD OR COLESLAW additional $1.00

~ CONDIMENTS ~
LETTUCE   TOMATO   HOT PEPPERS   GREEN ROASTED PEPPERS   ONION
PICKLES   FRIED ONION   SAUERKRAUT   SAUCE   KETCHUP   MUSTARD
MAYONNAISE   OIL   VINEGAR

CHEESE (American, Swiss, Provolone, Mozzarella, Cheddar)
BREADS (Rye, Seeded Bun, Kaiser, Grinder Roll, White)

ALL SANDWICHES/GRINDERS SERVED WITH CHIPS & PICKLE
.75 extra for bacon on any sandwich and $1.00 extra on any grinder

★★★★★ PHONE TO GO (860) 489-0600 ★★★★★

The History Of T.H.S. Swimming
Part 3 - The Turbulent 1960s

(New article. May 15, 2017. This article is the natural, and chronological, followup to the first 2 parts of the history of THS swimming that appeared in *Ye Olde Torrington Days*. That history started in the winter of 1930 and continued, despite major gaps and leapfrogging years, up to 1959. And that's where it left off. Sidebar 1: Because there were so many meets, events, and wonderful swimmers, it was impossible to get everything/everyone in. Apologies. Sidebar 2: When I cite individual times, they are the times I could find which were published. I have no doubt that many of these swimmers went faster in practice or in meets where they didn't finish first, and hence did not get what was their best times officially recorded. Apologies again. . . And now: On your mark, get set. . .)

When the decade of the 1950s ended, there was a golden aura hovering over the old 20-yard, Torrington YMCA pool. A rainbow mist through the chlorine saturated air that was already disappearing as the calendar pages flipped over to a new decade, a new swimming era at THS. Gone were the super stars, the All-Americans. Missing would be the names of Ostrander, Wall, Pinny, Will, Koplar, Baker, Killiany, Gemelli, Gilson, Mills, et al. . . Joan Rosazza's 1956 Olympic accomplishments would never again be equalled by another Torrington swimmer, female *or* male.

But, there were still Red Raiders who swam, swam well, and were determined to win. And it started during the winter of 1960 when senior backstroker John Hubbard was named captain. Along with Hubbard, that 1960 team featured only 3 other senior natators: Tom Mettling, Bill Hoffman, and Maurice Doolittle. It was a young team, but one in which many had swum for the YMCA and were Renny Belli trained. There were high hopes for a successful season.

The year began with an easy win over Wilby: 56-22. The Raider "Ducks," as they were frequently called, won 9 out of 11 events. The only individual event they lost was the 100-yard Breaststroke in which THS freshman Mike Marciano got out touched in 1:14. Henry Hoffman won the 100 Backstroke in 1:09:8 beating Captain John

Hubbard, who came in third. NOTE: Both Hoffman and Hubbard, The H&H Boys, were physically tall teens (Hubbard was 5'10" and Hoffman taller), and when they got really moving in that old, small, 4-lane Y pool, there was a LOT of wave turbulence and backwash off the gutters. It was akin to trying to plow a field during an earthquake. . . The winning times were noticeably slower in that first meet than the performances of previous Raider teams. For example, the 160-yard Medley Relay of Hubbard, John Eichner, Raoul Rebillard, and Reece Hoben won in 1:31.1. This time was nearly 5 seconds slower than the 1957 team of Mills, Baker, Killiany, and Gilson (1:26.2). BUT, a win is a win, is a good thing, especially when the team relied so heavily on underclassmen.

(Above the 1960 THS swim team. Front Row, L-R: Maurice Doolittle, Raoul Rebillard, Bob Zande, Tom Mettling, Captain John Hubbard, Ron Peasley, Joe Germano, Terry Dwan, Reece Hoben, Dennis Languell. Middle Row: Managers John Alaimo and Kevin Purcell, Dee Dee Dwan, Tom Mead, Bill Hoffman, George Ossola, Charlie Vierps, Bill Benisch, Todd Nelson, Vic Radzevich, Manager Tom Roman. Back Row: Dennis Santore, Jack Gatesy, Bob Mills, Jack Campetti, Gerry Ringstad, John Eichner, Robert "Ro" Lamoin, Bill Dranginis, Gary Batchelder.)

As that 1960 season progressed, times got faster, rookie *and* veteran swimmers stepped up. In the very next meet, Hubbard went a 1:06.3, and this time he won the 100 Back, and Hank Hoffman took third. Hubbard would not be beaten again by Hoffman for the rest of the season. Eventually the captain would drop his time to 1:04.6 for a new Torrington Y pool record, though Ray Ostrander would still hold the THS record at 1:01.4.

Observation: This was a era in which the weak teams were really weak, and strong teams really strong. For example in the meet against Croft from Waterbury, Kirschbaum edged out Torrington's Tom Mettling in the 100-yard Freestyle. The winning time was 1:03,

(Above, the 1960 seniors. Standing, L-R: Maurice Doolittle, Captain John Hubbard, Tom Mettling. Kneeling: Managers Kevin Purcell & Tom Roman.)

i.e. a slow time even given the era. . . On the other hand, against Crosby, a perennial powerhouse with their own pool, Garrity of Old Ivy won the 100 Free in 54.9, a time which would stand up as fast for many decades.

The Crosby meet furnished one of the most exciting moments of 1960. Both teams came into the Torrington pool undefeated, and with only the last relay left, THS trailed 36-34. It was winner-take-all time. Good News: Coach Charlie Duggan had saved his best freestyle quartet for this last 160-yard Freestyle Relay. Hopes were high; the Torrington stands packed with noisy well-wishers. And going into the anchor leg, things looked rosy. Junior phenom Raoul

Rebillard took off with a 2-yard lead in the short 40 yard sprint. BUT, Crosby had Ray Synder who had won the 40 Free earlier in 18.5. Ray Synder: An Old Ivy legend who in a few short years would be coaching his alma mater to many more victories and championships. . . He caught Rebillard on the first lap and nosed ahead by a foot in the last 20 yards. Crosby won the relay in time of 1:18.5 (19.6/man) and the meet. It was THS's first loss of the season. Sidebar: In 1956, the 4-man Red Raider team of Wall, Will, Koplar, and Ostrander had churned a blistering 1:13.5, i.e. a full 5 seconds faster. In other words, things were fast in 1960, just not *as* fast.

The 1960 team finished 8-3-1 and took 4th in the State Meet. The highlight of the year came at the 13th Annual Yale Swim Carnival when the 400-yard Medley Relay (an event normally swum only by collegians and Olympians) of John Hubbard, John Eichner, Raoul Rebillard, and Charlie Vierps nipped Greenwich in the stretch to win the spotlighted event in a state record time of 4:16.7. Coach Charlie Duggan enthusiastically told reporters, "This was the best Torrington High swimming in several years."

The following year, 1961, things again looked rosy to start the season. Though the team did not have the depth of speedsters the previous decade had, the squad had senior Captain Raoul Rebillard (on right with Coach Duggan) and junior Charlie Vierps, both capable of winning state championships.

Things started off fast and perfect. Before anyone could splash the chlorine out of his eyes, the Raiders splashers were undefeated at 8-0. The victories came against Wilby, Croft, New London, Bristol Central, Bristol Eastern, Windham, Manchester, and Hartford Public. With the exception of Windham, which was only defeated by 7 points, all the other scores were lopsided routs. It didn't last. The toughest meets came last and dealt the Raiders 3 consecutive loses as they fell to the UConn frosh, Crosby, and Sacred Heart. The final record was 8-3.

During the course of the 1961 season, times improved dramatically. For example, early in the season Captain Rebillard, by far the team's best overall swimmer, won the 160-yard Individual Medley (I.M.) in 1:54.5. By the end of the season, he'd improved to 1:48.0 for a new school record. Sidebar: In 1961, the Individual Medley was a *new* event in Connecticut duel meet competition. Previously it had only been swum during the high school State Meet and at the college and Olympic level. A decade earlier, it had consisted of only 3 strokes: back, free, and breast/butterfly (when the latter two were interchangeable).

Rebillard also brought down his 100-yard Butterfly time from a 1:01.8 to a 59.3. In doing so he broke Ray Ostrander's school record

(Above, Raoul Rebillard demonstrates his butterfly technique in the outside lane of the old Y pool. Note the high body position, the relaxed hands, and his prodigious wingspan.)

of 59.5 and established a mark that would not be beaten for a decade-and-a-half. Rebillard won the state title in the 100 Fly and took 4th in the New England's. Sidebar: Rebillard went on to swim at the University Of Maryland, became an ACC champion, and was called by Maryland coach Bill Campbell, "The most talented swimmer I ever coached."

Others who improved during the winter of '61 included THS's premier freestyler, junior Charlie Vierps. Charlie, or "The Bear" as he was affectionately called because of his husky build, early in 1961 won the 200 Free in 2:07.3. By the end of the season he lowered that time to 1:58.3 which, while not faster than Ray Ostrander's school record of 1:56.9, was fast enough to set a new Crosby High School pool record. He also lowered his 100 Free from a 57+ to a 54.8. Charlie Vierps wound up being the most accomplished THS swimmer in 1961, as he won not only the state title but also the New England championship in the 200 Free. . . The other big improvement and victory came at the Yale Swim Carnival where the 400-yard Medley Relay team of Jack Gatesy, Mike Marciano, Raoul Rebillard, and Charlie Vierps won the grueling event and scattered the previous state record, which THS set in 1960, by over 7 seconds! They finished in 4:09.6 (old record 4:16.7).

Although there was no THS girls swim team in 1961, and would not be for almost 3 more decades, there were many female swimmers who were excelling on the YMCA team in that '61 season. Below are a few. Left-Right: Melissa Mettling, Claire Dwan, Mary Ann Germano, and Mary Gilson. These teens won races, won championships, and were coached by Sue Mignerey Kearney.

When the following THS swim season rolled around in January 1962, unbeknownst to anyone, it would be the last time a THS swimmer would win a state title for many years. It would also be Charlie Duggan's last winter poolside. But, the business at hand that January was not about individual losses; it was about winning swim meets. And win the team did. In the opening meet against Wilby, the Raiders won 10 out of 11 events and swamped the Wildcats 66-21. Only the diving was lost. Sidebar: Gone were the 2 most recent THS diving stars: Reece Hoben and Joe Germano, both lost to graduation in 1961. Before them THS had Erwin Killiany and Glenn Gemelli, i.e. a streak of almost a decade of top tier divers was over (actually over the year before in '62), done in mainly by an antiquated plank the YMCA called a diving board. Diving for the next few years would prove to be an up-and-down affair...

(Below, Charlie Duggan and his 1962 co-captains: freestyler and butterflier Charlie Vierps and backstroker Jack Gatesy.)

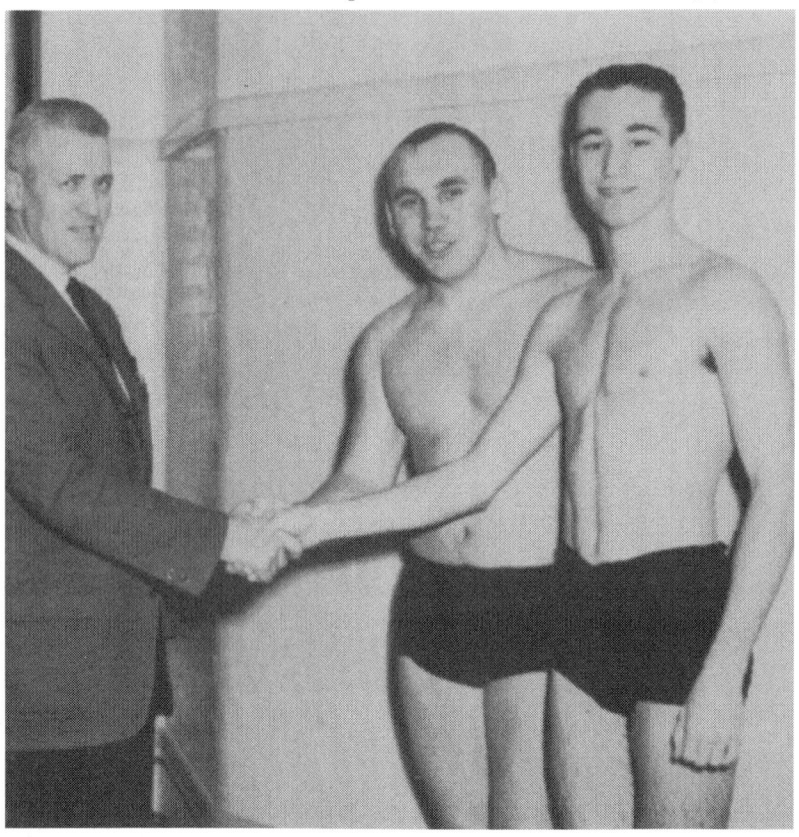

That '62 season mirrored the previous 1961 one, i.e. the weak teams were clobbered, and THS lost to the Waterbury powerhouses Crosby and Sacred Heart finishing 8-2. In the duel meet season, there were a number of outstanding memorable moments. Senior sprinter Bill Benisch churned an 18.8 in the 40 free. Sidebar: Benisch had the blond good looks of Troy Donahue, which didn't hurt attendance at home meets... Junior Mike Marciano became the first 100-yard Breaststroker in THS history to break the magic barrier of 1:10, pushing through to a 1:09.7 against Avon Old Farms, then hitting a

1:08.7 against The Hearts. . . Co-captain Vierps himself hit the wall in 59.8 in the 100 Fly against Avon, thus becoming only the 3rd THS swimmer in history to break a minute in the event. He'd be the last for almost 10 years. At the end of the season Charlie "The Bear" Vierps won 2 State Titles in his specialties: the 100 Fly and the 200 Free. He did it with an extremely powerful arm stroke and a pace that never seemed to slacken while his barrel chest plowed low through the water. In freestyle he *never* used flip turns, though most did by 1962. Vierps preferred the safety of an open turn in this era before goggles and having to touch the wall before starting the turn. . . **Postscript**: Charlie Vierps went on to swim for Maryland like Ostrander and Rebillard before him. Post-college, Charlie joined the Army, became an artillery Captain, married a German girl, and returned to Torrington where he died in 2009. He was a great and friendly guy. He's in the THS Hall Of Fame.

(Below, Vierps in the center takes off in 1961 at the start of the 100 Free against Manchester HS. Vierps won in 57.0. On the far left is fellow Raider George Ossola. Note the absence of lane lines in the old Torrington YMCA pool, and the fact that for a 100-yard race, which was 5 laps, the swimmers had to start at the shallow end, which meant a *very* shallow starting dive.)

Co-captain Jack Gatesy started the 1962 season flirting just outside Ray Ostrander's THS 100-yard Backstroke record of 1:01.4. But the West Point bound senior persevered, and in the New England's shot to a 1:00.7, which was good for the THS record. NOTE 1: Gatesy had a straight arm stroke, a long arm stretch, and a tremendous turnover rate, i.e. it wasn't the prettiest stroke in the pool, but because of Gatesy's iron-clad will and determination, it was usually the fastest. NOTE 2: Gatesy was always up on the latest and always looking to perfect it.

Bill Dranginis: "In 1962 we were swimming Sacred Heart in the old Y pool. Jim Farrar was their coach. As the Medley Relay was about to start, Jack Gatsey just stood up on the gutter with his back to the pool. He had practiced that start and was going to start standing up. Mike Berger, a sophomore and future HS All American backstroker for Sacred Heart, was starting to climb into the pool and Coach Farrar told him to do what Jack was doing. Berger had never tried it and didn't want to. They went back-and-forth for a couple minutes. Farrar did not want to give us an edge. Berger finally started on the gutter and did OK with it. (He won in 1:01.8.) Berger went on to swim for UCLA, and Jack ended up as the number one backstroker for West Point. Jack actually missed States that year to take an entrance exam for West Point."

Sidebar: In Connecticut schoolboy swimming history, one would be hard pressed to find anyone who was better than Mike Berger, i.e. Jack Gatesy raced against *the* absolute best. Berger swam the 40 Free in 17.4 (.1 off the national record) and was the first Connecticut high schooler to break 50 seconds in the 100 Free (49.6). While in high school he swam a 1:53.9 200 Free and a 55.4 100 Back. He held 8 individual state records and was part of 4 relay state records. Someone once called him the fastest thing in Connecticut waters since the Nautilus. At UCLA he was part of their National Championship 1967 team and part of that team's 400 yard Medley Relay record quartet. He was described as a tall, cocky kid. He got married, started a family young, and eventually worked with troubled youth. He was 60-years-old when he died of alcoholism.

THS finished 5th in both the State Meet and the New England's in 1962. Not great finishes given the standards that THS teams of the 1950s set. BUT, much better than anything that was to come for a long time... Coach Charlie Duggan, no doubt, saw the handwriting in the water, and, as so many coaches often do after a winning season, decided to hang up his stopwatch.

The Duggan swimming era was over. *But* there was a lot more Red Raider swimming yet to come.

✥ ✥ ✥

The new high school was nearing completion in that winter of 1963 when the Raider ducks took to the water under new head coach Ed Evers. Evers, like Duggan before him, had absolutely no swimming experience or knowledge. But he was an athlete himself (baseball and golf primarily, basketball on the side), and like all good athletes was willing to learn. He was a quick study.

The BMOD (Big Man On pool Deck) in 1963 was Captain Mike Marciano. Marciano was a high spirited, good natured leader who was just as quick with a mischievous smile/remark as he was off the blocks. But Marciano just didn't *look* mischievous; in fact, he *was*. Example 1: In the autumn of 1962 he traded a Yale warmup jacket that he had misappropriated, a.k.a, stolen (a jacket that was rumored to have belonged to Olympic gold medalist and Yale student Steve Clark), to me in exchange for my 125 pound weightlifting set. The swap took place at the Marciano home on Calhoun Street where I was good friends with Mike's younger brother, Buddy. Lest anyone be too shocked, this "misappropriation" of other team's apparel was not unique to THS or to the swim team alone. I myself had my complete THS warmup suit stolen a few years later at the State Meet when the underclassman in charge of watching our gear while we warmed up, drifted away. To this day I think a Naugatuck swimmer grabbed it (the Greyhounds were hovering close by). I also recall *so* many of our large warmup jackets on the football team "disappearing" that Coach Duggan told us that they had *better* be returned and *soon!*. . . Thievery, sad to say, was a game we played back then, as did our rivals. One 1963 swimmer told me that when he got to college and roomed with other swimmers, they had a sign on their apartment wall which read, "Never have so few, stolen so much, from so many." Apparently this tradition was widespread and went across state lines. Perhaps it's akin to the tradition of losing boats in rowing giving up their jerseys to the victors. In swimming it just lacked formality and verbal agreement. . .

Example 2: In probably a never-before, and never-since happening, the premier swimmer and captain was ineligible for the first few meets of the season due to academics. Mike Marciano didn't train *or* swim against competition till the February 1 meet against Buckeley. Sidebar: Captain Marciano also was a heavy smoker and could often

(Below, Captain Marciano with Coach Evers in the old THS coach's office. Mike had a great deal more swimming experience than the rookie coach, and hopefully has given the spiffy dressed coach some sage advice.)

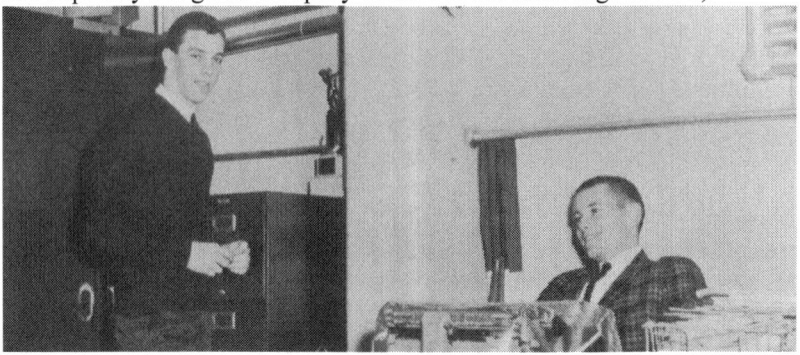

be seen standing in front of the YMCA puffing on a cigarette. This was against swim team rules because it was reputed to "cut down on an athlete's wind." To get caught meant suspension from the team. Moreover, smoking around practice time was a risky thing to do since a smoker never knew when the coach, or any other school official/teacher, might materialize. Certainly, Marciano was not the only THS swimmer in 1963, or before, or after, to do this, especially in an era when most adults *and* young adults smoked. But in many respects because of Marciano's expansive, extroverted personality, he was the most highly visible smoker that season.

In the winter of 1963, THS was in double session with upperclassmen going to school in the morning, and freshmen in the afternoon. The swim team practiced afternoons right after school for a couple of hours, M-F. This had been the SOP for years, which meant freshmen could not practice with the team.

Ed Holmes: "My freshman year (1961-'62), we had afternoon classes, and I was unable to practice with the varsity. Coach Duggan still wanted me to swim with the varsity, stating that I could practice with the Y team at night. I'm not sure how I could have made the away meets. I decided to swim just for Renny (Belli) and the Y my freshman year."

(Above, the 1963 seniors. L-R: Mike Marciano, Billy Finn, Dave Chait, Bill Dranginis, Vic Radzevich, Ed "Chub" Ruwet, Gerry Ringsted, Jack Campetti, and Gary Batchelder. NOTE: It appears in this picture as if Marciano is the shortest, and Batchelder the tallest. This was NOT the case.)

In 1963, Coach Ed Evers offered 4 freshmen swimmers the same deal that Holmes had been offered the year before, i.e. practice on-your-own right after school (5 p.m.) a few days a week, i.e. it was not a M-F deal, nor a 2 hours a session workout. But the 9th graders could be on the THS team and *could*, if they accumulated enough points, earn a varsity letter. Walt Chaberek, Jim Hoffman, Joe Rinaldi, and I took Evers up on his offer. And though we 4 frosh were often working out alone without even the Y team around, and Evers only occasionally popping in to check up on things, we did contribute to the team's success and helped establish the continuity of young swimmers.

With Captain Marciano unavailable through the month of January, it fell to others to fill in for Marciano's specialties: 160-yard Individual Medley and the 100 Breaststroke. Teddy Holmes, Ed's brother, won the IM in 2 meets going a 2:04. I filled in for another few going a 1:55. In the breaststroke, Marshall Waldron, Joel Ruwet, and I filled in during various meets with the sophomore Ruwet going a 1:16.5. . . Though Marciano was certainly missed, the team went 4-1 during his absence, losing only to powerhouse Crosby.

(Right, Ted and Ed Holmes, with younger sister Kathleen, the brothers looking sharp in their Red Raider jackets.)

Everyone stepped up during Marciano's absence including a pair of rookie divers: Gary Batchelder and Victor Radzevich. *The Torrington Register*: "Novice diver Vic Radzevich finished second (against Middletown) for the second meet in a row, after taking up the event only a few weeks ago." Radzevich starred on both the football and track teams and was said to be utterly fearless on that stiff old YMCA board, one time in practice doing a front double flip on a dare. As the ceiling was too low to get enough height in the traditional way, Radzevich took a running start, pounded the end of the board, and shot off almost vertical to the water. He traveled 10 yards down the pool as he completed the 2 rotations and hit while still tumbling in a tucked up position. It wasn't pretty. But it *was* funny, gutsy, coordinated, and Radzevich *did* win the dare.

When Captain Marciano finally did return on February 1, he turned in 2 stellar performances going a 1:06 in the 100 Breast and a 1:53.4 in the 160-yard IM. His 1:06 was a new THS record, shattering his old record of 1:07.5. It stayed a record for an entire decade until Jay Cilfone came along in the early 1970s with a more modern stroke and better training. Sidebar: Marciano's time is particularly noteworthy because he swam it using the old wide-styled arm pull and frog kick. It's also remarkable because he swam it his first meet back when he was supposedly in his worse shape because of not training. Inexplicably, he would not beat that time for the rest of the season, not even come close, almost as if the superior performance took everything he had left for 1963.

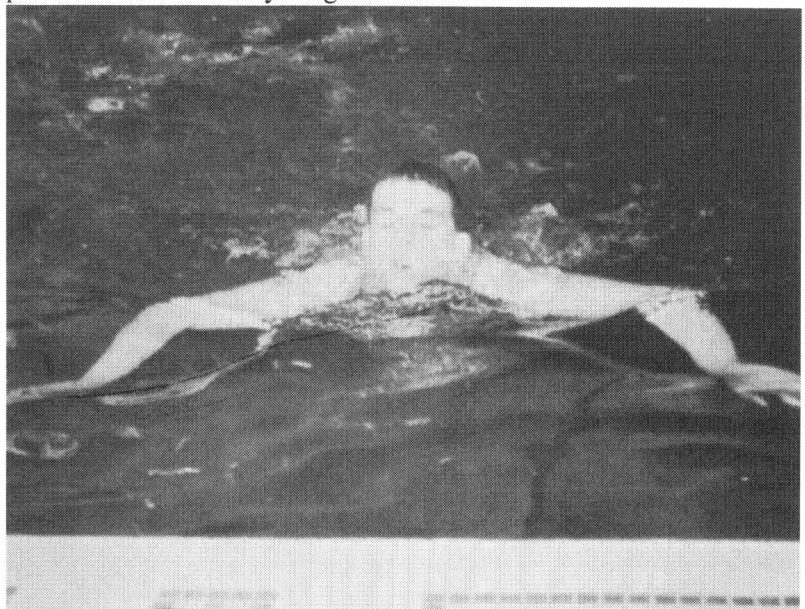

(Above, breaststroker Marciano coming into the wall.)

Mike Marciano was the only state-caliber swimmer on the team. *But*, there were many others who did the yeoman's work and contributed to the winning season. For example in this same meet against Bulkeley, Bill Dranginis (right) furnished one of the most dramatic races to date. Columnist Owen Canfield: "The most exciting event of the evening was the 200-yard freestyle race. Bill Conlon of Hartford and Bill Dranginis of Torrington were virtually neck-and-neck for 9½ laps of the 20 yard pool. Conlon, with a great closing effort, managed to pull ahead at the end and win it in 2:09." Dranginis later won the 100 Free in 58.4.

Another keystone moment in that THS vs Bulkeley swim meet was the first ever swimming of the 400-yard Freestyle. Never before had a distance of that magnitude been swum in a Connecticut high school meet. Owen Canfield: "Freshman Walt Chaberek of Torrington displayed amazing endurance and beautiful form in winning the 400-yard freestyle grind. Chaberek put everything he had into the final 40-yard span, finishing in a time of 5:23." The race was *not* reported in the finish summary, it's uncertain if it counted in the final point tally, and would not be swum again in the 1963 season. However, all that is irrelevant. Walt Chaberek was the first 400 Free winner, and he had himself a THS record.

Five days later there was a 59-27 lose to Sacred Heart, which was reported as a "dreary evening" for the Raider ducks. Two days after that, the Raiders journeyed to Hartford Public HS, and won that meet easily: 61-28 with Billy Finn winning the 40 Free in 19.8 and Walt Chaberek taking the 200 Free in 2:20.8. Noteworthy: At some point during the meet, one of the THS swim team members drifted away (usually happened during the diving) and swiped a brass nozzle from a firehose in a deserted hallway. This was the sort-of unheralded, unreported, non-talked about swim team tradition mentioned earlier, i.e. swiping things. It had never caused a ripple before. A fire nozzle. No big deal. However, this time all hell broke loose. A Hartford Public official called THS Principal Richard Williamson and demanded that the fire nozzle be returned. Was it a bluff, i.e. how could anyone know for certain that a THS swimmer had taken it? Much ado about very little?. . . Coach Evers laid it out as an ultimatum to the swim team, and the fire nozzle was anonymously turned in. Happiness. Smiles all around. Or at least the remainder of the season wasn't cancelled.

There wasn't much left, but what was left *was* important. It was a duel meet against Windham High for the Northern Division Championship of the State Swim League. Sidebar: Connecticut was divided into 2 divisions in swimming: Southern and Northern. The winners of each would meet for the State Title. Though THS had lost to *both* Crosby and Sacred Heart in the Northern Division, neither of those schools were eligible because they refused to swim each other over a dispute regarding where the meet would be held. If Torrington could beat Windham, they'd be swimming for a state title!

Ironically, the meet was at a neutral, but familiar, site: Hartford Public High School where the fire nozzle had been recently swiped, and returned.

The meet got off to a great start with the 160-yard Medley Relay of myself, Mike Marciano, Ed Holmes, and Bill Finn winning in 1:29.7. After that, it was a see-saw battle with Coach Evers juggling his lineup and sometimes having swimmers swim events they had never done before. For example Bill Dranginis, who had never swum the 100 Breaststroke in 4 years of THS swimming, now swam and won the event in a fine time of 1:14. . . The score stood 43-37 with Windham up 6 going into the final event: the 160-yard Freestyle Relay. It was *the* cliché ending of winner take all, i.e. whoever won the relay, won the meet *and* the Northern Division Championship. . . It was close, but at the wall it was Windham by a foot in 1:18.

I remember that the bus ride home was surprisingly noisy and loud (can't keep a good team down) with the seniors leading one cheer after another, e.g. Let's hear it for Mike!. . . Let's hear it for Coach!. . . All went silent when I finally yelled, Let's hear it for the last relay that blew the meet!. . . I quickly found my seat surrounded by bulky 12th graders who, rather than rough me up, pointed out that I had blown the 100-yard Backstroke when I blew a turn. It was true. My moment had come, and sunk. It takes a team to win. Everyone. A humbling thought and moment for a frosh.

Good News: Before hitting the road and leaving Hartford Public HS, the same Raider who had originally stolen the fire nozzle, stole it again! This time it would not materialize until a key moment 3 years later.

The 1963 team finished 6-3 and didn't do well at the State Meet. Mike Marciano won the Service Cup and Bill Dranginis was awarded the Varsity Club plaque at an awards assembly (picture below) in the old THS auditorium near the end of March.

(Above, March 1963. L-R: Paul Christina, Jim Amrich, Tony Toro, Hi Ruwet, Mike Marciano, Bill Dranginis, Larry Alibozak, Arthur Batchelder)

The swim season was over. And it was time to move into the new high school!

1963 Postscript: Because, as I said before, I was good friends with Mike Marciano's brother Buddy, I kept up somewhat with the world of Mike. A couple of years after graduation Mike decided he wanted to swim for the University of Southern California. He took the SATs and scored over 700 in math (Mike might have been a jokester, *but* he was also a *very* smart guy.) He was told that if he could get his 100-yard Breaststroke time down to 1:02, he'd get a full ride. Mike drove out to California, trained with the USC team, told us later he got his time down to 1:04, then said the hell-with-it. He bought a brand new 427 Corvette, drove it cross-country, and cruised the Farm Shop the first night of his return. Naturally we were all agog. The man definitely knew how to make an entrance... Mike for the rest of his days lived large. He had big jobs, like Director Of Data Processing at Royal Typewriter. And small jobs. He loved women, loved to party, but always kept a generous heart. He died in September 1998 at 53-years-old. In some ways he was *the* archetype for talented swimmers who also liked to cultivate a wild side. I consider him one of the all-time great THS breaststrokers.

✦ ✦ ✦

T.H.S. SWIM SEASON WINTER 1964

New school, same old antiquated pool. Swimmers in the winter of 1964 found themselves in a puzzling conundrum. On one hand the far seeing and generous taxpayers of Torrington had approved a new high school that the students were now in. On the other hand, the short-sighted and frugal (some would say *cheap*) taxpayers had voted down in *three* separate referendums a new pool to be included in the facility. In a pre-season article the *Torrington Register* reported: "The team has been working out since the middle of November, but it is still handicapped by a lack of practice. With no pool of their own, the boys have been using the Y pool, but the hours at which it is available would discourage most mentors and swimmers alike."

Coach Evers, now in his second season, told the press: "Our boys have to have a lot of desire to practice under the conditions we have here. We get to use the Y pool, but don't get in the water before 8:30. The kids get out of the pool at 10, and I hope most are home before 11. It's tough when a boy has to go out in the middle of the night for practice."

And that was only 2-3 nights a week. The one other practice came every Saturday at 6-8 a.m., i.e. 5-6½ total hours of practice a week at off-*off* hours.

Nevertheless, a dedicated squad took to the 1964 waters determined to do the best with what they had and to *hopefully* produce a winning season. Anything beyond that, e.g. an NVL title was out-of-the-question, and the boys knew it, though it was an unstated/not talked about thing. (Right, troubled Red Raiders. Image done by Mary-Jo Murphy in 1964.) As far as the State Meet went, it would just be a pleasant bus ride with no realistic hopes of putting anyone, much less the team, on the medal podium. This was no longer 1954, i.e. many high schools now had their own pools and plenty of practice time. Desire and stroke technique only go so far in swimming. Once the latter two conditions are met, it's practice, practice practice, i.e. conditioning, conditioning, conditioning. . .

The student newspaper ran an article in the March 20, 1964, issue featuring the swim team co-captains. The season was over by then, but it was nevertheless, a fitting tribute to the two aqua-leaders.

THE X-RAY

Introducing Swimming Co-Captains

Bob Amrich, who is a good all around athlete, is one of the co-captains for this year's swim squad. This past year Bob did a commendable job in swimming the free style and relays. Bob also holds his own with the books as well as with sports. He is pursuing a College Course consisting of: College English IV, Col U.S. History, Col. Physics and Solid Geometry and

Besides being a good athlete and a scholar, Bob also finds time for clubs, such as the Spanish Club and National Honor Society. For the future, Bob is planning on going to college to pursue an engineering career.

Ray Revaz, who came to the swim team in his Junior year, can remember this year's swimming with pride. Although he saw first place only a few times, he was always in the second or third spot in the freestyle. Ray is pursuing a General Course consisting of: General English IV, Genral Physics, General U.S. History and Senior Problems. Ray's also a member of the Boy's P.E. Club.

In his spare time, Ray likes most sports, with skating and baseball topping the list. After his graduation from THS he plans to go on to a technical education.

In reality, the season *almost* realized the expectations, i.e. it was neither a winning *nor* a losing year. The team finished 4-4, and there were some memorable moments.

(Above, the 1964 team. Front Row, L-R: Ed Holmes, Bobby Cahill, John Fitzgerald, Lou Carillo, Joel Ruwet, Ray Revaz, Bob Amrich, Tom Parnell, Cliff Curtis. Middle Row: Coach Ed Evers, Fran Marchand, Fran Sesko, Rich Coralli, Duane Nelson, Buddy Sokolik, Tony Picone, Bill Marchand. Back Row: John Klein, Ted Holmes, Rick Porritt, Buddy Marciano, Rich Beloski, Paul Bentley, Don LaRocco, Joe Rinaldi, John Franculli. . . Note: The water is reflecting on the front row swimmers, i.e. they are not naturally striped.)

The most memorable moment for me personally occurred in the opening meet against Hall High School of West Hartford, which we won. I remember being surprised when Coach Evers told me I was going to swim the 400-yard Freestyle, which was now a new, official event. I knew distance was not my forté and had my serious doubts. But Coach said to swim it, so. . . I was behind for most of the race (pacing myself, doing open turns, and just hoping to finish). I later learned that the head cheerleader, Rose Richard (right), who was in the stands (also the Belle of her class), said to no one in particular, 'If Paul wins, I'll give him a date.' I found this out right after the meet, and debated about asking her out for weeks. But alas, no guts in the dating department, and no precedent back then for younger guys to date older girls. I played it safe in this situation and swam *with* the current, so to speak. Sidebar: I came from behind in the race itself and won in 5:01.7, which while not impressive, was a new THS record (see p. 218). This time would be shattered in the coming years by both Bill Ryan and Fran Marchand. But for 1964, it stood.

(Above, the pool deck during a swim meet in 1964. On the bench waiting to swim, L-R: Bobby Cahill in a sweatsuit, Co-captain Ray Revaz, Marshall Waldron, Terry Ruefli, Co-captain Bob Amrich. . . Note the closeness of the pool itself and the fans. Behind Revaz, in the stands, is Jean Ruwet. On the other side of the pillar, 8th graders Chris Germano, Frank Bentley, Tom Husser, Bill Ryan, and Roger Carillo. It was not an uncommon occurrence for younger swimmers to attend high school meets to support the team and to see what awaited them. Fortunately, the Y conditions didn't scare off too many future Raider ducks. . .)

In that same first meet, Bobby Cahill won the 100 Back in 1:07.5, and Eddie Holmes grabbed the 100 fly in 1:04.3. In the Wilby meet Ray Revaz won the 40 Free in 20.8 and the 100 Free in 58.7, and I copped the 160-yard IM in 1:51.2. In the last meet of the year against Hartford Public HS at the local Y pool (Note: No fire nozzles were stolen by the visiting Owls.) Co-captain Bob Amrich won the 200

Free in 2:18.6 and Ed Holmes finished the 100 Fly in a fast 1:03.9. During these home swim meets, senior Hartley "Bud" Connell was our meet announcer. **Bud Connell**: "I used to announce, 'Swimmers take your mark.'. . Give a dramatic pause. . . Then, 'Mr. Starter, if you please!'" Maybe the THS team of 1964 didn't have stars, but we *did* have showmanship!

(Above, Coach Evers in the background left, puts the '64 team through a workout. Just taking off are, L-R: Bob Cahill, Bob Amrich, Ed Holmes, and Ray Revaz. Note the wooden blocks used to prop up the board and get it out-of-the-way.)

One of the best moments in the winter of 1964 occurred after a Friday night, home swim meet. A bunch of us swimming sophomores went to Bill Marchand's house on Migeon Avenue where we were joined by other classmates including a bevy of females, a.k.a. a party. But this party was different from previous ones. On January 20, 1964, an album called "Meet The Beatles" had been released, and when we heard it for the first time that night, we were thunderstruck. Played it over-and-over the whole evening. The British were here, and nothing would ever be the same again. It was *the* night the 1960s arrived for me. There were troubled times and turbulent waters ahead. But with The Beatles playing in the background, maybe we could, and would, survive. . .

✣ ✣ ✣

The winter of 1965 rolled around with nothing changed. The same out-of-date pool, the same constricted practice hours, the same we-know-we're-not-going-to-win-many-but-let's-do-the-best-we-can-and-not-get-embarrassed attitude. The squad consisted of 6 seniors, 10 juniors, 8 sophomores, and 5 freshmen. The only gold in 1965 was Captain Ed Holmes. Coach Ed Evers in a pre-season *Register* writeup called Holmes "the most dedicated swimmer I've ever coached." And Captain Holmes was. While the rest of us worked, I think pretty hard, Ed always worked harder. Set the standard, *not* by talking, but by *doing*. Leading by example. Captain Holmes' best event was the 100-yard Butterfly, and his best time going into 1965 was 1:02.5. Coach Evers told the press that he expected Holmes to crack the one minute barrier before the season was out. It was a lot of pressure on the senior. Could he, *would* he?. . .

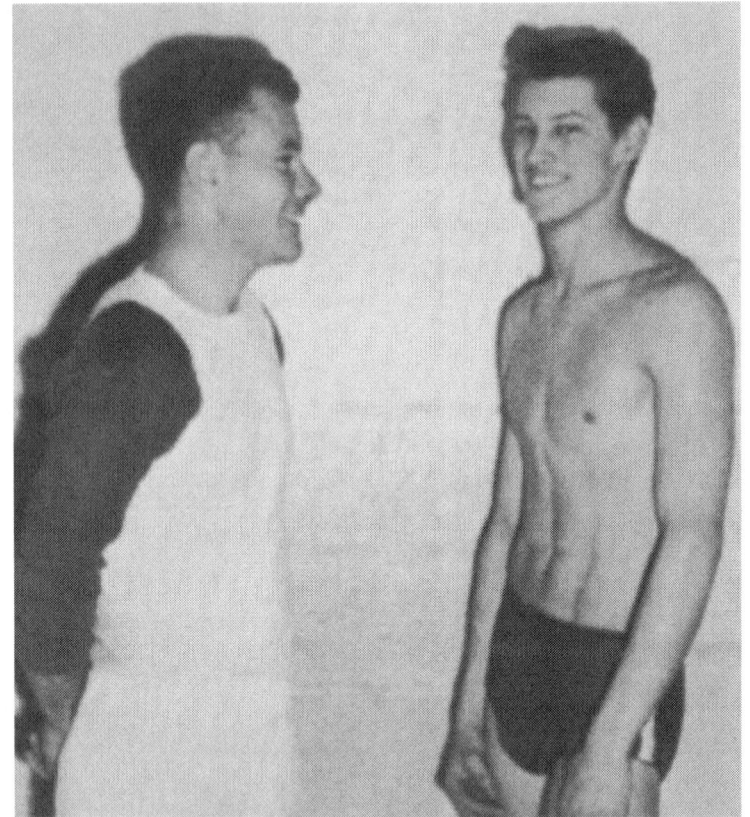

(Above, Coach Evers and Captain Ed Holmes take a moment together.)

The opening meet against Naugy at the new Naugatuck HS 25-yard pool (Yes, the Greyhounds had their own new facility compete *with* pool.) proved an ominous start to 1965. We were clobbered 71-24, and the only winners were Ed Holmes in the 100 Fly (1:02), me in the 100 Breast (1:11.9), and Walt Chaberek in the

400 Free (5:01.6). Chabarek's time was a new school record by tenth-of-a-second. It was a very good time, but it wouldn't stand long. Sidebar: Because we were never in tip-top condition, racing in a 25-yard pool such as Naugatuck's was always an odyssey. Those 5 extra yards per lap seemed endless. Just when your inner odometer said you should be hitting the wall and turning, the pool just kept going, and going. . . It also increased the distance in the IM (consisting of 2 laps per stroke) from 160 yards to 200. Those 40 extra yards were usually swum by us 20-yard pool trained IMers with anchors dragging on the bottom.

The next meet was against Old Ivy, a.k.a. Crosby at their pool in Waterbury. Sidebar: The old Crosby pool was also a 20-yarder like Torrington's. BUT unlike the Raiders, the Crosby ducks got all the training time they wanted. A 5'5" Ivy swimmer named Norm Reich was the best distance swimmer in the NVL simply because he not only swam for several hours a day, 6-7 days a week, he also swam year-round. This was mind boggling in 1965, i.e. *no one* swam year round. The swim season was 4 months long. Period. We regarded news of Reich's training regimen as pushing the boundaries of fair play, i.e. almost cheating. Needless to say, it paid dividends. Against us, the diminutive Reich went a 1:59.4 in the 200 Free and and a 4:18 in the 400 Free, i.e. in the latter event his winning time was 42+ seconds faster than the THS school record. . . This Crosby meet also saw the advent of a new event: the 60-yard Freestyle. From now on, the sprint event in 20 yard pools would no longer be the 40 Free. One more lap was added, for who-knows-what-reason. Crosby's Bob Hyner won it in the smoking record time of 29.1. . . The only 2 THS winners were me copping the 100 Breast, and Ed Holmes winning the 100 Fly. His time of 1:01.2 moved him closer to cracking the minute barrier.

One outstanding memory I have regarding the Crosby meet was that during the diving, someone wandered off and discovered that the Crosby athletic storage closet was unlocked. Before long, some of us who were not diving were in there misappropriating, a.k.a. pilfering, cheerleader pompoms and small megaphones. On the bus ride home, while Coach Evers sat in the front of the bus and never turned around, those in the back led cheers with real cheerleader equipment. Definitely took the edge off the loss.

Croft was up next. Captain Ed Holmes was out sick, but others stepped up and THS came away with a victory. Bobby Cahill won the 100 Back in 1:07.2, Joel Ruwet grabbed the 100 Breast in 1:13.4, and I took Holmes' place in the 100 Fly and won in 1:04.5. . . The thing I remember most about this meet was Norm LaFrance. LaFrance was a fine Croft freestyler (won the 200 in 2:06.6 and the 400 in 4:53.2), and a sharp, likable guy who went on to become an M.D. BUT, he was also extremely good looking and one of our cheerleaders, who just happened to be in the stands, took an interest in him. When I found out, I approached LaFrance, whom I knew through swimming, and botta bing, botta boom, the Croft beau and the THS belle were soon off on a date. I don't think it ever amounted to much, but romance at swim meets was a very real thing in the old Torrington Y pool.

(Below, the Raider ducks in 1963. Cheerleader Sharon Faita, looking pensive, sits behind her then boyfriend Ed "Chub" Ruwet. Talking to Chub, with his back to the camera, is Billy Finn. Ray Revaz is in the foreground wearing glasses, and Cliff Curtis is in the background looking at the photographer.)

Girlfriends at swim meets were a pretty standard occurrence. Karen Perzanowski came to my meets. Todd Benjamin's girl friend, Eunice Froeliger, was actually the announcer for 3 seasons:

1965-'67. I only remember "romance" causing a problem one time when one of the opposition divers struck up a conversation with a pretty Torrington gal. This was not unusual due to the closeness of swimmers and fans, as can be seen in the photo on the opposite page. What was unusual on this particular occasion was that the diver became physically aroused, and his next dive was a back flip. He was red-in-the-face as he walked out to the end-of-the-board, pivoted around, and raised his arms for balance. Normally a diver pauses in this position before starting the dive. But this aroused diver no sooner raised his arms, then he sprang upward and uncharacteristically blew the flip. Naturally, we Raiders were laughing our asses off. He climbed out of the pool, hung his head, and wrapped himself in a towel. He also stopped talking to the Raider coed, but the damage had been done. Unintended mission accomplished, and we could use every break we could get back in those days. If it took a pretty miss to get a rise, so to speak, out of the opposition, great! No problem. Love conquers all.

In 1965 we had a couple of senior divers: John Klein and John Fitzgerald. Though neither had a lot of experience, they were both gutsy and scored points for us.

(Above, John Fitzgerald doing a front dive in layout, a.k.a. a swam dive. Judge Renny Belli, watching intently, is seated on the left. Directly under "Fitzy" in the background is longtime announcer Eunice Froeliger. How she wore a blazer in that sweltering pool area and never broke a sweat is a mystery to this day.)

The next meet against Wilby was won convincingly 58-37, i.e. we did to Wilby what the better teams did to us. Swimming an event I didn't normally swim, the 100 Free, I won in 56.9. Bobby Cahill won Backstroke, and in his first ever Varsity win Jim Hoffman won the 100 Fly in 1:09. Sidebar: Hoffman had swum freshman year, taken sophomore year off, and had returned for this his junior year. Unknown to us, he would quit swimming after this season, so his lone 100 Fly win was, in actuality, his swan song.

The most impressive winner against Wilby was Captain Ed Holmes who swam the 60-yard Free for the first time ever and set a THS record at 30.3. It was a record which would stand for 2 years.

Holmes Sets Record In THS Swim Meet

Senior Captain Ed Holmes set a Torrington High School record in the 60-yard freestyle, 30.3 seconds, as Coach Ed Evers' squad picked up second win of the season, 58-37, over Wilby in the YMCA pool.

Next up was the first *ever* Naugatuck Valley League Meet, i.e. never before had all the high school swim teams in the NVL gathered to compete. The meet was held in the old 20-yard Crosby pool, which, while having a larger seating and deck area than the Torrington Y natatorium, *still* was not large by modern standards. We swimmers were cramped pretty tightly around the pool's perimeter.

The meet turned out much as expected. Crosby swimmers won 7 events and far out-distanced second place Sacred Heart. Torrington was third, followed by Wilby and Croft. Ansonia did not have a swim team in the 1960s, Naugatuck was temporarily out-of-the-league, and Kennedy hadn't been built yet. . . Individually, Captain Ed Holmes (above) was the only Raider winner, taking the 100 Fly in 1:00.7. This put him on first team All-NVL. Holmes didn't beat the magical minute barrier, but he came *awfully* close. Second team NVL honors went to myself in the 100 Breaststroke as I was edged out by Dave Roach of Wilby who won in 1:08.5. *And* to our 160-yard Medley Relay quartet of Bobby Cahill, Joel Ruwet, Jim Hoffman, and me, which placed second.

(Above, L;R: Bobby Cahill, Captain Ed Holmes, Jim Hoffman, Joel Ruwet, and Paul Bentley. . . NOTE: Swimming is often a family affair, and everyone in the above photo had either a sister *or* brother who also swam competitively.)

There wasn't much left to the 1965 swim season. We were sunk by both Sacred Heart and Conard HS, the latter a state powerhouse. Such a loss only confirmed to us that going to the State Meet would be a nice sociable bus ride, but nothing more. Example: Paul Liniak of Conard won the 100 Fly in 55.3 and Goldkamp the 100 Free in 52. These times were far beyond what we Raiders were capable of.

In late February we beat Bulkeley of Hartford. Captain Holmes won the 100 Fly in 1:01.2, Joel Ruwet took the 100 Breast in 1:13.9, Bobby Cahill the 100 Back in 1:08.7, freshman Chris Germano won the diving, and I took the 160-yard IM in 1:49.7. . . The other individual winner was junior Joe Rinaldi who finished the 60-yard Free in 31.6. Though a 3 year Varsity swimmer, Rinaldi had won only one other individual race before (100 Fly in 1:19.4, freshman year). Unbeknownst to us at the time, Rinaldi would not win again. He wouldn't swim the next year due to a football injury, so like Hoffman, 1965 would be his swan song too. Sidebar: The majority of swimmers don't win races. *But*, like Hoffman and Rinaldi consistently did, they grab second and third places *and* fill relays i.e. they score points, which was/is invaluable in helping the team.

The season ended with a 4-and-6, won-loss record, the worst in THS swimming history since 1942. Under better training conditions, with a modern facility, this would have been depressing. But we knew we'd done the best we could with what we had. Still, none of us undergrads were looking optimistically ahead. . .

A Couple Of Additional 1965 Shots

(Above, freshman Bill Ryan on the far right, showing a very quick reaction time, and junior Paul Bentley next to him take off in the 160-yard IM against Bulkeley. Bentley won, Ryan took 3rd. . . Timer on the left side in the white t-shirt is Frank Janis. Behind Ryan sitting down is Eunice Froeliger. Standing in front of her are timers Renny Belli and Erwin Killiany).

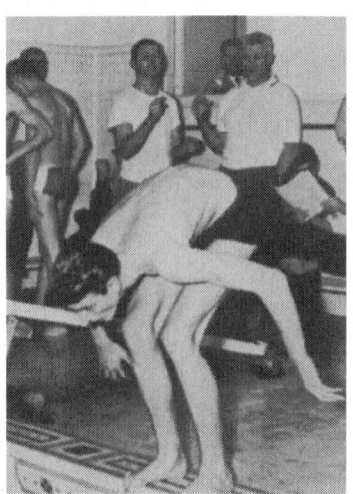

(Left, the rangy Joel Ruwet, an excellent breaststroker, gets set to take off. Behind him can be seen timers Erwin Killiany and Charlie Duggan.)

✢ ✢ ✢

The 1966 season. My senior year.

Coach Ed Evers: "Captain Paul Bentley, whose best event is the Individual Medley, is our squad's utility man and can swim any event I ask of him. I expect Bentley to break the school record in the Individual Medley."

(Above, Captain Paul Bentley and Coach Ed Evers)

Breaking Raoul Rebillard's 1961 school record in the 160-yard IM was one of the major goals I had in 1966. And it was important to me to break it. I knew a winning season was unlikely. I also knew that with the level of talent in the NVL and State, there was no possibility of any honors/championships at season's end for either the team *or* me. My personal focus was that IM record, trying to set a good example for the underclassmen (at least in the pool), and perhaps along the way having a little, maybe a *lot* of fun.

Ed Evers was the only high school coach that anyone on that '66 team had ever known. We liked Coach and respected him because, like us, he was doing the best job he could with what he had. *And*, he was just a damn good guy.

Mike Hogan (then a sophomore): "I looked up to Paul Bentley on that team. So good, and naturally gifted. He and Bill Ryan were the two most 'natural' swimmers I ever knew. It was great swimming with them. . . I admired Mr. Evers – he was tough, quiet, but always fair, and when you did well, he'd let you know it. So much integrity. People don't know the effect they can have on another person's life, especially during the formative years. Bentley and Ryan taught me about strength, diligence, persistence, and competition in the best sense of the word. And they were models I could look up to and was never disappointed in."

(Above, the 1966 senior swimmers tread water in front of the diving board. L-R: John Franculli, Paul Negruzzi, Todd Benjamin, Captain Paul Bentley, Bill Marchand, Don LaRocco, and Joe Rinaldi. NOTE: Freestylers Walt Chaberek and Rick Porritt were absence for this photo, while Joe Rinaldi disappeared from the swimming scene right after it.)

The season started off with losses to Wilby and Crosby. The good news was that many were swimming well and scoring points, e.g. there was a squadron of winning sophomores: Frank Bentley 1:08.5 in the 100 Back, Mike Hogan 1:14.7 in the 100 Breast, Bill John 100 Fly in 1:08.1, and divers Chris Germano and Duke Wall. The Raiders had good overall depth and points were consistently scored by veterans Walt Chaberek, John Franculli, Rick Porritt, Todd Benjamin, Fran Sesko, et al.

Early in the season, Crosby coach Ray Synder approached THS coach Ed Evers with a unique offer. Synder knew he had no IMers who could knock off the best from Kennedy (now built and replacing Croft) and Sacred Heart. He also knew that THS would *not* be in the running for the Valley title. So he proposed to Coach Evers that if Evers (and Paul Bentley) were willing, that Bentley could train with the Crosby team. Synder knew that THS got little practice time, and figured that if Bentley could get himself into good shape, he'd win the IM, take points from Kennedy and Sacred Heart, and thus help Crosby to win the NVL title, while also helping Bentley himself. . . When Coach Evers explained the proposition to me, it was briefly tempting. Most of the Waterbury swimmers who were now beating my teammates and me, we had successfully handled in our junior and intermediate YMCA years. It hurt my pride and my sense of athletic fairness to know we were being beaten simply because of a lack of pool time and conditioning. *But*, to drive round-trip to Waterbury every day just because of pride and to forsake my teammates in the process was unacceptable. I told Coach Evers to tell Coach Synder, Thanks, but I'd stay in Torrington.

The top sophomore and distance specialist, along with junior Fran Marchand, was Bill Ryan. Sidebar: Bill's older brothers Dave and Ed had been on the THS swim team during the glory years of the 1950s. Dave had been a champion freestyler, mainly on the relays, while Ed swam varsity for 4 years: 1956-'59. It was a swimming family, and now it was Bill's turn. He didn't disappoint. Against Hartford Public Ryan started by winning the 200 Free in 2:10.7, and for an encore shattered the THS record in the 400 Free finishing in 4:39.9. (Left, Coach Evers congratulates Bill after the 400.)

Like all swim seasons, that winter of 1966 furnished some light, funny moments. On our bus rides home from away meets, some of the seniors (*not* me) who controlled the back of the bus took to mooning cars out the rear glass. It was funny in a sophomoric way, and because it was only done when it was dark out, there was little/no chance of IDing the culprits *or* the asses... Against Kennedy in their sparkling new 25-yard pool, senior Don LaRocco took the final turn in the 100-yard Fly, pushed off the wall, took a couple of strokes, and stood up. He loudly announced to all those present, "I can't go on!" We laughed like hell. In Boulder's (as we called him) defense, 25-yard pools really kicked our butts. And yet while we laughed because it was simply funny, we also inwardly sympathized with Boulder because we knew what he was feeling, i.e. we'd all, at one-time-or-another, felt like quitting a race. . . . Senior Todd Benjamin, who lived on Brightwood Avenue, claimed that for the 6 a.m. Saturday practices, he'd walk down Pythian

(Above, the start of a 1966 race. Todd Benjamin is closest to the camera; Rick Porritt is next to him. Note the "homemade" wooden starting blocks. These were new in 1966. They would be pulled back after the race started. Note also the different arm positions of the swimmers. There was no one accepted method of starting except to hit the water flat in a sort of belly-flop and to start swimming as soon as possible. Photo compliments of Eunice Froeliger.)

Avenue opposite his house, cross North Main, start up North Elm, and where Prospect Street intersected he'd hop a milk truck and ride it all the way down Prospect to the Y. Obviously it saved time and energy, which at 6 a.m. we all needed. I suppose this particular anecdote would have been funnier if Benjamin had fallen off. But even if it had happened, he was a tough kid who would have bounced up and not missed practice. . . We got a rookie on the team who thought he was a hotshot freestyler. I watched him swim, and the next time he boasted, I casually said, "I'll bet you $1 that in a 40-yard race, I can swim a circle around you." He hesitated. The team members laughed and egged him on, and he finally took the bet. I gave him the inside lane, took the lane to his right, and when someone said, "GO!" I sprinted ahead. Had him by a body length at the 10-yard mark and crossed over in front of him. I let him pass, swam behind him and came up his right side again. I hit the 20-yard wall ahead of him and thus completed the "circle" with 20 yards to spare. Everyone laughed, and he learned the lesson that there's a big difference between being a good *recreational* swimmer and being a good *competitive* swimmer.

Going into the final meet of the season, the team stood 3-6, i.e. even with a victory, a winning season was not possible. And much to my personal concern I had not yet beaten the school record of 1:48 in the 160-yard Individual Medley. Had swum a 1:49+ several times. Fairly close, but no. . . This was now *it*. The meet against Hall HS. Last try. Four years had come down to this. . . Flashback one week. With 7 days till my final attempt at Rebillard's record I wracked my brain trying to think what I could do. Could not get in better shape. Not enough time. Then it dawned on me that the only thing I *could* control, that *might* make a difference, was my weight. I'd been swimming at around 175 pounds, which was a lot on my 5'9" frame. Many on the team were packing too much weight, but there was no one around telling us we should lose it. Many thought the husky Johnny Weissmuller (Tarzan) was the swimming ideal. So for the week preceding the final meet I starved myself. For example, on grinder day in the cafeteria, I didn't have a single meatball sub when normally I'd eat 2. The weight started to drop, a lot of which was superficial water loss. Still. . . In a time trial that week in practice (Coach Evers seemed as anxious as I was), I went a 1:48.8. Coach was disappointed, but I wasn't. I knew I had more in reserve, which was a feeling I hadn't had in years.

Meet Night. I didn't warm up. Frequently didn't. Was naturally very loose. Believed warmup would only tire me out, which it probably would have. Coach Evers went along with all this, much to my relief. **Fran Marchand**: "I used to see Bentley in the drying room (a tiled space between the showers and locker room) doing pushups before a meet. I couldn't believe it. When I asked him about it, he said he needed to get the blood flowing." Sidebar: No one else ever adopted my pushup routine or my no-swimming-warmup "system," and I would never recommend it. BUT, it seemed to work for me. Each individual has to know his/her own body. And I felt I knew mine.

We took the opening relay, and jumped out to an early lead. Soon it was IM time. My parents and girlfriend were in the stands. I didn't

see them. Old time officials like Renny Belli, Frank Janis, and Erwin Killiany were timing. They all knew the situation, and wished me luck, I think. I wasn't hearing anything. At the gun I jumped into an early lead and was never challenged. It was me vs the clock. I swam hard, but controlled, and when I hit the wall at the end, I knew it was the best IM swim I'd ever had. But was it enough?. . . I looked up. Renny Belli glanced at his stopwatch and said, "1:47.7" And he smiled.
(Below, Coach Evers congratulates me. . . NOTE: In 1966, along with starting blocks, a center lane line was added and can be seen in this picture. It did little/nothing to keep down the chop. Mainly it was there to separate "us" from "them," i.e. THS swimmers swam on the "home" side, where I am in the picture. The opposition swam on the visitors' side.)

Personal Confession: Part of the reason I wanted the IM record so badly, in addition to having shot for it for 4 years, was that it was held by Raoul Rebillard, and I honestly thought I was a better all-around swimmer than he was. I'd seen him swim and believed that 3 of my strokes were better than his, and my fly nearly as good (I'd gone a 1:02). Stay high in the water, get a skimming undulating rhythm going, and really use the lower body to drive forward. I suppose that might sound cocky, but to me it was just knowing my abilities and being confident in them. . . But, if it *was* cocky, then so be it. I certainly wasn't the only THS swim captain in the 1960s who was. As long as a swimmer was "one-of-the-guys" too, a smidge of cockiness didn't hurt. . .

The next-to-last event in that meet was the 100-yard Breaststroke. Before the race, the head official, Mr. Maurice Hoben, came up to me and said, "In the last meet when you swam the breaststroke, I noticed you used an slight dolphin movement underwater on the turn. If you do it tonight, I'll disqualify you." He was nice about it, and he was right. I had learned that if I arched my back on the push-off, when I pulled down with the one underwater stroke you were allowed, that I could simultaneously dolphin the lower half of my body and get a slight forward push. It wasn't much, but in a close race it could be the difference. . . Going into the final turn I was in a dead heat with Grillo from Hall who had earlier won the Fly in 1:02. He was a tough swimmer and competitor, and I didn't feel confident I could take him on the last lap. So, despite Judge Hoben's earlier warning, I used the dolphin movement on that last turn. We sprinted stroke-for-stroke the final 10 yards, and when we pushed for the wall, Grillo hit first in 1:08.5. I was a fraction-of-a-second behind. . . I was happy with the time, but disappointed with the loss on this my final duel meet *ever*. Then Judge Hoben came over and told me I was DQed. Said he had warned me. No argument there. Beaten *and* DQed. Not a good way to end a swimming career. **2017 Sidebar**: That movement would be legal today. **1966 Good News**: Our last relay won, which meant we took that close last meet by 5 points. Which meant we finished the season 4-6, same as last year, i.e. one of the worse swim records *ever*! But not *the* worst (other than '42). . .

We took dead last in the NVL Meet, and the only 2 things I remember about the State Meet at the old UConn pool, were that the place was freezing. And that someone stole my sweatsuit. I had put an underclassmen in charge of watching the warmup suits, and he wandered off. To this day, I'm positive a Naugy swimmer swiped my THS togs. The Greyhounds were sitting near us and looking very shady and guilty. Truth be told, I couldn't complain. Freshmen year I had swiped a Jonathan Law sweatsuit (which was actually a large, yellow, terrycloth bathrobe). It was now MY time to freeze my ass off. Needless to say, my swims went poorly as did our overall team performance.

Only thing left was the winter awards assembly at the end of March in the THS gymnasium with the entire school gathered. . . Flashback to that fire nozzle from Hartford Public that was stolen by a swim team member for the second time in 1963 (p.219). It now materialized at that awards assembly. It had been given to me at some point after 1963 by the thief himself. In winter 1966 I had it engraved to Coach Evers and now presented it to him in front of the whole school. With the swim team smiling and happily looking on, Coach stepped forward and accepted it good-naturedly, though looking back I think he had too much dignity and sense of rightness to ever really enjoy it. A few years ago he told me that he didn't know what had ever become of it.

I got the Service Cup at that assembly, and before long, THS was over for the Class Of 1966. Vietnam was heating up. Protests were beginning on the home front. The turbulent '60s were in full swing. . .

Bentley   Those Glorious Torrington Days

✣ ✣ ✣

Raider Ducks Splash Tomorrow

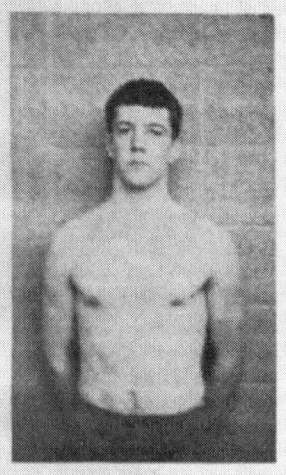

Tomorrow night, the THS Swim Team will meet Hartford Public in Hartford for the first meet of the year. Next Wednesday the 21st, E.O. Smith will come to Torrington for the first home meet. The squad has been practicing for about six weeks and Coach Evers, in his 5th year as coach, expects a good season provided the team puts in enough practice. Returning lettermen are: Capt. Fran Marchand, Bill John, Frank Bentley, Mike Hogan, Bill Ryan and Duke Wall. Also, Fran Sesko and Tony Picone show great promise.

Leading the swim team into a promising season is senior Fran Marchand. Fran is enrolled in a college course consisting of College English IV, Economics, Chemistry, and Senior Problems. Outside activities which he enjoys are camping and skiing. An active member of Thespians, Fran worked diligently as chairman of the stage crew to construct the intricate set of Green Grow the Lilacs.

Fran's plans for the future include college where he plans to study business.

When asked about the outlook for this season, his reply was, "Very good!" T.H.S. students are behind the team and wishing it a winning season.

Nineteen sixty-seven. It was a young, but talented team. Captain Fran Marchand, freestyler and distance specialist, would be leading the Raider ducks. Marchand led by example and had the reputation of being the hardest worker on the team. He was a positive person, and as others looked up to *him*, he looked up to his *coach*. (Left, a profile from the Dec. 1966 X Ray.)

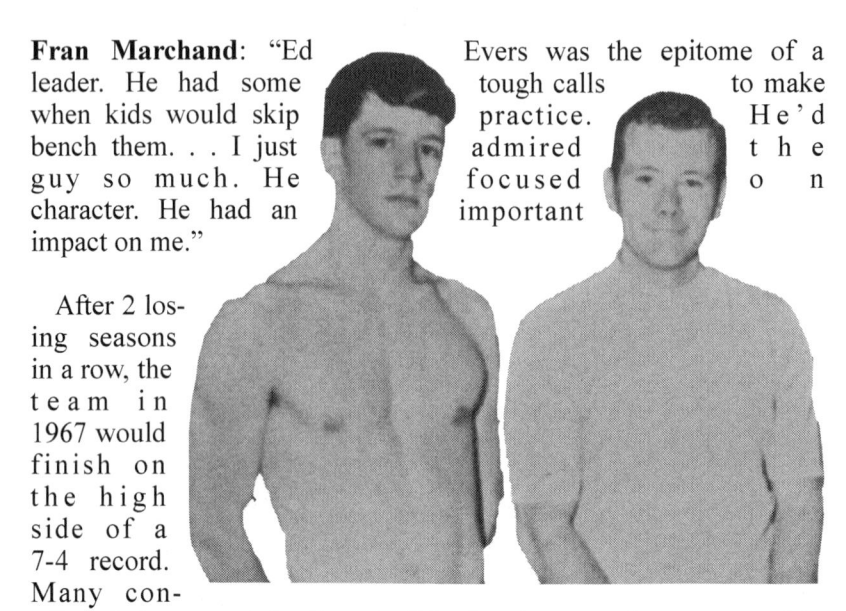

Fran Marchand: "Ed Evers was the epitome of a leader. He had some tough calls to make when kids would skip practice. He'd bench them... I just admired the guy so much. He focused on character. He had an important impact on me."

After 2 losing seasons in a row, the team in 1967 would finish on the high side of a 7-4 record. Many contributed, but certainly Captain Marchand was a large part of it. Marchand usually swam the 200 & 400-yard Freestyle and won them both. Against undefeated Kennedy, Captain Marchand set a new THS record in the 400 Free finishing in 4:32.8. This time shattered Bill Ryan's record by 7.1 seconds!... Not to be outdone, Bill Ryan himself in that same meet eclipsed Ed Holmes' school record in the 60-yard Free by a tenth-of-a-second, finishing in 30.2. Ryan was proving that he could not only excel in the distant races, but also go very fast in the sprints. This was, and still is, a rare ability.

Sidebar Irony: The winner of the 100 Back (60 seconds flat) in that THS vs. Kennedy meet in the old Torrington Y pool was Kennedy sophomore Newell Porch. Porch would be back in 6+ years to take over as head coach of the THS swim team. *But*, for now he was the enemy, the loyal opposition...

Distance swimming wasn't always such a winning proposition for Captain Marchand. He had not swum competitively before high school, and got quite a surprise in his first official swim. **Fran Marchand**: "My first meet ever I swam the 400 Free at Hartford Public. Everyone was clapping. I was so happy. Coach told me, 'They're clapping because you finally finished.' I was dead last... Another time as a freshmen my bathing suit started coming down. There was my ass showing. I had just learned how to do a flip turn, which made it worse. Every time I came off the wall, I'd try to pull it up. Ed Evers was shaking his head. My mother was so embarrassed."

The only other 2 senior swimmers on the team in '67 were Tony Picone and Fran Sesko. Both were journeymen who did not win races, but who *did* garner points. The lone exception was the Picone winning the 100 Fly in 1:14.8 against E.O. Smith.

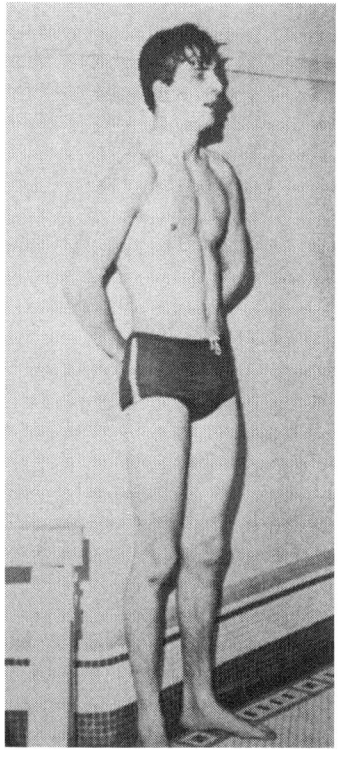

(Above, Tony Picone beginning his arm recovery in the butterfly. Note he's wearing a nose clip. A number of swimmers wore these during the 1960s, most notably backstrokers. It restricted breathing but *was* effective in keeping water out of the nose.)

(Left, Fran Sesko standing ready for action. Sesko swam all 4 of his THS years.)

Other commendable performances in 1967 included Fran Marchand churning a 2:03.9 in the 200 Free, juniors Billy John going a 1:07.7 in the 100 Fly and Mike Hogan finishing the 100 Breast in 1:13.3, while freshman Doug Traub copped a first in the 60 Free in 32.2. Captain Marchand himself was the benchmark of consistency in the 400 Free almost always finishing in the 4:30s.

While there was not a girls THS team in 1967, an important part of the boys team was Eunice Froeliger, who was the announcer at the home swim meets for 3 years.

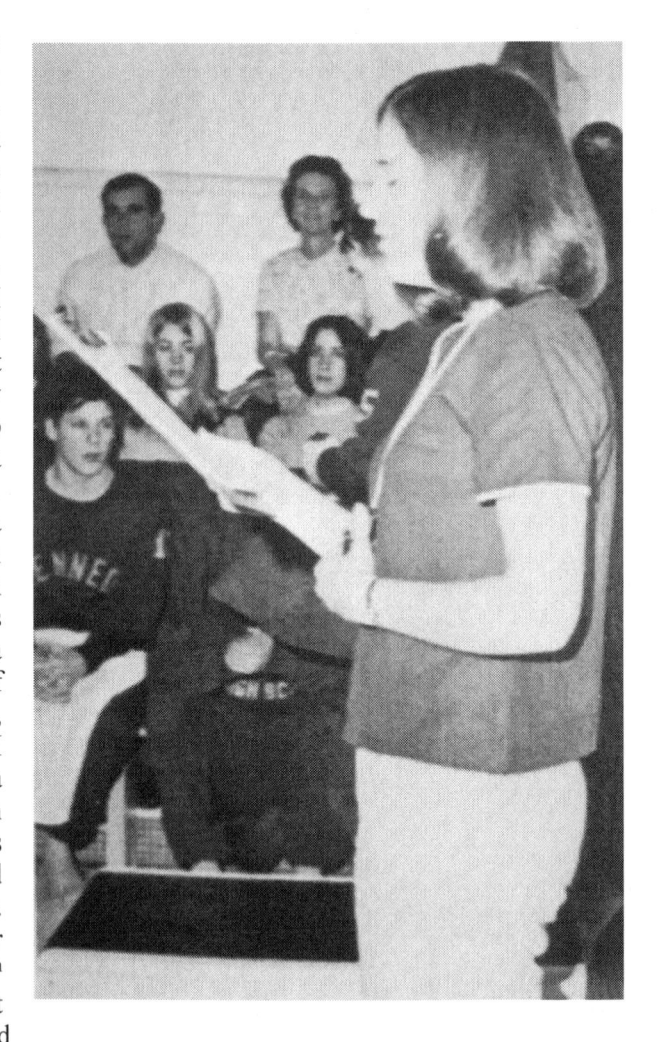

Eunice Froeliger: (Right, announcing at a THS home meet.) "I started swimming competitively when I was 9 or 10. I tried different things initially but ended up being a breaststroker. Being on a sports team with a bunch of girls was certainly a highlight of my young life, and while I think I was a strong team member, I was not a record setter or a star. I remember winning a 5th place trophy at a New England AAU swim meet somewhere in Massachusetts in the 200 medley relay with Carolyn Gatesy doing the backstroke leg, Patti Cahill butterfly, me breaststroke, and I can't remember who anchoring. That was a big deal to me. I think that was in 1967 during my senior year of high school. I found the trophy recently in a box with the swimmer on top broken off just below the knees. . . The girls team practiced on Tuesdays and Thursdays and the boys on MWF (Mmmm! yes, a disparity but that's how it was). . . I think it was during my senior year that some of us 'special' girls got to have an extra practice with the boys – it may have been toward the end of the season, maybe when we were preparing for the NE meet. And it may have been on a Saturday. . . I don't remember how being the announcer came about, but I worked as the girl's locker room attendant and was a very active 'Junior Leaderette,' and so I was at the Y a lot. I think it had something to do with Coach Evers. We may have talked, and he may have recognized my interest. Todd (Benjamin) and I met at the Y – he must have been there for high school swim practice, I don't think he ever did much else there. He became the 'love of my life' during my junior and senior high school years. I guess in that context, you could say Todd was a 'byproduct'!"

Bill Ryan: "Eunice was a lifeguard at Burr Pond when I was one as well. The Burr Pond crew went to her cottage at West Hill a few times to drink beer and sing songs, like Dylan's "Girl From The North Country." I had a crush on her. Not only because she was gorgeous, and I saw her in a bathing suit a lot, but also because I thought *she* thought I was funny. She always said, 'Oh, Billy,' which endeared her to me even more. (Nothing ever came of it.) I remember that she was our swim meet announcer. She put her own humorous spin on the announcements, as she did with just about everything I ever saw her do."

In 1967 Eunice Froeliger was awarded a varsity "T" for her 3 years of announcing at THS swim team meets. As far as I've been able to determine, Eunice Froeliger was the *first* female to earn a varsity letter in Torrington High School sports history. The fact she should have won one for actually swimming and couldn't because of the era, doesn't lessen or negate the fact that Eunice Froeliger was the *first*. And *that* is a *very* big deal. . .

1967 Postscript: Captain Fran Marchand went on to swim for the University Of Vermont, and when his college and competitive swim years were over, he returned to Torrington, and in 1971 took over the

YMCA girls swim team. Early on he met a "smart alecky" (his words) girl on that squad. Her name was Sarah "Sally" Traub (THS '72). Eventually they married, had sons (thus combining the aquatic genes of the Marchands and Traubs), and raised some of the finest swimmers Torrington has ever seen.

✥ ✥ ✥

1968. The Summer Of Love was over, and it was time to make a winter splash. Co-captains on that team were veterans Bill Ryan (on right) and Mike Hogan (on left).

Bill Ryan: "Coach Ed Evers was a great coach. He also coached the THS golf team my senior year after Hugh Franklin's Dad gave it up. Despite Mr. Evers not being a swimmer, he was an excellent judge of athletic talent and was a motivator. He cared about ALL the swimmers. When we were going up against a weak swim team in a dual meet. Mr. Evers would make sure that the younger swimmers on the team, or the ones not quite as fast, were entered in events where they could do a best time, earn some points, and contribute strongly to the team win. I admired him for that. He was a good man and good coach. Oh, and a great strategist. He did his homework and knew what events to put us in for the best possible advantage. He knew the other team's strengths and weaknesses and how we matched up to them. That took doing some homework."

Mike Hogan: "In my Junior year things came together for me. I did well and took up a new event, the Individual Medley. At the end of that year, Bill and I were elected co-captains for our senior year. Unfortunately, sometime between spring and late fall 1967, something gave way in me, mostly related to health issues. I was a strong, hard-working, dogged kid willing to make up with work what didn't come naturally. But early in the fall of my senior year, I was burdened with a recurring strep throat, fevers, fatigue, and the vague intimations of the asthma that would break through in my thirties and change my life for many years. My swim times were mediocre. The energy, the drive seemed to desert me. It just wasn't there. I did the best I could, but the season was something of a disappointment."

(Above, the 1968 THS swim team. Front Row, L-R: Pete Jennings, Paul Simko, Jim Rubino, Tony Urban, Armand Persechino, Jimmy Buonocore, David Strogatz, Gary Newth. Middle Row: Sam Stevens, Pat Gallagher, George Pellegren, Bill "Skip" Meyer, Doug Traub. Back Row: Coach Evers, Edmond "Duke" Wall, Frank Bentley, Bill Ryan, Mike Hogan, Bill John, John Bianchi, Fred Brenker.)

Despite Mike Hogan's health issues his senior year, he continued to swim and to push through his physical and mental ennui. In doing so, he set a sterling example for the team. Many seniors turned in winning performances and posted very good times: Bill John 1:03.5 in the 100 Fly; John Bianchi 1:10.8 100 Breast; Bill Ryan 1:07 100 Back, 24.3 50 Free, 2:03 200 Free; Frank Bentley 26.3 50

Free; and Mike Hogan himself 1:13 Breaststroke, 1:08.1 Fly, and 1:56.7 IM. . . Meanwhile, senior diver Duke Wall took *many* first places. . . **Bill Ryan**: "Duke Wall owned that diving board. He used to push off the ceiling with his left hand when doing the front dive with a half twist in layout. Sometimes he did it, sometimes not, and I think he got away with it from the judges. Funny, no?"

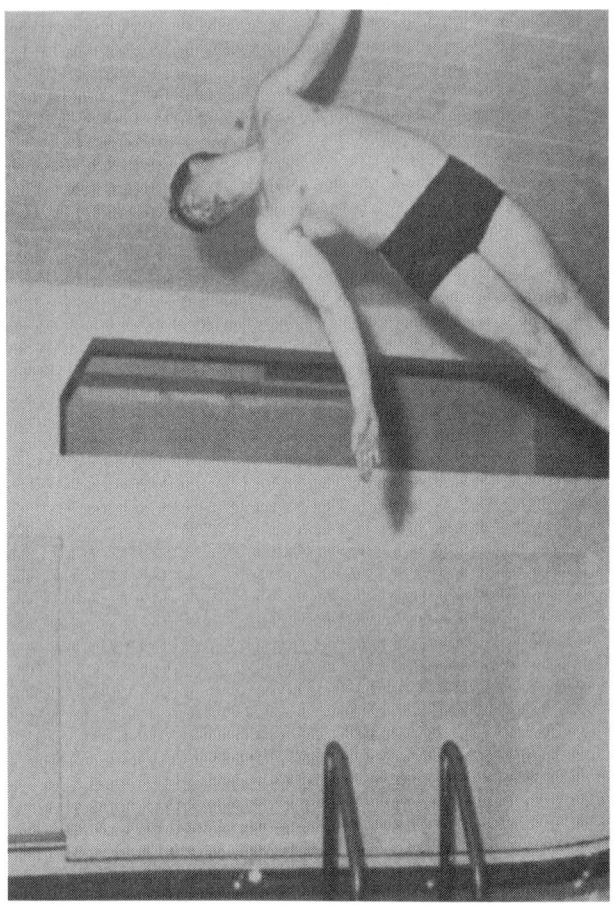

(Left, Duke Wall at the apex of his dive reaching in his patented way for the ceiling. . . Note that the audience gallery on the visitors' side has been bricked in. This was the start of construction changes involving the new 25-yard pool addition.)

The underclassmen also contributed greatly. Sophomore Paul Simko raced to a 2:13.6 200 Free. Junior Pat Gallagher did a 58.2 in the 100 Free, while classmate Sam Stevens marked a 1:07 Backstroke. Best of the underclassman was sophomore Doug Traub. Three meets into the season against Xavier, Traub swam a 30.2 60-yard Free tying Bill Ryan's school record set in 1967. Neither Traub nor Ryan would swim the 60 Free faster in '68, and when the season ended, they co-held the record.

While 1968 embraced many fine team and individual performances, the swimmers themselves were *still* handicapped by an antique facility and a lack of practice time. Somehow though they managed to keep their spirits up.

Frank Bentley: "I was brought up swimming on the Y team from an early age. Maybe it was all those long, all-day meets that soured me. I'm not sure how I lasted 4 years on the high school team, considering I was burnt out by the time I entered high school. . . I remember the 20-yard, 4 lane pool at the Y. The fans were right on top of you, crammed in at the meets. And oh! how hot it got. . . The Saturday morning practices were the worst. I was no angel in high school, and after a Friday night at Wright's, having consumed a few frosties, it wasn't much fun getting up on Saturday. There were many times I wanted to quit, but I hung in and stayed the course. I loved Coach Evers, respected him highly, and I never wanted to let him down. . . My funniest memory was in my senior year. We practiced Friday night and had the NVL meet the next day. I should've gone home and hit the sack early. But of course I went up to Wright's. When I went to leave, I discovered my car on fire. It so happened that our diver, Dukie Wall, went out to my car and had a cigarette. Well, you can guess what happened. All of my swimming gear was burnt. A fitting end to my swimming career."

Dave Strogatz: "A distinct memory from my freshman year (1968) – we had early morning practices on Saturdays, maybe starting as early as 6 or 6:30. I remember walking into the old YMCA lobby in the darkness of an early winter morning, and you could make out these shadowy, lumpy shapes on the ping pong tables. They were upperclassmen, lying on the ping pong tables, getting some final moments of rest and recovery after Friday night recreation. Frank Bentley may have been one of those guys half passed out on the ping pong tables, Duke Wall another candidate! It was a lesson from my older teammates on balancing interests in-and-away from the pool."

Many on the '68 team, and on the teams from most THS years, hit high school having had many years in the pool. It was not unusual for swimmers to quit their senior year. For those who persevered, who felt an obligation to themselves and to the team and hung in there, a good part of what got them through was comradery *and* some lightheartedness.

(Below, the '68 seniors taking a break. On the board, L-R: Co-captain Bill Ryan, Duke Wall, Frank Bentley. Standing: Co-captain Mike Hogan lighting up the camera, George Pellegren, John Bianchi, Bill John holding an old-style kick board. Reclining on the right, fully at ease, is Tony Urban.)

Undoubtedly the biggest meet of the year was against Conard HS. The West Hartford school hadn't been beaten by anyone in 4 years, and they traditionally trounced THS. *BUT*, Conard was weaker this year, Torrington stronger, and the meet was at the Torrington Y.

Bill Ryan: "Torrington's 'Band Box' of a swimming pool was a tough place for visiting teams. Especially for those teams that swam in larger 25-yard pool with official height diving boards. Our YMCA pool was 20 yards long, and 6 feet deep in the deepest end where the diving was held. Diving was off of a board that was stiff, short, and close to the water. The ceiling was too low and the water too shallow for a regulation board. There were no 'floating lane dividers' to keep swimmers swimming straight. The lanes were skinny and the waves Titanic with no lane dividers to dampen the swimmers' wakes. The shallow end was three feet deep. Doing a flip turn there was like doing one in a bathtub. Many swimmers scraped the bottom coming off the shallow end turn. We had a definite home-pool-advantage."

From *The Torrington Register*: "Conard High's swim team from West Hartford came into Torrington last night with an impressive string of straight victories with no defeats. After a swim at the YMCA against Torrington High's Raider Ducks, Conard High left with its first defeat in four years. THS won 52-43. Four key men in Coach Ed Ever's biggest victory in six years were Duke Wall, Bill John, Mike Hogan, and John Bianchi, all taking first positions. Not taking first but being credited by Coach Evers for an outstanding job in the 100 yard freestyle and on the 400 yard freestyle relay was Pat Gallagher. Gallagher took second in the 100 yard freestyle, one of the key spots that THS didn't expect to capture."

(Below, nothing says "victory" like throwing in Coach.)

With 3 meets to go, THS met Hartford Public and won. The most noteworthy swim in that 9th team victory occurred in the 400-yard Freestyle Relay, a *new* duel meet event in 1968. Previously it had only been swum in special meets such as the Yale Carnival. The relay team of Bill Ryan, Frank Bentley, Pat Gallagher, and Doug Traub won with a time of 3:41.4, averaging 55.35/man. This just missed the THS record of 3:40.1 set by Tom Wall, Kevin Gilson, Don Will, and Ray Ostrander in 1956 (it was a state record then).

With 2 meets to go THS stood 9-4 on the year. It was the best season in 5 years. The next-to-last meet was against Whethersfield, and it promised to be an easy time. Frequently in meets that are a foregone conclusion, coaches enter swimmers in events they don't normally swim. Against Whethersfield, Bill Ryan convinced Coach Evers to let him shoot for the 160-yard Individual Medley school record. Though not normally an IM swimmer, Ryan was *very* proficient in all the strokes, and Evers gave him the nod. Ryan swam a great race and hit the wall in 1:48.3, a mere .6 off the record. NOTE: The 160 IM would only be swum a few more times in school history, and Bentley's record of 1:47.7 would not be beaten.

The final meet of the year was against Hall HS. Hall came in at 11-0, while THS stood 10-4. It was the most victories for a THS swim team since 1959. In the opening 160-yard Medley Relay, Torrington got out touched, and that split-second difference provided the ultimate outcome. THS lost 48-47 and finished the year 10-5. . . Noteworthy in that meet was Billy Ryan's winning of the 100 Free in a torrid 52.9. It was the fastest any THS swimmer, other than Ray Ostrander, had *ever* gone. Faster than Tom Wall, Kevin Gilson, Charlie Vierps, et al.

When Bill Ryan received the Service Cup, it was a fit ending to the victorious 1968 season.

✣ ✣ ✣

The end of the decade, of the swinging and turbulent sixties. It was 1969. War and revolutionary changes were shaking the world. In Torrington there was a new swim team coach *and* a new pool.

ANTHONY TURINA   WILLIAM RYAN

Service Club Cup Winners Selected At High School

The New Coach. Jack Kohler came to the THS swim team from Chicago with 15 years of swimming experience. He was the first THS swim coach to come to the position with an appropriate background. He was also the assistant football coach.

The New Pool. In 1969 a new 25-yard, 6 lane beauty opened. It was built behind the Y where the old parking lot next to EJ Kelley's was previously. John Ocain in *The Torrington Register*: "Sports fans who haven't seen the new pool should make it a point to attend an event there soon. . . It is listed to seat over 300 fans, and they don't have to worry about getting wet like the sideline fans did at the old pool. Also, the diving board must be a joy for the boys to perform on. Quite different from the old pool where more than one diver bounced off the ceiling."

Sidebar: Though the old 20-yard Y pool was still in good shape in 1969 and filled with water, it was no longer the "main" pool and was only used then, and for the next couple of decades, for family swim, swim parties, and miscellaneous activities. Eventually the water temperature was raised and the pool was used only for physical therapy. Today in 2017 it's drained, and the inside of the pool and surrounding deck are used by the YMCA for storage. As of 8 months ago, when I saw it last, the inside of the pool and deck were crowded with such things as archery targets, chests, desks, cabinets, signs, crates holding this-and-that, a boat, stacked chairs, stacked lumber, drums of ?, 5-gallon buckets, a large fan, et al. The pool and deck tile, as well as the paint on the walls, still looked good, though the ceiling tiles were peeling in places. NOTE 1: I wanted to include a picture here of the old Y pool being used as a storage area, but when I asked permission of the Northwest YMCA executive director, I was politely denied. NOTE 2: The fact that the old Y pool is being used for storage shouldn't sadden anyone, i.e. it's the evolution of a building. It's a great, utilitarian thing that the area can *still* be used, even though the pool has outlived its usefulness.

New pool, new coach – what was the 1969 season's outlook? Preseason article in *The Torrington Register*: "Kohler admits this won't be one of Torrington's stronger teams, but that the prospect for a successful season look good." The article cited a healthy number of returning lettermen: Jim Rubino, Paul Simko, Pat Gallagher, Doug Traub, Bill "Skip" Meyer, Pete Jennings, and Fred Brenker as an upbeat sign, though the article also noted that "Sam Stevens and Glenn Newth are currently ineligible." Still, despite the basketball team chalking up a streak of losses at this time, the swimming outlook was bright.

The experienced and quick breaststroker Fred Brenker was named captain, and there was no reason to think that the team, with a full roster of veterans, a knowledgeable coach, and a new pool (where the swimmers were now going to get double+ previous practice time) would have anything *but* a winning season.

Captain Fred Brenker (left): "Coach Jack Kohler was a great guy. He knew stroke technique. No coach I'd had before did."

Doug Traub: "Jimmy Buonocore and I liked to snow ski. Coach Kohler didn't want us doing that. Said it would tighten us up... He made us keep a diary of what we ate everyday, and he'd critique it. My mother had to change what she cooked... He was fanatical."

Jim Rubino: "1968-'69 was the year we moved to the 'big pool.' Ed Evers had given over the coaching reins to Jack Kohler... The 25-yard pool got us in the same arena with Kennedy and Naugy. Training made for a mental change. Biggest change though was going to a 1-meter board. Mark Jennings was a freshman, and he flourished with the change. He became one of the states elite."

Under their new, highly motivated coach, the Raiders met Plainville HS in December, a few days before Christmas. The holiday glow was in the air, and the Raiders won. Doug Traub swam a very fast 100 Free in 52.9 tying Billy Ryan's best the previous year. Captain Brenker won the Breast in 1:12.6, Paul Simko copped the 200 Free in 2:15.6, Pete Jennings swam to victory in the 400 Free in 4:57, sophomore Dave Strogatz took silver in the 100 Fly, and freshman aerial acrobat Mark Jennings won the diving.

The elation was short lived. Soon after, the THS swimmers got dunked by Naugy 76-19. Two Bright Spots: Fred Brenker won the Breast and lowered his official season's best to 1:11.6. Mark Jennings again won the diving.

Against Crosby in Old Ivy's 20-yard pool, Doug Traub (on right) broke the THS school record by .2 in the 60-Free going a 30.0. **Doug Traub**: "I remember swimming the 60 Free and doing 2 turns (instead of one as in the 50). I remember the closeness of the bottom when flipping in the shallow end. The timers had to move to the shallow end for the finish, and they didn't like it. . . I also remember a lane line which did nothing. It was like trying to swim in a washing machine because of the waves."

Next up was Kennedy, and THS suffered its 3rd lopsided loss in a row, 75-20. Junior Doug Traub the 50 Free in 24.5, and Kennedy senior Newell Porch won the Backstroke in 1:02.1. He was showing no mercy to a team which would soon be his.

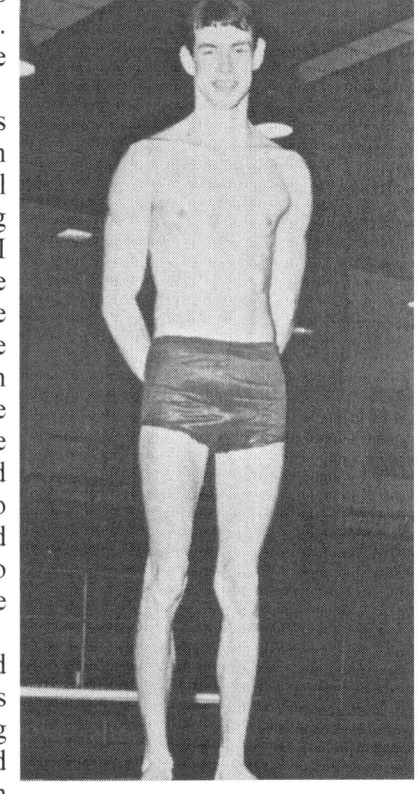

Then, disaster struck.

Several swimmers were suspended for the remainder of the season. Their offense? Playing cards in the locker room during the diving.

Jim Rubino: "There was one event that stands out. It occurred in the locker room rather than the pool. At one of the early season duel meets during the diving, a few guys went to the locker room and played cards. When Kohler found out, he kicked them off the team. One of those was a good freestyle swimmer whose dad was on the Board of Education. They were never allowed to return. The card playing incident left most of us disappointed in that I don't think there was a team rule that was broken. A one meet suspension seemed more appropriate."

Board Backs Swim Coach

At an "emergency" meeting of the Torrington Board of Education Sunday afternoon, members of the board backed up the THS swimming coach on a decision he had made to suspend members of the school team.

Coach Jack Koehler suspended several members of the squad observed playing cards while a diving event was going on during a meet.

Two letters were received from parents of the boys involved, one of them requesting something be done and the other stating he felt it was up to the coach to run things the way he saw fit.

As a result of the board meeting, the suspensions stand.

The suspension decision was appealed, but the Torrington Board Of Education backed the coach. (On left, the news article.)

Sports writer John Ocain felt the suspension was valid and said in print: "Jack Kohler is a man of conviction, and he is to be commended on his stand against reinstating 3 boys who were suspended from the THS swimming team for doing something they had been told not to do. A lot of people may think his treatment was too harsh, but you can bet your bottom dollar it'll be a long time before any other boys will do something that they were told not to by Mr. Kohler... It is a coach's job to build men and character, as well as athletes, and Kohler's action will go a long way toward doing just that."

Whether or not a person then *or* now thinks the punishment was too harsh (and I do), the fact is, it had a tremendously negative impact on the team.

Jim Rubino (on right): "Kohler was judge & jury, and he lost the team then...We suffered both as a team and as individual athletes."

It showed. Instead of a winning season in a new pool under a new coach, the team finished a dismal 3-8, i.e. the worst THS swim record since 1942... Fortunately, there were some very good individual performances.

Captain Fred Brenker: "I'd gotten my 100-yard Breaststroke time under 1:10 in the small pool, but it took longer to get under 1:10 in the 25-yard pool. I did eventually. I liked the smaller pool and missed the extra turn (4 turns vs. 3). Turns were the best part of my breaststroke. I could really hold a turn a long time."

Doug Traub got his 50 Free time down to 24.1. The next year, in 1970 when he was a senior co-captain, he'd break 2 long-standing THS records. Traub would beat Tommy Wall's 1956 50-yard Freestyle record (23.8) by going a 23.5. And Doug Traub would beat Ray Ostrander's 1957 100-yard Freestyle record (51.7) by going a 51.3 in the NVL Meet. **Doug Traub**: "I was a skinny 120 pound runt.

I remember getting up on the blocks against guys who were 150-160 pounds, and they were mortified when I beat them."

Sophomore Dave Strogatz in the final meet of the year against Whethersfield went a 1:08 in the 100 Butterfly. (Below, Strogatz in 1969.) He'd go a 1:00.9 the next year as a junior, and as a senior in 1971 would churn a very fast 59.8, while splitting a 25.6 for his 50-yard leg in the Medley Relay.

But all that was reserved for future days.

The 1969 swim season, the final year of the decade, came to an end with Jack Kohler leaving THS and the swim team. Captain Fred Brenker thought it was "politics" and that Kohler had drawn the ire of a BOE member over the fact that Brenker himself was the lone captain. Others thought it involved the card playing suspension. . . Whatever the reason, the new decade of the 1970s would usher in a highly qualified and ultimately a greatly loved coach: Ken Reall. And the decade would see every record on the THS record board broken.

❖ ❖ ❖

While the THS boys swim teams of the 1960s were winning some, losing some, and in general doing the best with what they had, the teenaged Torrington girls were swimming on the YMCA team and experiencing much success. In 1969, names that were making the press included: Bebe Mettling, Doree Mettling, Lisa Bossarelli,

Colleen McLaughlin, Leslie Killiany, Diane LaPorta, Janis LaPorta, Diane Pergola, Pam Cilfone, Michelle Gallicchio, Cheryl Begey, Pat Palker, Patty Tomala, Katherine Marchand, et al.

Since 1958, the most outstanding boy and girl swimmer on the YMCA team was honored with the Renny F. Belli Award. The inscription on the plaque states: "Awarded to the most progressive male and female swimmer who demonstrates overall leadership, skill, and sportsmanship during the course of the season."

The 4 females pictured on p. 209 *all* won the Renny F. Belli Award. Below are some of the other outstanding female swimmers who were honored during the 1960s with the annual Belli Award.

Jean "Gigi" Buonocore

Sue Chait

Carolyn Gatesy

Pat Cahill

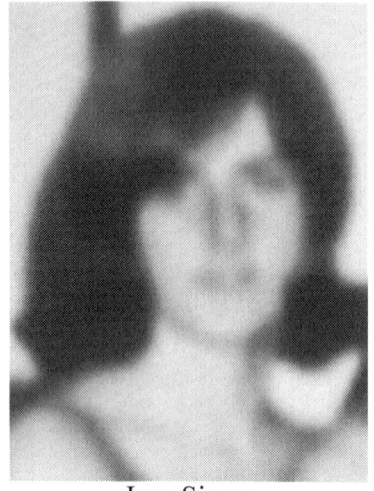

Jean Singer

Lisa Bossarelli

Dorothea "Doree" Mettling

Bernice "Bebe" Mettling

✣ ✣ ✣

It was over. The turbulent 1960s. Looking back, there's no doubt that from the perspective of won-loss records and best times, the decade didn't remotely compare to the 1950s. Yet, the swimmers of this decade kept the THS swim team going through poor swimming conditions and helter-skelter social times. The decade was loose, *but* at the same time focused. Swimmers like Rich Beloski and Jimmy Hoffman would be arguing one minute over who was the greater musical talent: The Beatles *or* The Beach Boys. And the next minute be swimming their hearts out. Some of us twisted-and-shouted and knocked-ourselves-out in New York State, at Wrights, and on a dozen back roads in Torrington. BUT, we showed up for practice and pushed hard (2, 4, 6, 8 - who do we appreciate? Torrington, Torrington, rah-rah-rah!). . . Of course, there's no dividing line in space-time. Just as THS swimming in 1969 had fallen on hard times, recovery would *not* be instantaneous. The coming years would blur together; THS swimming would be slow to recover its former glory.

BUT, it would recover. Change would be slow, another Golden Era was half a dozen years away. But it was coming. . .

In Memoriam - Rest In Peace

Charles "Charlie" Vierps: 1943-2009

John Eichner: 1943-2016

Gerald "Jerry" Belli: 1944-2016

Michael "Mike" Marciano: 1945-1998

Gerard Ringstad: 1945-2013

Theodore "Teddy" Holmes: 1946-1991

Anthony "Buddy" Marciano: 1948-2011

Paul Negruzzi: 1948-2001

James "Jim" Hoffman: 1948-1997

Edward "Buddy" Sokolik: 1949-2001

William "Billy" John: 1950-2014

Lisa Bossarelli Traub: 1953-2011

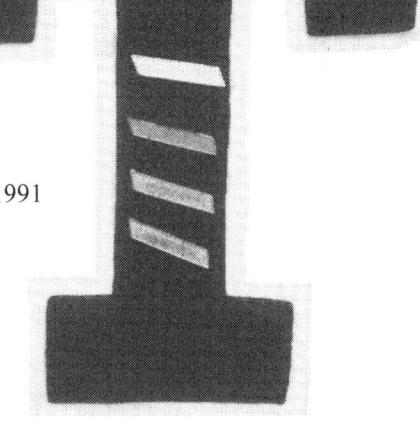

Epilogue

And so we come to the end of the Torrington road for yet another go-round. Writing this book occupied a *lot* of my winter and spring. And while it was fun researching and *great* talking to people who, in some cases, I hadn't talked to in decades and who, in other cases, I had *never* talked to before, it's time to slap a "fini" on these pages.

I apologize for the length of the T.H.S. swimming article. It obviously got away from me. Trouble was, because it's a subject close to my heart and deep in my memory, lots of recollections gushed out. That, and other articles, would have been even longer if certain key people had returned phone calls or emails. They did both themselves *and* their teams/groups/businesses a disservice by not acknowledging the little things that only an insider would know.

But, it's always that way. Quelle dommage.

I'm certain there's not an article here that's not missing key people. Apologies. It was unintentional. Hopefully, I *did* include enough people/players to assuage any major sense of omission.

Do I have yet another "Torrington" book in me? Possibly. Maybe. Could be. . . Time will tell.

Till then, I'll leave you all with a couple of images. The first shows a 2011 reunion in Florida with Coach Ed Evers, my brother Frank, and me. It was *great* seeing Coach again. I'll let you sort out who's who. . . The second picture speaks for itself.

Fini.

Bentley   Those Glorious Torrington Days

All roads lead to Torrington.
Peace and harmony to all.
          Paul Bentley
             Spring 2017

Made in the USA
Lexington, KY
12 August 2018